Other Books by Stephanie L. Fowler

Crossings

*Chasing Alice: How the Life, Murder, and Legacy
of an English Teacher Changed a Delmarva Community*

INTO THE NIGHT

INTO THE NIGHT

A JAILBREAK AND DOUBLE HOMICIDE ON MARYLAND'S EASTERN SHORE

Stephanie L. Fowler

Copyright © 2025 by Stephanie L. Fowler

All rights reserved. No part of this book may be reproduced in any way without the written permission of the author.

ISBN 978-1-62806-458-2 (print | paperback)
ISBN 978-1-62806-459-9 (print | hardback)
ISBN 978-1-62806-460-5 (ebook)

Library of Congress Control Number 2025913027

Published by Salt Water Media
29 Broad Street, Suite 104
Berlin, MD 21811
www.saltwatermedia.com

SALT WATER
MEDIA

Cover art used with license from istockphoto; author photo by Kelly Russo
Interior images used with permission and proper citations

www.stephaniefowler.net

This book is dedicated to the three men of the
Wicomico County Sheriff's Office
who died in the line of duty:

Samuel A. Graham

Albert L. Kelly

Glenn R. Hilliard

and to those who remember them and carry their stories.

PARTS OF MARYLAND, DELAWARE, AND THE EASTERN SHORE OF VIRGINIA

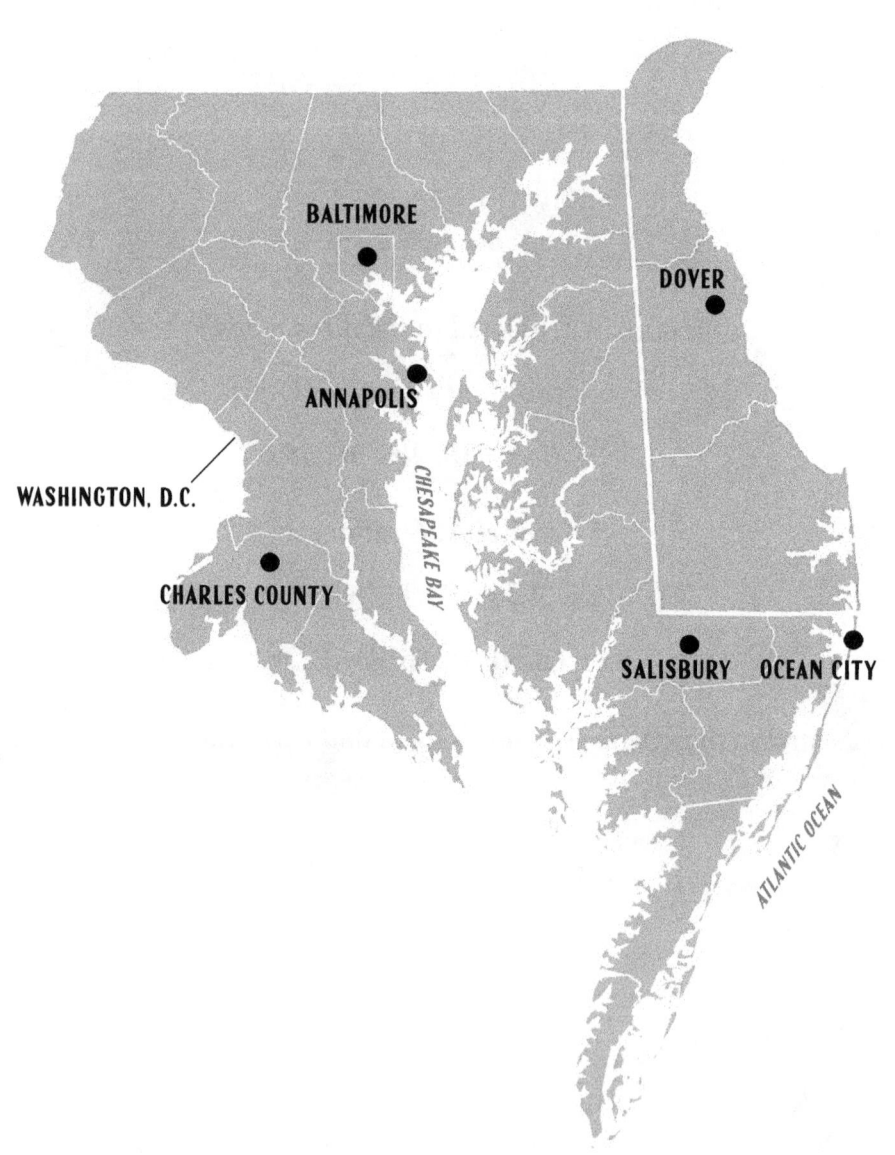

– CONTENTS –

Author's Note i

PART I

Prologue: Bud 1

Trial By Fire 5

Samuel Adams Graham 20

The First Two Murders at the Courthouse 35

Big Sam and Sheriff Jesse Pollitt 42

A New Sheriff in Town 52

PART II

The Evolution of a Hurricane 65

"A Story of a Series of Most Unfortunate Circumstances" 67

Delinquents in a House of Refuge 79

Prison Breaks and Sweet Potato Pies 96

Crownsville State Hospital 107

Clifton T. Perkins State Hospital 120

Crime on the Rise 128

The Cut 136

Albert Lee Kelly 141

The Tempest Draws Near 146

PART III

Foolproof 159

Chaos in the Chamber 169

Manhunt 178

The Immediate Aftermath 183

Lingerings of the Exposé 197

A New Sheriff in Town (Again) 200

The Grand Jury and Joseph 204

LSD and Thorazine 207

The Murder Trial of Joseph James Bartholomey, Jr. 214

PART IV

Donna and Erick 267

Another Murderer Named Bartholomey 273

The Furman Decision 277

The Trial and Sentencing of Ethan L. Bartholomey 279

The Rest of the Story 282

Epilogue: Ghosts 297

Acknowledgements 303

Sources and Select Bibliography 306

Index 316

– AUTHOR'S NOTE –

I did not set out to write this book. It was supposed to be a short story in a collection of other short stories about the Eastern Shore, a sequel of sorts to my first book, *Crossings*. My research began in the summer of 2010 when I interviewed my grandfather, Bud Fowler, who was the deputy on duty in the courthouse the night Wicomico County Sheriff Sam Graham and jailer Albert Kelly were killed in December 1968. The story fascinated me, and I plunged headfirst into newspaper accounts and Freedom of Information Act (FOIA) requests, which yielded a stunning amount of documentation, including the entire transcript from Joseph J. Bartholomey, Jr.'s murder trial in 1969. This mountain of information took time to sort and understand thoroughly. And so, I began chipping away, bit by bit, making notes and timelines and writing preliminary drafts.

Then, something terrible happened. In early September 2011, Alice Davis—my high school English teacher and writing mentor whom I deeply respected and admired—was murdered by her husband. This had a profound impact on me and changed how I feel about true crime and telling these types of stories. They cannot be for mere entertainment. There must be a reason, a genuine purpose for writing about them. For me, it became about telling people who Alice was, what happened to her, and why she mattered. I didn't want her legacy to be lost. So, I decided to put the story of the sheriff, the jailer, and the prisoner on a back burner, and, instead, I wrote *Chasing Alice*, the story of Alice Davis. Writing that book made me realize the heart of true crime stories does not and cannot exist in the gory details ... no, the heart of the story exists in the people who are at the center of these terrible events.

After publishing *Chasing Alice* in September 2020, I decided to knock the dust off my original files and notes about the double homicide and refresh my memory of what I had and where I had left off. When my mother asked me what my next book was going to be, I told her I intended to write about the murders of Sam Graham and Albert Kelly at the old courthouse. She wrinkled her nose and asked, "Are you only going to write about murders now?" It was a fair question and I still haven't landed on an answer. Where I find myself is this: when I revisited the files and documents of this case, I was unable to look away from the issues of mental health and prison conditions, of broken families and generational trauma and abuse, of the ever-present struggle between the good guys and the bad guys ... the very things that, more than fifty years later, still play out on our evening news. Change the date on this murder to last week and you'd completely accept it as a new yet terrible headline.

During the writing of this book, in the summer of 2022, another member of the Wicomico County Sheriff's Office was killed in the line of duty. Corporal Glenn R. Hilliard was shot and killed by Austin Jacob Allen Davidson. Our community was horrified and heartbroken ... another senseless, violent death in which a good man was taken too soon. Until that night, Sam Graham and Albert Kelly were the only two in-the-line-of-duty deaths for the sheriff's department and I was already absorbed into every detail of that crime. When the news broke about Corporal Hilliard, I couldn't help but research who Austin Davidson was. I realized, with chilling dismay, that he was a near carbon copy of Joseph Bartholomey, the killer of Sheriff Graham and jailer Albert Kelly. Here we are again. Lessons unlearned. Lives irrevocably changed. The similarities were uncanny and one thought took shape in my mind: the more things change, the more they stay exactly the same.

This book in your hands took years to pull together. It was long hours at my writing desk, sorting through details and documents, seeking to find out who these people were and what happened to them, searching for ghosts in the remnants of a lost story. It was an endeavor for truth and justice, an attempt to usher into the light the worst of what we do to one another and perhaps try to understand how these things happen. This is a cautionary tale.

In this book, I have done my best to ensure the research here is true or as near to true as I can ascertain. If there are any conflicts, then I will explain in a footnote. Any dialogue in quotation marks has been obtained directly from a source like a newspaper article, an interview, medical/psychiatric records, or the trial transcript while dialogue in italics is my best approximation based on available documents. All dollar amounts will have an associated footnote, and for this, I used an online inflation calculator maintained by the Official Data Foundation. I also rounded up or down accordingly. The Wicomico County Jail is also referred to as the Salisbury jail and the penthouse prison. When writing about race, I followed the recent conventions of capitalizing Black, White, and Indigenous. This practice acknowledges race and ethnicity as proper nouns. To differentiate between Joseph Bartholomey Jr. and his father, Joseph Sr. during the early years, I use the name "Jimmy," which was a family nickname. Once Joseph Jr. turns eighteen, his father essentially drops out of the narrative and I switch to using Joseph instead of Jimmy. Albert Kelly's family now spells their last name as "Kelley" so I have used both spellings where appropriate. Additionally, for privacy and other reasons, I changed the names of a few people connected with the case, none of which alters the story in any factual way.

And one last note: I appreciate your readership and the time you spend with *Into the Night*. There are so many good books out there and I am grateful you chose this one. Thank you.

Stephanie L. Fowler
July 2025

PART I

– PROLOGUE: BUD –
SUMMER 2010

My grandfather remembered the double murder. *He was there that night,* he said.

Eighty-five and declining, Bud Fowler sat in his electric scooter with green oxygen tubing draped down the front of his chest. It snaked across the carpet of his living room, leading to a centralized oxygen system in the den. Emphysema and a small lump of cancer in one lung—a reminder of too many Kent cigarettes in his younger years. By this point, though, he could get cantankerous, but that was to be expected from a man who looked like a terminally ill version of Walter Matthau when he starred in a movie about grumpy old men.

His name was Delbert Earl Fowler, but he always went by Bud and, honestly, he looked like the kind of guy you'd call Bud. In his younger years, he was just an inch or so shy of six feet tall with a sturdy frame, a head of thick, wavy black hair, kind blue eyes, and a genuinely sweet smile. The fourth of five children, Bud was born into a dirt poor family in either late October or early November 1924. Since no one remembered the exact date, he chose his birthday: Halloween. The Fowlers were originally from Fort Dodge, Iowa, but for a brief time, the family lived in Anaheim, California. This is where Bud was born, but their time on the West Coast didn't pan out, and the Fowlers returned home to Iowa. His father was a skinny, dark-haired man who worked odd jobs to keep his family going: a horse and wagon milkman, a brick digger/cleaner/

reseller, a gypsum mill worker, even a stone layer under Roosevelt's Work Projects Administration. Often, Bud's father would take him and his brother out on the Des Moines River, looking for mussels and clams; local merchants would buy the shells to make buttons, which provided a little extra income for the family. Bud's mother was a heavy-set woman who, whenever she was away from Iowa, always became homesick for Fort Dodge. She died of acute pancreatitis on her 44th birthday. Bud was twelve. Despite his mother's wishes for him to be a minister, young Bud dreamed of one day being a Royal Canadian Mountie. Unfortunately, being an American nixed that plan, but he continued to hope that one day he'd be a police officer with a shiny badge, ready to save the day.

My grandfather was a simple, composed man governed by rules and family. A Navy seaman turned Army sergeant who became a sheriff's deputy. He fell in love with my grandmother, Elizabeth, or Libby as we called her, the first time he saw her and promptly married her six weeks later. His cars were immaculately kept. He obeyed the speed limit as if Moses himself had written it on those stone tablets. Black coffee and polished shoes; spearmint Lifesavers and Jesus. Bud was as straightforward as they come.

Now, as I sat close to him, notebook and pen in hand, all I could see was just how frail my grandfather had become. His chest was that of a bird, fragile and thin. Each inhalation pulled against his clavicles, heaving his lungs against his rib cage underneath his white Hanes t-shirt. His legs withered inside a pair of over-worn trousers. Veins like bulbous earthworms rested on the bones of his large hands. The heavy menthol of Vick's VapoRub overpowered his Aqua Velva aftershave. In the two years since my grandmother's death, his decline had progressed rapidly, producing a stark contrast to the stalwart man I'd known all my life.

My heart sank. *Would this conversation be too much for him?*

As I listened to him begin to recount the end of his military career and the beginning of his time as a lawman, I felt the past rushing up behind me. This house, a modest rancher built in 1963, sat at 501 Elberta

Avenue, right on the corners of Elberta and Allenwood Drive, near Salisbury University. A large magnolia tree graced the backyard with its fragrant blossoms and generous shade. Bud and Libby's house was neat and clean and always smelled like he had just brewed a fresh pot of coffee, a scent my sister and I remembered from spending time with them watching *Golden Girls* or *Wheel of Fortune* and eating more junk food than our mother would have ever allowed. The back bedroom, where we slept as little kids, had luxurious emerald green shag carpet, a magenta silk comforter on the bed, and a bookcase full of Danielle Steel paperback novels. Blanche Devereaux would have undoubtedly approved.

We were shifting the past into the present now. I quickly refocused. Bud had a plaque on the wall in honor of his service with the Wicomico County Sheriff's Department. He retired in October 1987, when I was eight years old. The realization dawned on me ... I knew very little about his time as a lawman. I had never thought to ask him about it until this day, when I had chosen the worst moment of his career as the entry point: the murders of Wicomico County Sheriff Samuel Graham and jailer Albert Kelly by a prisoner named Joseph James Bartholomey, Jr.

I scribbled my notes in blue ink as he recalled that Sunday night in December 1968. The old jail was located on the top floor of the Wicomico County Courthouse along with the apartment where the sheriff and his wife lived. Bud was working the desk downstairs in the basement of the courthouse when a trustee came to get him. (A trustee, he explained, was a low risk prisoner who had been given some privileges.) The trustee told Bud that the sheriff and the jailer had been shot and a prisoner was making his escape. They ran to the elevator, found it was jammed, but they made it to the jail as quick as they could. Bud found Sam. He couldn't see Albert. He touched Sam and knew he was gone. Dorothy Graham, the sheriff's wife, knelt down with Bud and they huddled together over his body.

My grandfather's eyes flickered. Ghosts had entered the room.

Bud said he stayed at the scene until late, getting home around 3:00 a.m. When he hadn't arrived by midnight, Libby grew worried and called in to the department. Another deputy told her what had happened, how a routine evening had turned into a nightmare. The bodies of Samuel Graham and Albert Kelly were taken to the hospital. A manhunt had begun. There was nothing left for Bud to do but go home ... and so he did, with the blood of the slain sheriff on his uniform.

Later, when I received the trial transcripts, I read that, ten months after the murders, my grandfather testified to leaving the scene around midnight and he testified to seeing Albert. I realized then that piecing together this story was going to be a challenge. Memory is a fragile thing. We forget. Our perspectives shift. After forty-two years, my grandfather had a few things wrong, but I believed the heart of his story. He liked Sam Graham, he said. He wasn't just his boss, but a man Bud respected. The murders of Graham and Kelly represented an inconceivable fracture of normalcy, a crisis when justice and fairness were lost and danger unmasked itself in the form of a scrawny young drifter with empty eyes and a stolen gun. My grandfather never expected such a thing to happen. Even after all this time, the events of that night in the jail still caused him consternation.

There are moments in a writer's life when they know a story will haunt them, compel them to put it onto the page ... stories that will not yield to time. This is just such a story for me. A sheriff and a jailer. A prisoner with a gun. A cold December night in 1968 when a jail once extolled as the safest and most impregnable in the entire state of Maryland became the scene of a grisly double murder, stunning the people of Salisbury and Wicomico County and leaving them in shock and inconsolable heartache only to be swallowed up by the devastating aftermath which inevitably follows such a tragedy.

As I stared at my grandfather, caught between the past and present, I had a feeling this story was going to haunt me until I wrote it. The only thing I did not know was just how much bigger it would become.

– TRIAL BY FIRE –
THE BIRTH OF WICOMICO COUNTY AND ITS COURTHOUSE

On Sunday, October 17th, 1886, S. Frank Toadvine fed and checked the horses in his livery stable near East Camden Street and Dock Street in Salisbury, Maryland. Seeing that everything was as it should be, he closed the stable door behind him. It was about 6:00 p.m., and the sun had already slipped below the horizon. From the south, a crisp autumn breeze rolled through town, carrying the familiar sound of the ringing bell at St. Peter's Episcopal Church welcoming parishioners to the evening service.

Autumn on the Delmarva Peninsula is a splendid affair. Cornflower blue skies replace the oppressive haze of those thunderous Mid-Atlantic summer days that threaten to roast alive every man and beast who dares to step out of the shade of the pines and maples. It is a time to take a deep breath and fill the lungs with air so clean and cool it might just cure what ails the soul. It is a time of change on Delmarva. Caught between the mighty Atlantic Ocean and the majestic Chesapeake Bay, this is a place of rich, rural landscapes carved by the timeless wisdom of the tides. Three of the oldest states in the union—Delaware, Maryland, and Virginia—are gathered here on this 170-or-so-mile stretch of flat land. The histories are as deep as the watery horizon is long; her people are salty and proud, God-fearing and loyal, and they are governed by and blessed with all four seasons of Mother Nature's grandeur. Icy, barren winters thaw into lovely springs of wild blossoms and dogwoods, followed by hellishly hot and humid summers, eventually giving way to the cool and delightful days of autumn.

But this would be no ordinary fall evening in Salisbury. These were moments of calm before an unimaginable chaos. Had S. Frank Toadvine been smoking in his stable? Had he carelessly tossed out a match or failed to stub out a lit cigarette or cigar? He would later deny any such wrongdoing, but within minutes, the entire stable was aflame and the fire began to lay claim to other nearby buildings.

The church bell at St. Peter's now rang at a feverish pace, transforming itself into a frantic alarm. The fire department responded quickly with their Silsby engine and reels of hose. Replacing the bucket brigade, this vital piece of new equipment was purchased after a July 1879 fire destroyed the lumber mill. The Silsby was to be the town's saving grace, but seven years of disuse had allowed rust to gather in the engine's machinery. Every frenzied effort made by the firemen to get the Silsby to pump water was fruitless. Townsfolk gathered around to help. As they toiled and failed, the stables were consumed in the full bloom of fire while the horses, hogs, and cattle trapped inside perished in a tortuous death.

Dock Street[1], now fully engulfed in flames, provided an easy avenue for the fire to overtake Main Street, and soon every building on both sides were burning. It did not confine itself there. The blaze was spreading with plague-like fury. Telegrams for help were sent to Crisfield, Maryland and Wilmington, Delaware. The horror came immediately: without the Silsby, the people of Salisbury realized there was nothing anyone could do to stop the fire. Help would never come in time to save them from the impending disaster. The inferno was far too intense for a bucket brigade. Barrels of whiskey and kegs of gunpowder exploded. The detonations were deafening. Shrieks rang out in the burning streets. The sky itself must have seemed alive with a blistering orange glow presiding over heavy blankets of smoke, choking and suffocating everything

---

1 Dock Street is now Market Street.

within its reach. Bedlam reigned. The guttural roar of the fire and its indiscriminate savagery were punctuated by the screams of horses and small children. For the people of Salisbury, it must have seemed like the world was ending in an unyielding maelstrom of fire and smoke and heat and wind. So great was the fire that people as far away as Talbot County could see its glow in the blackness of the October night sky.

For four hours, the fire ate and ate; it gorged itself on rooftops and lumberyards, general stores and residential homes. Even the church, whose bell first rang the alarm, burned. Gone were the newspaper offices, the opera house, a Catholic church, a Methodist church, the bank, and the hotels. The people of Salisbury fled their homes and businesses with only the clothing on their backs. Family heirlooms and life-savings: there were many who lost every single thing they had. Five hours after it started, the reinforcements began to arrive—first, Crisfield at 11 p.m. and then Wilmington at midnight. The town of Pocomoke also sent aid. One can only imagine the visions of horror that greeted them. In the midst of all this, someone had managed to fix the Silsby and it was pumping water. The firemen began working but it was too late. The damage was already done.

When dawn broke on Monday morning, the scene was apocalyptic. An entire city, once teeming with people and commerce, was nothing more than mounds of ash and blackened debris. Brick chimneys rose up like bony fingers from a shallow grave. Wisps of gray smoke drifted through the morning's light, carrying with them the stench of burned livestock and the cries of injured animals. Broken glass crunched underfoot. People in torn, mired clothing staggered through the city's charred remains looking for signs of life or any useful scrap or item that might have been spared. All said, twenty-two acres had been scorched and not a single business remained. The initial estimates placed damages anywhere from $800,000 to a million dollars.[2] The source of the

---

2 $800,000 to a million dollars in 1886 is roughly equivalent to $27 million to $34 million in 2025.

Unknown men pose in the rubble after the Great Fire of 1886 burned all of downtown Salisbury. The courthouse is visible to the right of the photograph.

Image courtesy of the Edward H. Nabb Research Center for Delmarva History and Culture, Salisbury University, Walter C. Thurston Jr. Photograph Collection

terrible, all-consuming fire of 1886 would forever remain a mystery. Astonishingly, no one died. As for S. Frank Toadvine, he lost his three horses, his livery stable, and even his home two streets away.

As the smoke began to clear, the townsfolk saw a wondrous, almost miraculous sight. Standing sentinel on the horizon was a single surviving structure: their stately courthouse. (Well, make that two, technically. The little jail—nicknamed the Red Bird—situated behind the courthouse also survived.) Despite catching on fire several times, the Wicomico County Courthouse was saved only by the Herculean efforts of a bucket brigade formed by townsfolk. Each time it caught, those flames were extinguished before any major damage was done. Some of the luckier people in town had managed to shove various bits of furniture inside the courthouse, hoping the mighty brick building would offer some protection. And much to the amazement of the bleary-eyed townspeople, it did.

The cinders died out, yet the specter of the inferno loomed over

The Wicomico County Courthouse after the Great Fire of 1886

Image courtesy of the Edward H. Nabb Research Center for Delmarva History and Culture, Salisbury University, Walter C. Thurston Jr. Photograph Collection

the people and the town. The Great Fire of 1886 was catastrophic. Two days later, the *Baltimore Sun* newspaper filled column after column, inch after inch, with a sobering chronicle of Salisbury's conflagration, which included firsthand witness accounts as well as a list of each and every home, business, and structure lost. To build again would require money and vision; it would require help and hard work. Friends and neighbors. Businessmen and politicians. The road ahead must have seemed insurmountable, but with winter approaching, the people of Salisbury cast their eyes upon their magnificent courthouse.

Completed in 1878, it was a marvel to behold: three stories of deep red, pressed brick with tall and slender windows capped by decorative white keystones and a clock tower on its northwestern corner. Horizontal lines of black brick offered an attractive accent that drew the onlooker's eye upward toward the gables of its dark gray mansard roof. The courthouse was the grand Victorian Gothic vision of a Pennsylvania architect named E. M. Butz, and it caused a stir around the peninsula. Before construction was even complete, a newspaper in Smyrna, Delaware, some seventy miles away, reported that the building would be the "handsomest structure of the kind on the Eastern Shore." And indeed it was, surely deserving of its prominence on Salisbury's growing skyline. It sat in the heart of the downtown district as the very pride and joy of the newly formed Wicomico County in the postbellum years of the Civil War.

Wiping the smoke and tears from their eyes, they knew this is where they would begin again.

• • •

Before this story of murder on Maryland's Eastern Shore can begin, the stage must be set and made ready. Soon, the lawmen and prisoners will make their entrances and exits in this tragic tale, but first, step back in time and the scene first opens on an empty plot of dirt and wild grasses. A quiet meadow of nothing. Then a man named Humphrey built a dam nearby for his mill and created a lake that washed up within a stone's throw from that inconspicuous spot. Now, people came and went, passing by with increasing regularity ... so much so that a popular tavern was built upon this lot. Stagecoaches rattled to a stop in front of the old clapboard inn. The large porch and brick chimneys like bookends must have made Byrd's Tavern a cozy and welcome sight for weary travelers, but nothing could make this place pleasant for the slaves sold here. In time, the tavern was torn down and the land was free again, but only for a moment. This would be the birthing ground of a grand courthouse, a monument to bear witness to the times and people of Wicomico County.

In 1865, the Civil War was over, its battles hard-fought and relegated to history, but the people remained divided. The scourge of slavery had been cast out but the deep-seated resentments and hostilities remained. The boil had only been reduced to a simmer. Maryland had remained in the Union, but many of her people, especially those on the Eastern Shore, were sympathetic to the Confederacy. In the 1860 election, the people of Somerset and Worcester Counties cast more than 5,500 votes ... only two were for Abraham Lincoln. It had been arduous work to save the country. On the Eastern Shore, that task fell to Unionist men like John W. Crisfield of Somerset County to keep Maryland in the hands of Honest Abe Lincoln.

In the little city of Salisbury, the people were divided by more than just their political ideologies. They were physically living on a dividing line between Somerset and Worcester Counties, the two lower counties of Maryland's Eastern Shore. To transact their business, they had to travel roughly thirty-six miles roundtrip to Snow Hill in Worcester County or roughly thirty miles roundtrip to Princess Anne in Somerset County. It was a headache and a hassle, and as their bustling port town grew, so did their need for independence. Talk began of forming a new county and, when Maryland amended its state constitution in 1867, the citizens of Salisbury got their wish. So named for the dark, brackish river that runs through it, Wicomico County was then carved out of portions of Somerset and Worcester Counties and Salisbury was made its center and seat. The word *Wicomico* is said to be a shortened form of the Indigenous word *Wighcocomico*,[3] which means "where houses are built." It is possible that when English settlers asked the Indigenous people where they had landed, they may have responded with *wik ahkamikw* to tell them, "This village is where we live." Such places have been lost to time as European settlers claimed more and more territory in the New World.

Being situated at the beautiful headwaters of the Wicomico River, Salisbury quickly went from a remote trading post, as it was in its earliest days, to a bustling town of the nineteenth century variety. Stables, shops, taverns, and homes popped up along its narrow and angled

---

3 The word "Wicomico" has several variations and/or interpretations. For a better understanding, I consulted with Keith Cunningham, a linguist from the Nanticoke Indian Tribe, as they have done extensive language work. Other sources say that it comes from *wiko mekee* meaning "a place where houses are built" and may have referred to a village or villages along the Wicomico River while additional sources say Wicomico can be roughly translated to "pleasant dwelling."

streets; commerce flourished. Wicomico County seemed destined to boom yet the immediate elation of the citizenry was tempered by the enormity of the tasks ahead of them. The new county was a blank slate without a single piece of chalk: no elected officials to make decisions, no money or credit to make necessary transactions, and no proper place to conduct government business. The first issue was solved in November 1867, when the first slate of representatives were voted in: judges, county commissioners, a clerk, a state's attorney, a surveyor, and a sheriff, who was a farmer from Quantico named William Howard. There was a great deal of work ahead of them. By the census of 1870, the county boasted a population of almost 16,000 souls, and they needed a place to handle the county's affairs.

What they needed was a courthouse.

Five prominent men came together and each committed $5,000[4] for the building of a majestic courthouse worthy of the people of Wicomico County. But only one man actually made good on his promise and the fundraising slowed considerably. In the meanwhile, the elected officials used the second floor of a general store as their town hall; the first floor was reserved for groceries and hardware sales. For their courtroom, they used the second floor of a drug store. Prisoners were sent to Princess Anne. Then, in 1874 or 1875,[5] the county commissioners purchased the site on which the old Byrd's Tavern sat to build the new courthouse and a new jail. The inn's namesake, John Byrd, was rumored to have been killed by a Union soldier and that the tavern had a sinister past as a slave market where Black men, women, and children were held in cages in the basement and in the rear of the establishment until they were sold or traded. The tavern was completely torn down and cleared away to make room for the courthouse and a jail. Construction began on the

---

4 $5,000 in 1867 is roughly equivalent to $108,000 in 2025.

5 Some sources say the land was purchased in 1874 while other sources offer that a levy and/or legislation was passed in 1874 and the site was actually purchased in 1875.

resplendent courthouse: the first floor held offices for the clerk and register of wills while the courtroom was located on the second floor.

By 1878, the people of Wicomico County had all the trappings of a real county: they had elected officials, money in the bank, and the most beautiful courthouse for miles. They had railroads and newspapers; streetlights in Salisbury were powered by oil and gasoline. Steamboats ran up and down the meandering waters of the river. Indeed, Wicomico County was a growing and prosperous place to live and work.

• • •

Two years after its completion, the Wicomico County Courthouse had a famous visitor.

On the evening of February 24th, 1880, Frederick Douglass visited Salisbury for a lecture at the courthouse as part of a fundraiser for a local Black church known as the John Wesley Methodist Episcopal Church. This church was special to the Black community—it was one of the oldest on the shore, dating back to 1837. Black congregations had been gathering there in Salisbury since the original structure of red painted pine slabs was built in 1838. The fundraiser for which Douglass was in attendance was to help garner enough funds to expand the church's footprint.[6]

Tickets for his speech were sold in advance at a price of fifty cents.[7] Douglass, then a United States Marshal for the District of Columbia, had been in Baltimore visiting Dr. Henry J. Brown, an outspoken and courageous leader in post-Civil War political arena about Black liberation and rights; Brown's voice was so important that he was appointed to a committee to speak at the 1867 Maryland Constitutional Convention, the same one that birthed Wicomico County. When Frederick Douglass arrived in Salisbury, he was hosted by Solomon T. Huston, who was to

---

6 The expanded church is today the Chipman Cultural Center.

7 $0.50 in 1880 is roughly equivalent to $16 in 2025.

Salisbury as Dr. Henry Brown was to Baltimore. Solomon Huston was a man of wealth and means and fervently spoke out for the Black citizens of the area, leading the charge for religious, educational, and political causes. One can imagine Douglass found men of similar minds in Dr. Henry J. Brown and Solomon T. Huston.

Frederick Douglass, in his early sixties with white hair blending into his gray-white beard, was escorted to the courthouse by the Grand United Order of Odd Fellows where, at 8:00 p.m., he gave a profound and well-documented speech called "Self-Made Men." Douglass was born into slavery in Talbot County on Maryland's Eastern Shore, but now he stood before this racially mixed audience as a nationally recognized orator and author, a United States Marshal, and a leading mind in the fight for Black equality. He spoke in the courthouse for two hours to the citizens of Salisbury, who assembled themselves in segregated areas across the aisle from one another. Among his many points, Douglass argued the only road to individual success is work and that there could be no substitute; whether a preacher, a plowman, or a professor, a man's greatness was dependent on his own orderly mind, upright morals, and spirit of determination as well as the support of his community and fellow man; and that given a level playing field, the Black community could and would thrive in this reunited America. He quoted Shakespeare, Paul Laurence Dunbar, Robert Burns, and Thomas Jefferson, and his words rang out in marvelous fashion through the halls of the Wicomico County Courthouse.

His speech was both praised and criticized by the *Salisbury News and Advertiser*. On February 28th, 1880, an unnamed reporter wrote of Douglass: "He talked slow and distinct, and with a clear voice, fine articulation ... His points were well taken and appropriately applied, occasionally breaking out in strains of eloquent allusions to men and events. We heartily agree with most of his points taken, while we most emphatically disagree with him on one point upon which he dwelt with some degree of force and feeling. That was the justification of a feeling of animosity in the hearts of negroes against their former owners for the barbarism and cruelties of slavery, for we here undertake to say, and challenge successful contradiction, that the four millions [sic] of slaves in the United States at the date of the emancipation proclamation [sic] were the most intelligent, most happy, most healthy and the best looking four millions of negros [sic] under the canopy of heaven."

Curiously, although the headline for the reporter's article was "Marshal Douglass' Lecture," only eight and a half sentences of the twenty-five he wrote concerned the actual lecture or Frederick Douglass himself. The remaining words were a longwinded defense of slavery and finger-pointing at the North and the Yankees, proof of those ever-present and still simmering Confederate resentments that encumbered progress for the freed Black population ... which was one of the very points Frederick Douglass was trying to make.

That evening would prove to be a historic moment for Salisbury and its grand courthouse, one that would be noted for decades to come.

● ● ●

In the late 1870s, while the county courthouse and jail were under conversation and construction, the town leaders were using a temporary jail. This two-room structure was built in 1873 over a wharf on the Wicomico River. That shed of a jail cost the town $300[8] and, as one could imagine, it was not ideal.

The new two-story red brick jail opened in 1877 and was located a few hundred feet to the east of the stately courthouse. Beyond that was Humphrey's Lake, which would later be filled in permanently. Square, squat, and flat-faced, the Red Bird (as it came to be known) had six narrow windows across the front and at least four on each of the other sides. A white, octagonal cupola had been plunked down on the roof. On the south side, there were quarters for the sheriff and his family; the

---

8 $300 in 1873 is roughly equivalent to $8,000 in 2025.

north side of the jail and the second floor was for prisoners. While the notion of a sheriff living in the same building as the jail may seem outlandish by today's standards, this was a fairly common if not standard practice of the time. These lodgings were often considered a part of their compensation. Many jails across the Delmarva Peninsula housed both prisoners and the sheriff (or warden) and his family. The *Star-Democrat*, a newspaper out of Easton, Maryland, made a lonely notation on August 20th, 1878: "Salisbury jail has but one prisoner." But more than lonely, the Red Bird was a tough place to be, as many a prisoner would learn.

In 1923, a prison inspector named Joseph F. Fishman published a fiery book titled *Crucibles of Crime: The Shocking Story of the American Jail*. This 300-page tome included appalling descriptions as Fishman lamented emphatically and in thunderously bold and often overwrought prose about prisoner conditions and treatment. The Red Bird did not escape his castigatory pen: "It consists of four or five stone vaults on the second floor of the sheriff's home. The largest of these is about fourteen by ten or twelve, and the others ten by ten or ten by eight. The sheriff's wife said that sometimes there are so many prisoners that it is necessary to crowd 16 and 18 men into one of these chambers. There are no special quarters for women or children. They often have women prisoners ... The women are simply put into any of the vacant cells. Not only are there no bathing facilities, but there is no water at all on the floor, and the prisoners simply wallow in filth. There is the usual cold, dirt, vermin and darkness. There are no cots. The prisoners sleep on foul mattresses on the floor. Two or three blankets are in each cells [sic] and when there are more prisoners than blankets the excess just do without regardless of what the weather may be. What bitter fights must must [sic] rage at these times it is easy to imagine."

While his description of the Red Bird is bleak, it was also common. Fishman found these conditions from Alaska to South Carolina, from Texas to New York ... from sea to shining sea. He recalled a trip to Sing Sing prison in New York in January 1922 where it was so cold he could

The Red Bird

Image courtesy of the Edward H. Nabb Research Center for Delmarva History and Culture, Salisbury University Walter C. Thurston Jr. Photograph Collection

see his breath as he talked. In Cleveland, jail officials spent $1,200[9] on bed bug spray and the combination of human stench and pesticide made the air unbreathable. Arizona jails did not separate prisoners with tuberculosis from otherwise healthy prisoners. A prisoner sitting in a jail in Princeton, West Virginia, had the worst case of syphilis Fishman had ever seen: the man's tongue was gone and most of his mouth was nearly missing as well, yet he shared a single drinking glass with the other inmates. In Key West, prisoners who need to relieve themselves shared iron buckets and emptied them each morning. Several girls in a Gainesville, Georgia jail were entirely naked in their cells save for a thin slip that hung around their waists. The jailer and anyone from the town could wander by their cells for a look. Fishman believed every pig, horse, and cow had better living quarters than any sad soul who found himself in the jail in Waco, Texas.

Maryland was the only state to receive its own chapter in Fishman's book and the portrait he painted was ghastly. The jail in Chestertown was described as having an inch of watery filth on the floor on which the prisoners slept. There were no cots or beds, just dirty mattresses, deplorable isles in a lake of sludge of unknown origins. There was no light in the cells. In Cecil County, women were left in windowless stone vaults, which froze in winter and roasted in summer. When Fishman asked the Queen Anne's County sheriff about why there were no bathing facilities

9 $1,200 in 1922 is roughly equivalent to $23,000 in 2025.

in the jail, he was told there was no need—prisoners rarely stayed for more than two to three months. In a jail in Hagerstown, prisoners slept on crossed iron slats with a county-issued blanket as their only source of bedding material. Fishman was led by a prisoner with a candle down a dark corridor in the Westminster jail to get a look at the bathroom which was an unlit room containing two toilets and several buckets of human waste. Prisoners there slept directly on iron cots or the concrete floor. In every jail, vermin and bugs were as plentiful as the foul odors, the bitter cold or the intolerable heat, and the never-ending darkness.

At the Red Bird, waiting for a sentence became a sentence of its own and some prisoners opted to take matters into their own hands. One of the first documented escapes from the Red Bird happened on May 28th, 1894. The *Baltimore Sun* reported that a prisoner who had been arrested for robbery escaped by sawing through the bars on his cell. Another prisoner in the same cell decided to stay.

Year after year, prisoners succeeded in breaking out of the Red Bird. They sawed at the bars in the windows. They used blankets knotted together to shimmy down from the second floor to freedom. They removed bricks. They fought their jailers and took advantage of padlocks being left undone. Once in a while, their attempts were thwarted, often by luck alone, but the Red Bird was no fortress. On a rare occasion, prisoners would resort to a different sort of escape plan: in June 1924, a man from Louisiana who was being held for drunk and disorderly conduct, was found hanging from a blanket tied to a heating pipe. The jailer pulled him down and the man survived. His story was a sad one: he had saved $58[10] dollars from picking berries and potatoes only to have it stolen from him after he got drunk. Of his suicide attempt, he told a judge that he tried to take his life because he felt like a failure and a disgrace to his wife and children. The judge dismissed the case.

The constant jailbreaks frustrated county officials and it was a problem without an immediate solution. Reporting on one of the escapes,

---

10 $58 in 1924 is roughly equivalent to $1,100 in 2025.

the *Salisbury Times* noted, "County authorities declare it is virtually impossible to prevent a well-planned break unless an all-night watch is maintained." In one case, the exasperation lead to the indictment of Wicomico County Sheriff Ralph C. Duffy and his turnkey because a notorious bootlegger simply walked out of the Red Bird one August night in 1928. The charges were dropped, but the sting of embarrassment persisted, especially when the bootlegger reappeared a year later to pay his fines.

The Red Bird was a damned sieve. And everyone knew it.

Grand juries in Wicomico County had repeatedly recognized it was no longer suitable but nothing had been done, or could be done, to correct the situation. One grand jury in 1924 suggested the Red Bird be torn down entirely to make room for a better building. In 1929, a state jail inspector urged rebuilding or overhauling the Salisbury jail because it was in such terrible condition. In 1932, another inspector submitted a report to Maryland Governor Albert C. Ritchie in which the Red Bird was deemed to be in "very bad" condition: "filled to capacity, there being eight White men in one room, a colored woman in another, and nine colored men in the other two rooms. In order to accommodate this many, it is necessary to use several sets of double-deck beds in each room. This shuts out a considerable amount of light and ventilation and makes them more difficult to keep clean." The Red Bird was by no means alone in that assessment: every jail on Maryland's Eastern Shore was listed as either "very bad" or "bad." That report served to further highlight the desperate need for a new jail, a call that had been echoed for nearly a decade and a call that would finally be answered in 1935 by President Franklin D. Roosevelt when the Wicomico County Courthouse would see major renovations that also included the demolition of the Red Bird.

Times were changing.

– SAMUEL ADAMS GRAHAM –
ORPHAN, RAILROAD MAN, AND CHIEF DEPUTY

Resting along the banks of the Quantico Creek, an offshoot of the Nanticoke River in western Wicomico County, there is a village known as Quantico. It is a place like many others on Maryland's Eastern Shore, where landscape and history come together to tell you old, old stories. Giant black walnut trees and full crepe myrtles shade the maintained red brick sidewalks. The homes are reminiscent of earlier colonial and salt box style or the modest farmhouse familiar to the Eastern Shore. On warm summer evenings, the buzzing of crickets and katydids coalesce into a natural rhythmic backdrop while the well-tended graveyard at St. Philip's Episcopal Church holds a solemn silence. Quiet and lovely. The serpentine Quantico Creek runs nearby and may be the source of the town's name, derived from the Indigenous words meaning "long river." Another possible derivation is that this place was at the "limit" or "as far as" the "evergreen trees" would "extend."[1]

This hamlet is a window into time: once an outpost during the Revolutionary War, it was also home to one of the earliest post offices, dating back to January 1808. When Methodists needed refuge, they found it in a log cabin meeting house built in 1784 in Quantico. During the Civil War, sentiments there ran with the Confederacy as

---

1 Again, I consulted with Keith Cunningham, a linguist from the Nanticoke Indian Tribe, for this word. Other sources say that it means "the dancing place" but that interpretation comes from a Moravian missionary and may not be accurate based on current etymological studies. Cunningham states most names are "prosaic and practical, denoting some feature of the geography that would be important for someone navigating or making their livelihood from it to know."

slavery played a major role in the town's farming and milling enterprises. When White townsfolk burned down a Black church, a band of encamped federal troops made them rebuild it. As a new century dawned on Quantico, visitors refreshed themselves at the hotel, renowned for its meals and hospitality. Men of distinction, born and reared near the creek banks, went on to become judges, doctors, a state senator, and the first duly elected sheriff of Wicomico County.

In the early twentieth century, the town grocer was George W. Graham. Born in May 1868,[2] he was one of six children born to Leah and John Tubman Graham. He was six years old when his father died in early 1874. George was accustomed to the hard labor of rural living: by the age of twelve, he was working as a farmhand. By his early 30s, he attained a managerial position at a local mill. Through the strength of his hands and back, he had been prosperous enough to purchase his own home on Main Street where, in 1900, he lived with his two sisters and a brother-in-law. By the 1910 census, 42-year-old George Graham had seen a few life changes: he was now the town grocer and he was married to a woman named Ella, who was six years his junior. They alone lived in his home on Main Street.

The couple did not remain childless, however. On January 15th, 1920, the census was taken in Quantico and a new addition was listed in George's household: an adopted son by the name of Samuel Adams Graham. (His name may have been a nod to Samuel Adams of Massachusetts, one of the founding fathers of America and a signer of the Declaration of Independence.) Samuel Adams Graham was born on November 30th, 1906[3] in Easton, Maryland, but little else is known about his childhood. He remained with the Grahams into his early 20s when he was working as a hauler for a trucking company.

As a man, Sam Graham cut an imposing figure at nearly six feet tall and weighing in at a solid 230 pounds with broad shoulders, a barrel of

---

2 The exact year of his birth is unknown as several records show 1868, 1869, and 1870.

3 Some resources say 1907 but his gravestone says 1906.

Samuel Adams Graham

Image courtesy of the Edward H. Nabb
Research Center for Delmarva History and
Culture, Salisbury University,
Mel Toadvine Collection

a chest, and a noticeable belly gathering around his waistline. He had large brown eyes and brown hair (when he had it) as well as a ruddy complexion. Yet his face was inherently kind. Perhaps the impression came from the roundness of his cheeks and chin and the ever-present hint of smile on his lips. As big as a bear and as gentle as a kitten, that was Sam Graham.

The year of 1940 saw two important life events for him. First, on May 11th, 1940, the *Salisbury Times* ran an advertisement on the opening of the Commercial Personal Loan Company where it was announced that Sam would act as the manager of the branch located at 316 E. Main Street. The ad, which invited customers to try their friendly service, offered auto loans secured in just five minutes without the need for a co-signer. Then, three months later, on August 15th, 1940, Sam Graham, now thirty-four, settled down and got married.

• • •

Less than five miles away from the leafy hamlet of Quantico lies the small town of Hebron. In 1890, there was nothing there except a single home and one store until the railroad came through and soon it was growing. The volunteer fire company began hosting a carnival in 1926, and folks from around the county have been walking the lively festival grounds on summer nights while eating fried oyster sandwiches ever since.

There were three Holliday brothers—Linwood, George, and Joshua—and all were well-known merchants in their respective communities. Linwood worked in Whitehaven on the Wicomico River while George and Joshua sold their goods in Hebron.

Joshua Lee Holliday married Edith Dashiell and they had two daughters, Dorothy and Ethel. Dorothy Lee Holliday was born on September 14th, 1909 and two years later came Ethel Dashiell Holliday. The family was prosperous. Edith's name was regularly seen in the newspaper, which tracked all the comings and goings in the neighborhood. Joshua ran ads promoting his shop.

Both Joshua and Edith had an 8th grade education, and perhaps this might have inspired the career paths of Dorothy and Ethel as both women went to college and became teachers. Although Ethel started out as a school teacher, she later became a dietitian at Peninsula General Hospital, where instead of teaching children their three Rs, she taught folks how to eat right and balance their meals. Meanwhile, Dorothy graduated from Western Maryland College[4] and began working as a history teacher in August 1932 at Wicomico High School, which was situated close to the Salisbury Municipal Park. Then, schools were segregated by race and Wicomico High was for the White students while the Black students attended Salisbury High School. (Interestingly, the land on which Wicomico High School sat once belonged to Solomon T. Huston, the Salisbury friend of Frederick Douglass.) She put in roughly thirty hours a week and earned a yearly wage of $1,363.00.[5] Dorothy Holliday was active within the school. One newspaper article noted her as the treasurer of the high school's PTA. Although she was a single

---

4 Western Maryland College is now McDaniel College. The name was changed in 2002.

5 $1,363 in 1932 is roughly equivalent to $31,800 in 2025.

*Dorothy Holliday Graham
in the 1942 Wicomico High School yearbook*

Image courtesy of the Edward H. Nabb Research Center for Delmarva History and Culture, Salisbury University

woman, she wasn't a shut-in. She gave her time and talents to a local women's charity club and helped plan several Western Maryland alumni gatherings.

According to the 1940 census in Hebron, which took place prior to their weddings, both Dorothy and her sister were teachers approaching their 30s and living at home with their parents. This may have been a bit unusual in a time when women were expected to marry early, but nonetheless, they avoided the dreaded "old maid" label when they found their matches. Ethel was first, marrying a man named Robert Jackson, who was a deputy sheriff and warden of the jail in Princess Anne, in July 1940. Dorothy was her maid of honor; her own wedding just weeks away.

How and when Dorothy and Samuel Graham met is unknown. One possibility is that the match was made through friends, specifically a young attorney named William W. Travers, and his wife, Maude Larmore Heath, who was also a teacher. When William and Maude married at 6:00 a.m. on Thursday, June 28th, 1934, the only two people attending the early morning ceremony other than the minister were Dorothy Holliday and Samuel Graham. By the time of the Travers' wedding, Dorothy and Maude were already friends. They both had attended Western Maryland College and became teachers in the same county. The society papers noted that they played bridge together with other local ladies and those same gentle gossip columns revealed that both William and Samuel were in attendance at mixed functions. The Travers' wedding announcement was revealed in a coy headline on the front page of the *Salisbury Times*: "W.W. Travers, Attorney, And Miss Heath Are

Wedded; Guarded Plans From Friends." All their friends, that is, except for Dorothy and Sam who had breakfast with the newlyweds before the couple motored off to New England to celebrate their marital bliss.

On Thursday, August 15th, 1940, Sam Graham and Dorothy Holliday married at her parents' home in Hebron. The wedding took place at 2:00 p.m. with Ethel standing as her matron of honor and William Travers as his best man. After the wedding, they took a page from the Traverses and decided to honeymoon their way through New England. Afterward, they made their home at 203 Newton Street in Salisbury and settled into the routine of everyday life.

Dorothy Graham continued to teach at Wicomico High School. Her subject was World History and U.S. History and she held her students to a high standard ... so high that some students prayed they wouldn't be assigned to her class. One student referred to her as being "hard-nosed" for her strict and pragmatic way of moving through her course material. Others remembered her no-nonsense style of dealing with tomfoolery, to the point that many didn't even try any shenanigans in her classroom. Another student recalled the sound of her high heels clicking on the hallway floors, hoping she wasn't coming for them. Serious and focused, Mrs. Graham was no pushover. If opposites attract, then perhaps that might have been the secret to their marriage: she was tough and her husband was tenderhearted.

Sam's career as the manager of the Commercial Personal Loan Company was short-lived. By November 22nd, 1941, he was the manager of the West End Service Station, a job that carried him until he began working for the Pennsylvania Railroad in 1942. His size and strength surely came in handy during his years working with the railroad.[6]

The two couples, the Traverses and the Grahams, experienced a terrible tragedy in late November 1947 when Maude Travers died at age

---

6 His exact job is unclear. Different sources state his job was either a freight brakeman, a fireman, and even an engineer. It is possible he may have had more than one duty with the railroad.

thirty-eight. She had had cranial surgery the previous month at Johns Hopkins Hospital in Baltimore, but continued to suffer from severe headaches. It was a crushing blow for the foursome. The two couples were showing all the signs of upward social mobility.

Prior to her death, Maude Travers had been involved in a number of women's groups and charitable societies as well as an alumni group for Western Maryland College while William Travers was proving that he could advance through the ranks of the state's political machine. He had been a city solicitor, a Maryland State Senator, and just six months before her death, the governor appointed him as the Maryland State Tax Commissioner. In the years to come, William Travers would be named a judge in Wicomico County's circuit court system.

The Grahams were also headed up the county's social ladder, albeit a little slower than the Traverses. After 1942, the Grahams moved from Salisbury to Dorothy's hometown of Hebron. She was noted in the local paper for entertaining guests at nice dinners and large picnics; she hosted card parties at their home to raise funds for Peninsula General Hospital; and she held meetings for the Young Ladies Bible Class and the Women's Society of Christian Services at Nelsons Memorial Church, a Methodist church in Hebron. At Wicomico High School, Dorothy—now a ten-year-veteran of the classroom—was a strict yet respected teacher known for being rigorous about the course material. Many of her students were on the receiving end of one of her favorite sayings: "A word to the wise is sufficient." And God help the unwise student. Or a young lady with a skirt too short. Some students tried to avoid her gaze altogether. Despite her outwardly stern manner, she seemed to genuinely care for her students and offered to help them and mentor them along their high school years. She even lent a hand when the teens decided to perform an operetta.

During this time, from 1943 until 1949, it is likely that Sam's job with the railroad took him to Baltimore regularly, possibly even requiring him to live there. This shouldn't be taken as a sign of an unhappy marriage as they continued to see each other on weekends and took trips to Canada and the Poconos. Their life together returned to a more normal routine when Sam left the Pennsylvania Railroad and took a new job in Salisbury.

On September 8th, 1949, Samuel Graham was sworn in as the chief deputy sheriff for the Wicomico County Sheriff's Department. He took his oath in the historic courthouse, which was administered by Circuit Court Clerk Joseph W. T. Smith. It was quite a step for Sam, walking right into the second most powerful position within the department. When he was sworn in, the sheriff of Wicomico County was Jesse M. Pollitt, a friend of Sam's. While this sounds like preferential treatment, this was not an uncommon practice. Becoming deputized in this era was less about law enforcement and more about just applying for the job. There was no mandated training for deputies or sheriffs. Some men had a military background to help them prepare for and understand the role, but many men who became deputies had little to no law enforcement experience. All one needed to do was ask the sheriff. When Sam was hired, his annual pay was listed as $2,000.00.[7] It was a modest salary for a public servant's job.

· · ·

Chief Deputy Sam Graham was now a full-time member of the Wicomico County Sheriff's Department, which operated out of the county courthouse. But it wasn't just the old Gothic building that survived the Great Fire of 1886 anymore.

In 1935, President Franklin D. Roosevelt announced his New Deal program called the WPA or the Works Progress Administration.[8] The aim was to get unemployed folks back to work in the wake of the Great Depression by carrying out important projects like the construction of

---

7 $2,000 in 1949 is roughly equivalent to $27,000 in 2025.

8 It was later renamed the Work Projects Administration.

A photograph of the Wicomico County Courthouse as it appeared before the 1936 annex construction.

Image courtesy of the
Edward H. Nabb Research Center
for Delmarva History and Culture,
Salisbury University,
Walter C. Thurston Jr.
Photograph Collection

municipal buildings, roads, and bridges and beautification campaigns like painting murals and creating city parks and playgrounds. The first injection of nearly $5 billion dollars[9] launched initiatives all over the country, and Wicomico County stepped up to claim its slice of the New Deal pie.

By late March 1936, an architect's rendering of the proposed courthouse addition was prominently displayed in the window of White and Leonard, a well-established office supply store located at the corner of West Main and St. Peter's Streets. The posting of the architect's drawing was an opportunity for folks from all over to take in the impressive Art Deco vision that was to come. The plan included keeping the original Gothic courthouse from 1878 while adding on a massive annex containing three floors and a basement, which was partly at street level. The top level of the new building would be the new "penthouse prison" as well as a separate apartment for the county sheriff. One thing was clear: the county government had long outgrown the old courthouse.

Once construction began, the Red Bird was torn down and the

---

9 $5 billion dollars in 1935 is roughly equivalent to $116 billion dollars in 2025. For a modern perspective, it is on par with President Biden's Bipartisan Infrastructure Bill of 2022.

Looking west at the back of the old courthouse as construction was underway on the new annex. The Wicomico Hotel is visible on the left.

Image courtesy of the Edward H. Nabb Research Center for
Delmarva History and Culture, Salisbury University

Another view of the back of the old courthouse as construction was underway on the new annex.

Image courtesy of the Edward H. Nabb Research Center
for Delmarva History and Culture, Salisbury University

prisoners were moved to a building on Water Street.[10] It had once been the grand Orient Hotel, hosting the likes of President Grover Cleveland and a cache of dignitaries, but since the turn of the twentieth century, the building had changed hands a few times. It had been a boarding house, a fruit store, an antique shop, and even a private school. By the time the Red Bird's prisoners arrived, the old Orient Hotel was an undertaker's establishment.

On September 3rd, 1936, the superintendent of construction told the *Salisbury Times* that work was being rushed on the top floor in order to get the prisoners moved in. The cell blocks were being erected and riveting was to begin within days. The end of the article had an interesting note: "The new jail upon completion will be practically escape-proof. Built-in precautions to prevent passage of weapons to prisoners by visitors are provided, and a corridor will separate the cells from the windows."

Work continued through the end of 1936, with a few changes being made to the sheriff's quarters. The new addition was abuzz: workers were laying and sanding hardwood floors and the Wicomico County Bar Association was working on filling two rooms on the second floor of the courthouse with a massive law library. By mid-January 1937, county personnel had already begun to move into their new offices; and finally, three weeks later, the new Wicomico County Jail was ready to house the prisoners and the sheriff.

Upon its completion, the "penthouse prison" (as it would be called) was the crown jewel in Maryland's penal system. It was lauded as "escape-proof," "impregnable," "ultra-modern," and "state of the art." The *Salisbury Times* proclaimed: "No other county jail in the state can compare with it. Only the new cell blocks in the House of Correction are on [sic] this latest type." With the ability to house eighty to ninety inmates with room for more, the penthouse prison touted bulletproof glass, thick steel doors, and metal bars so strong not even one hundred

---

10 Water Street later became Calvert Street.

Workers build the new addition to the courthouse.

Image courtesy of the Edward H. Nabb Research Center for Delmarva History and Culture, Salisbury University, Walter C. Thurston Jr. Photograph Collection

hack saws could dent them. The jail's design ensured that segregation by race and sex was achieved; there were four cell blocks to house up to 32 "Colored" men, 12 "Colored" women, 28 White men, and 17 White women.[11] Stationary tables and chairs, beds, and benches provided the furnishings for prisoners. Their cells were located inside large steel cages and the cell doors were all controlled by a complex lever system. Slots in the cell doors were used for passing food trays in and out. On scheduled days, visitors sat behind bulletproof glass inside steel booths resembling a phone booth. Because the jail was located on the top floor, it could only be accessed by an elevator or an unmarked back stairwell near the second floor courtrooms.

---

11 In the 1930s, a Black person was more than four times more likely to be incarcerated than a White person. The breakdown of the segregated units could reflect this disparity.

A vintage postcard reveals the finished work of combining the original courthouse with the new addition. This view is looking west on Main Street. The top floor was the penthouse prison and sheriff's quarters while the door on the street level led to the sheriff's department.

Image courtesy of the Edward H. Nabb Research Center for Delmarva History and Culture, Salisbury University, Walter C. Thurston Jr. Photograph Collection

The sheriff had quarters on the same floor. The apartment was surprisingly spacious with a large kitchen, a pantry, a living room, a dining room, two bedrooms, and two storage areas. The sheriff's quarters straddled the old Gothic courthouse and the new; the old grand jury room had been repurposed into the new design. The final cost of the project—from the basement where the sheriff's deputies manned the desk to the new courtrooms to the county offices to the sheriff's apartment and the penthouse prison—was $200,000.00.[12]

The new courthouse was dedicated on Saturday, February 27th, 1937. Hundreds of people from Delmarva came to take a look and roam the halls and courtrooms. In the new Peoples Court Room, they were treated to stunning visuals: hardwood maple floors, walls and ceilings of painted plaster adorned with indirect lighting, a judge's bench made of

---

12 $200,000 in 1937 is roughly equivalent to $4.4 million in 2025.

beautifully stained wood, walls of walnut paneling, and Venetian blinds on the windows. It must have been a winsome scene to behold.

The ceremony kicked off with an invocation by the pastor of Allen Memorial Baptist Church. Three influential men of Maryland gave remarks: United States Senator George L. Radcliffe, United States Representative T. Alan Goldsborough, and State Comptroller William S. Gordy, Jr. The head of Maryland's Public Works Administration presented the building to Circuit Court Chief Judge Benjamin A. Johnson who had also been present at the cornerstone ceremony almost a year earlier. The ceremony was closed by a minister from Asbury Methodist Episcopal Church. It was a day of handshaking and wonderment as the citizenry of Delmarva walked the penthouse prison's freshly painted hallways, eyeballing every inch of the metal bars, bullet-proof glass, and concrete floors. The newspapers do not mention whether or not the prisoners were in their cells when the throngs of onlookers passed through, but it is entirely possible they may have been.

• • •

And so, this complex, from the old to the new, was the Wicomico County Courthouse where Chief Deputy Samuel Graham would report for duty and assist Sheriff Jesse Pollitt to the best of his abilities. Yet, there is one curious detail in that September 1949 *Salisbury Times* article announcing his new job. It stated that Samuel Graham was replacing Donald A. Parks, the current chief deputy of Wicomico County.[13]

Born in 1898 on Holland Island in Dorchester County, Parks was a World War I veteran and served with the 29th Division of the United States Army. Out of the military, he returned to the Eastern Shore of Maryland, where he worked for both the Wicomico County Sheriff's

---

13 His obituary in May 1973 lists his last name as "Parke." This is likely an error as his relatives are listed as "Parks."

Department as well as the Poplar Hill Correctional Camp where he was a guard. He was a family man with a wife and son, likely making their home in Bivalve, a waterside neighborhood on the Nanticoke River along the westernmost edge of the county. By the age of 33, Donald Parks was a sheriff's deputy: the earliest mention of him as such comes in an October 19th, 1931 article in the *Salisbury Times* in which he and another deputy along with several Prohibition agents got into a tussle with a bootlegger from Quantico.

Why is his name important? Because there have been four men murdered at the Wicomico County Courthouse and Donald A. Parks was connected to one of them.

– THE FIRST TWO MURDERS AT THE COURTHOUSE –

THE LYNCHINGS OF MATTHEW WILLIAMS AND GARFIELD KING

On December 4th, 1931, Matthew Williams, a young Black man from Isabella Street, arrived at the office of his boss, Daniel J. Elliott, around 2:00 p.m. Williams had worked for about eight years at the D.J. Elliott Crate and Basket[1] company located near 328 Lake Street in Salisbury. Born in Norfolk, Virginia, on February 8th, 1908, he had lost both parents by the time he was five years old. Matthew and his older sister were sent to live with their maternal grandmother in Salisbury. He attended school but dropped out to help his grandmother pay the household bills.

When Matthew Williams entered the office, Daniel J. Elliott was on the phone with another Salisbury businessman. Elliott was a wealthy man, having made his money in milling, lumber, canning, and box/crate manufacturing, and he was involved in a number of civic organizations. That winter of 1931, he was in his mid-sixties with a wife, two daughters, and a son. What exactly happened next is unknown as there were no eye witnesses, however, as soon as it happened, two narratives emerged about the events of that awful afternoon. One paints Williams as a murderer, the other as a victim.

---

1 The company name appears in various different ways. I used D.J. Elliott Crate and Basket as that is how his company name appeared in *Salisbury Times* advertisements prior to the events of 1931.

In the first, Williams went into his boss's office to discuss his low wages and the conversation turned into an altercation in which Matthew Williams shot Daniel Elliott and then turned the gun on himself. Daniel's son, James, was nearby and heard the gunshots. He found his father dead and Williams wounded. James Elliott said he ran for help, at which time, Williams got up and ran but James pursued him.

In the second, Williams went into his boss's office to discuss a loan he had made to Daniel's son, James. Matthew Williams was concerned that he had not been repaid and was likely asking for his boss's help with repayment. Williams was known as a frugal person and was said to have offered money-saving advice to other employees. This version of events goes on to say that James discovered his father and Williams together in the office, and either in panic or in anger, shot both men. Then, as Williams ran wounded from the office, James gave chase.

Shot and barely conscious, Matthew Williams was taken to Peninsula General Hospital where he was put into a straightjacket and placed in the "Negro Ward." In short order, there were a number of people surrounding Matthew Williams in his hospital bed including Wicomico County Sheriff G. Murray Phillips, Chief Deputy Donald A. Parks, Wicomico County State's Attorney Levin C. Bailey, Peninsula General Hospital physician Dr. Randolph Nock, and nurse superintendent Helen Wise. This is where Sheriff G. Murray Phillips allegedly took a confession from Matthew Williams.

According to Sheriff Phillips, he asked Matthew Williams about the murder of Daniel Elliott, and Williams said he had killed his former boss because he was angry about his pay. When he drifted into a state of unconsciousness, Dr. Nock brought him around by sticking a sharp instrument into his already injured face. This roused Williams who allegedly stated, "You better let me alone[.] I am going to die anyhow." The confession was accepted as the final answer and Sheriff Phillips left Chief Deputy Donald Parks in charge of safeguarding Matthew Williams.

The racial animosity percolating that night in Salisbury was not a new phenomena. In May 1898, a group of White men broke into the Red Bird jail. Their target was Garfield King, a young Black man who was just eighteen years old. King said he had shot and killed the son of a prominent White farmer in self-defense. The mob snatched Garfield King from his cell and lynched him near the Red Bird. As he hung in the air, members of the mob repeatedly shot at his body. The *Baltimore Sun* reported that the back of the Wicomico County Courthouse was pockmarked by bullets. No one was ever held to account for the murder of Garfield King.

To make matters worse for Matthew Williams, the Eastern Shore was already primed for another lynching. Less than two months prior, a Black man named Euel Lee[2] was nearly lynched in Worcester County when a White farming family living near Berlin, Maryland, were all found dead. Lee had worked for them and was found with some of their property. His lynching was interrupted and this left many on the Eastern Shore deeply unsettled, especially when a Baltimore lawyer who was an avowed member of the Communist Party intervened on Lee's behalf. The beast had not been sated in Berlin, but Salisbury was going to be altogether different.

As the news of Daniel J. Elliott's murder spread across the city, the tenor of conversation quickly shifted. Hundreds of people began to gather at the hospital, chanting a lynch mob's refrain. Several men pushed their way into the hospital and found Williams. Helen Wise, the nursing superintendent, reportedly told the men, "If you must take him, do it quietly." With that, the men threw a straightjacketed and unconscious Matthew Williams out of the window where hundreds of White people awaited the impending lynching. Some accounts said that Williams walked out of the hospital with the men. However, given what is known about his significant head injuries, it is unclear if he could have done so. He had been drifting in and out of consciousness and many felt he was likely to die.

---

2 He was also known as Yuel Lee and Orphan Jones.

What happened next to Matthew Williams is nothing short of calculated, brutal, sadistic torture. At 8:00 p.m., in front of a sea of two thousand people, the mob took him to the Wicomico County Courthouse, their symbol of justice and peace, a spot of land where slaves were once sold, the place where Frederick Douglass had spoken about what it takes to be a self-reliant man in this world if given a chance at fairness. They placed a rope around his neck and hung him from a tree. Twenty feet in the air. They dropped him. They lifted him again. Williams was unconscious. Lifted and dropped. Over and over. Twenty minutes. After his body hit the courthouse lawn for the last time, he was then drug behind a truck into the Black neighborhood near Poplar Hill Avenue. The dead body of Matthew Williams was tied to a light post, doused in gasoline, and set on fire for all to see. When there was no more damage to be inflicted upon the corpse of Matthew Williams, the crowd dispersed ... the beast now satisfied.[3]

Wicomico County Sheriff G. Murray Phillips cut down the body and dumped it in a field on the outskirts of town.

One cannot even begin to imagine the fear and horror felt by the Black community that night and in the days and weeks that followed. Matthew's family wanted to give him a funeral so a Black undertaker went to get him. He found the body and brought it back to his home, hiding it from view and from anyone who would seek to do it more harm. A prominent Black physician, Dr. Arthur Brown, went to the undertaker's home to examine the body of Matthew Williams. In addition to the damage done by the lynching, the dragging, and the burning, Dr. Brown also found two bullet wounds: one was at the back of Williams's head, just grazing his scalp, and the other was at Williams's right temple with the bullet exiting close to his left eye. For days afterward, very few Black people were seen on the streets of Salisbury. This was a nightmare come to life. It was a warning delivered with gloating.

---

3 Two days after the lynching of Matthew Williams, an unnamed Black man was found beaten to death. There is a possibility his death was related to the lynching.

Immediately, some officials demanded answers while others offered handwringing. The mayor of Salisbury gave a prevaricated statement to the *Salisbury Times* the day after the lynching: "A careful investigation shows that everything is quiet and no further trouble is anticipated. There is no indication of tense racial feeling and what has happened can be safely classed as indignation directed only toward the individual concerned. There never has been any trouble between the races here and there is not going to be now." Maryland Governor Albert C. Ritchie was in New York when he was informed of the Eastern Shore lynching and was quoted in that same article as saying, "When the investigation is completed I shall have something to say, but the matter is entirely too grave for me to talk about now, of course, I am shocked by the affair."

Different newspapers reported slightly varying accounts of that night, but never once was a ringleader named. It was simply a faceless, unknown mob. The call for accounting was never answered. A grand jury interviewed 124 witnesses to the lynching and not a single person interviewed said they could identify anyone involved. Offered and accepted was the old recitation about the mob of men being from other counties and cities, certainly not any of the fine folks from Salisbury.

But that wasn't entirely true. Someone did find out who they were.

• • •

While writing a book about the Matthew Williams lynching,[4] Dr. Charles L. Chavis, Jr., a professor from George Mason University, made an extraordinary discovery at the Maryland Archives in Annapolis. During his research, Dr. Chavis found the original investigative papers of the lynching which likely had not seen the light of day in more than eighty years. Filed away and forgotten, Dr. Chavis held a lost history in his hands.

---

4 *The Silent Shore: The Lynching of Matthew Williams and the Politics of Racism in the Free State* by Dr. Charles L. Chavis, Jr. was published in January 2022 by Johns Hopkins University Press.

Pasquale "Patrick" Anthony Petta was an undercover Pinkerton detective who had been assigned to the case at the behest of Maryland Governor Albert Ritchie and his Attorney General, William Preston Lane. Petta was a boxer from New York who went by the name of "Patsy Johnson," and he was able to successfully infiltrate various social circles in Salisbury in January 1932. As the locals became comfortable with the affable pugilist, their lips loosened on the details of the lynching. During candid conversations in their homes and restaurants and gyms, they spoke the names of the mob members and the roles they played, often bragging about their own involvement. What he learned was this: the men were locals, not the unknown rabble-rousers from out of town as the newspapers, politicians, and citizens of Wicomico had said over and over again.

Patsy Johnson played his part, befriending the men he met, listening to their tales, sorting out the myriad of connections, probing deeper whenever he could. He made meticulous notes and sent his reports back to his headquarters. He said he had uncovered many of the identities of the previously faceless. This is what Dr. Charles Chavis found in those old boxes at the state archive—an untold story was taking shape after more than eight long decades. He read Patsy's records of those weeks in early 1932, when the local men couldn't help but talk and talk and talk about it. For the first time in decades, the names of the men in the lynch mob were revealed, specifically a dozen men who were directly responsible and several of whom were prominent citizens. According to Pinkerton Detective Patsy Johnson, the man who provided the rope for the lynching was Salisbury Fire Chief Frederick A. Grier and three high-ranking lawmen—Salisbury Police Chief Nicholas Holland, Wicomico County Sheriff G. Murray Phillips, and his chief deputy, Donald A. Parks—were involved in the abduction of Matthew Williams from the hospital and delivered him to the courthouse lawn where he was lynched. Local men told Patsy Johnson that Sheriff Phillips and Chief Deputy Parks knew what was coming and that they had helped make it happen.

Detective Patsy Johnson fled town as the grand jury convened. Some of the witnesses called were men named in his reports. The efforts were futile, though. Nothing came of the grand jury. No indictments. No justice. Nothing. Patsy Johnson's detailed notes and reports went into boxes and were filed away.

Eighteen years later, Donald A. Parks resigned from the sheriff's department. And if Patsy Johnson is correct, he had eighteen years of enforcing the laws of the county with a man's blood on his hands.

Eighteen years.

And then his successor was named: Samuel A. Graham ... a good and honorable man who would be elected sheriff of Wicomico County and who would suffer his own bloody fate at that same courthouse ... the one that stood silent during the lynchings of Matthew Williams and Garfield King.

– BIG SAM AND SHERIFF JESSE POLLITT –
1950–1958

For newly minted Chief Deputy Samuel A. Graham, police work gave him a close-up of the oddities of everyday human life. In 1950, he was tasked with bringing a woman to court. The State's Attorney had sworn out warrants against the woman and her husband for not vaccinating their two sons. The mother argued, "The Bible says you must not mark the flesh." However, Sam was not able to bring her to court; instead, her husband appeared to tell the judge his wife and sons were sick at home with the chicken pox. He pled guilty and paid a $20 fine.[1] Then he had a case of a food thief: he investigated a break-in at Hebron Elementary School and another at East Salisbury Elementary School. The thief took twelve pounds of lunch meat, eight pounds of chicken, a couple of sweet potatoes, a large can of mixed vegetables, and four pounds of hamburger. The only thing left behind were fingerprints. (It would be another twenty years before McDonald's introduced The Hamburgler to the American public.)

Sam even went on a few raids. The Esquire Club was a notorious hotspot in Delmar known to local authorities. So ill-famed was the Esquire Club that a laundromat once referred to it in an advertisement about how to get a beer stain out of one's clothes. One night, Sam and Sheriff Jesse Pollitt along with two other deputies raided the

---

1 $20 in 1950 is roughly equivalent to $265 in 2025.

Rare is the photo of Sam Graham without a hat covering his bald head.

Image courtesy of the Edward H. Nabb Research Center for Delmarva History and Culture, Salisbury University, Mel Toadvine Collection

establishment. The club operator was selling beer after-hours and the deputies noticed several gaming tables, although they were covered up. When the case went to court, Sam testified against the club operator who ended up with a $500 fine and one-year sentence at the Maryland House of Correction.[2] Along with the club owner, two other men, noted as "Wilmington gangsters" in the newspaper, were also hauled into court for this raid. They had been charged with disorderly conduct. In a stunning moment from the bench, the judge referred to the two men as "wops"—an ethnic slur for Italian-Americans.[3]

Rather than taking a heavy-handed approach to police work, Sam Graham opted for an easier touch, a quality that would come to define his reputation as a lawman. Once, a down-on-his-luck man asked Sam for a dollar so he could get some food. Sam obliged and suggested he inquire about a job at a local mill. The man even stayed at the jail for a few nights, but when he appeared in court, presumably to face vagrancy charges, the judge did not have the same lenient heart as Sam. The

---

2 $500 in 1951 is roughly equivalent to $6,200 in 2025.

3 There is a prevalent falsehood around this derogatory term that "wop" means "without papers" or "without passport" in reference to immigration status. This is unfounded. Instead, it comes from the Italian word "guappo" meaning "swaggerer," which is to infer someone is a dandy, a bully, or a showoff. The "gua" has a "wah" sound instead of a hard "g" sound.

man got an eleven-month jail sentence. Another time, in June 1951, Sam pulled up on an illegal craps game. Four men were engaged in gambling in a pine thicket somewhere between Sharptown and Santo Domingo, which was a predominantly Black neighborhood. When the men saw Sam, they ran, leaving behind their cars, their dice, and thirty cents.[4] Sam did not give chase. Instead, he reached into their vehicles, took their keys, and drove one of their cars back to Salisbury, forcing the men to turn themselves in.

One hot July night at the jail, a prisoner told Sam, "I have heart trouble. I'd just as soon be dead as feeling like I am. I swallowed some razor blades." To which Sam immediately sent the prisoner to the hospital, later telling a reporter from the *Salisbury Times*, "We don't like to take any chances with prisoners who say they are sick … we don't fool with things like that." It didn't matter if it was a ploy—Sam wasn't taking any chances. He would not risk a prisoner's health.

Chief Deputy Sam Graham was also getting an education in juvenile delinquency. In August 1951, he drove two young boys, eleven and nine, to the Maryland Training School for Boys. The boys had started a fire at the Feldman Brothers storage building on East Railroad Avenue by sprinkling gunpowder on the floor and setting it alight. The fire caused $20,000.00[5] in damage and the boys were sentenced to stay at the reformatory school until they were twenty-one. Months later, three juveniles who had been arrested for petty larceny and ransacking automobiles around Salisbury escaped from the custody of a deputy when he attempted to move them from the penthouse prison to a car. The juveniles made it as far as a restaurant where they were once more apprehended. When asked about their escape, Sam told the newspaper that it "was not the policy to handcuff juveniles—looks bad." However, the juveniles were cuffed to one another as they were taken to the reformatory school. Everyone learned a little lesson there.

---

4 $0.30 in 1951 is roughly equivalent to $3.70 in 2025.

5 $20,000 in 1951 is roughly equivalent to $246,000 in 2025.

In February 1952, Chief Deputy Sam Graham was involved in a sensational case that made headlines in Maryland newspapers. An 81-year-old farmer named Charles Littleton stood accused of killing his 69-year-old wife, Mary Littleton, at their home near Jersey Road on the outskirts of Salisbury. Theirs was a small, four-room house covered in red tar paper on a farm they were renting. The Littletons were a poor American Gothic portrait: Charles was a slight man with oversized ears that stuck out from his gaunt face; Mary's white hair was pulled back from her round face, accented by large glasses and her thin, unsmiling lips.

On that cold February morning, Mary was found at the bottom of their back steps. Blood covered her dress and the concrete steps. Her glasses were smashed. Charles said he was in the corn crib when he heard his wife cry out just after 7:30 a.m., and he told authorities later he thought his wife had had a heart attack. A doctor arrived at the crime scene and, in his opinion, there were too many lacerations on her head to be a simple fall. An ax was found in a nearby woodpile and authorities presumed the red substance on it was blood. Charles said it was blood, but not his wife's. He had killed some chickens earlier, but when the lawmen asked him to produce the dead chickens, Charles could not. Chief Deputy Sam Graham and a Maryland State trooper took the ax to an FBI lab in Washington, D.C. for testing along with bloodied clothing and strands of gray hair. Authorities also found $600 pinned into her dress, an odd detail.[6]

Within a day, the autopsy revealed that Mary had skull fractures and eight lacerations to her head. By then, Charles was in the penthouse prison. Upon his arrival, he told the reporters that he wasn't feeling well, but Wicomico County Sheriff Jesse Pollitt was ready to talk, calling it "the most brutal murder I ever saw ... You could fall off the Washington Monument and it wouldn't cause cuts so deep."

A few days later, Chief Deputy Sam Graham read the charges to Charles Littleton as he stood in his cell. Big Sam was known to be rather

---

6 $600 in 1952 is roughly equivalent to $7,300 in 2025.

soft-spoken and the old man, perhaps a bit hard of hearing, couldn't understand him. Charles apologized and asked him to read it again. So Sam did: "... on February 21st feloniously, willfully, and deliberately premeditated malice aforethought did kill and murder Mary Littleton."

"I didn't do it."

"Is there anything you want to say?" asked Sam.

"I didn't do it." Charles Littleton repeated. Frail, old, and now incarcerated, he must have been an utterly defeated man.

The murder case went to trial in the spring of 1952. The jury heard testimony about how the couple argued over money and how Charles had once thrown a jar of strawberry preserves at Mary's head. Charles's conflicting accounts of that morning were recounted for the jury along with the presentation of the autopsy report, the ax, and blood evidence, which the FBI determined was human but insufficient for further analysis. But could such a woebegone wisp of a man find the strength to so brutally murder his wife? In the end, the jury deliberated for less than an hour and found Charles Littleton not guilty of his wife's death. The case remained unsolved.

Sitting at the defense table with Charles Littleton when the verdict was delivered was a young and upcoming lawyer named Richard M. Pollitt—the sheriff's son and a friend of Sam Graham's.

• • •

In January 1954, the *Salisbury Times* ran an article about the political whisperings on the Delmarva Peninsula. The front-page article spilled over onto a later page where there was this tidbit: "For sheriff, Samuel Graham of Hebron, a former deputy sheriff, has been telling friends he's going to be a Democratic candidate for sheriff." By 1953, Sam had resigned from the sheriff's department and had gone back to work for the Pennsylvania Railroad. Jesse Pollitt was still the sheriff and he had already filed his re-election paperwork.

Sam decided to make his running more than just a rumor, and for the first time, he waded into the political waters of Wicomico County as a Democratic candidate for sheriff, pitting himself directly against his former boss and fellow Democrat, Jesse M. Pollitt. Had the two men had a falling out? Sam had left the department, after all, and Pollitt was a popular sheriff. So why would Sam choose to run against him? Or maybe it was nothing more than a political change of heart?

The Pollitts were a prominent family with political ties, dating back to Josiah Wesley Pollitt, who was born in 1858. A judge in the Orphan's Court in Somerset County, he and his wife had several children, one of whom was Jesse. Early in his life, around 1910, Jesse Pollitt opened up a general store in the little village of Eden and then, fourteen years later, moved it to the slightly bigger little village of Allen. He was also a farmer and a postmaster—and a prolific cigar smoker—and in 1946, he campaigned for sheriff of Wicomico County and won. He moved his family into the sheriff's living quarters on the top floor of the courthouse, right next to the penthouse prison. Jesse's wife, Agnes, better known as Aggie, cooked all the meals for the prisoners. There is a Pollitt family legend that goes like this: there was a man in town who used to do his best to get arrested on Sundays because he knew Aggie Pollitt served chicken and dumplings on Sunday evenings. Apparently, the deputies began to expect his weekend shenanigans. Living in the sheriff's quarters came to feel somewhat normal for the Pollitt family.

Jesse and Aggie had four children, two sons and two daughters. One of their sons, Richard Malone Pollitt, born in April 1927, attended law school at the University of Maryland. He had graduated from Salisbury State Teachers' College[7] and set his sights upon a law degree. Richard frequently stayed with his parents in their apartment at the courthouse. Once, when he had to fill out a required form, he listed his return address like this: Dick Pollitt, County Jail, Salisbury, Maryland. Surely this

---

7 This school has seen several name changes through the years. It is today Salisbury University.

must have raised a few eyebrows for the folks back at the law school! Even Richard's young son, Rick, would recall in his later years visiting his grandfather, the sheriff, in his apartment for holidays and overnights on the weekends. Often, little Rick Pollitt would walk right into the jail and chat with the people who were locked up. Imagine the surprise of a prisoner seeing a six-year-old boy stroll up to the cell bars and ask, "Does your mother know you're in here?"

This anecdote, while funny in one respect, is shocking to a modern day sensibility about prison security. The penthouse prison was supposed to be impregnable ... but maybe it wasn't if little Rick Pollitt, unsupervised and unbothered, could simply stroll right in.

Sam Graham lost his 1954 primary bid for sheriff to Jesse M. Pollitt by 616 votes; Pollitt then went onto to beat his Republican opponent in the general election with more than seven thousand votes—the highest number for any candidate in the county. Pollitt's popularity was undisputed and Sam continued on with the railroad. However, in just four months time, Sheriff Jesse Pollitt would face an enormously uncomfortable moment in his political career. So much so that he might have wished he hadn't won. And it had to do with that impenetrable penthouse prison.

• • •

In February 1955, police officers in Wicomico County were investigating a series of burglaries and thefts. A 1953 Plymouth sedan was stolen from a used car lot. Whiskey, gin, and money were taken from the Red Men's Hall in Fruitland.[8] Candy and cigarettes were missing from James Conley's store. A safe at the Southern States Cooperative

---

8 The Improved Order of the Red Men is a fraternal organization that dates back to the early 1800s. Although it was for Whites only until 1974, the group's language, customs, and rituals are directly taken from Indigenous cultures. This stems from the founders' belief that they originated from the colonists who participated in the Boston Tea Party dressed as Mohawks.

on Vine Street was cracked and the $583[9] inside was gone. Another safe was busted at a propane company. Police found footprints but had few other leads. Then, a sensational headline appeared in the *Salisbury Times* on March 2nd, 1955, announcing the crimes had been solved: "Prisoners Escape, Commit Thefts, Return to Jail Here With Loot."

Yes. The thieves were prisoners from the "escape-proof" penthouse prison where Sheriff Pollitt lived just down the hall. They were breaking out, committing burglaries and thefts, and then putting themselves back in their cells before sunrise.

"It's so fantastic and ridiculous, you'll both call me a liar," Sheriff Jesse Pollitt told two reporters.

Here's how it went down: four men, ranging in ages from nineteen to twenty-one, jimmied the door to a cell in which no prisoners were kept. That cell was empty because it was missing a bar where a previous inmate had sawed it out, leaving an opening of almost a foot high by eight inches wide. Somehow, through a feat which would make any contortionist jealous, the four men squeezed themselves through this mighty small space, which led them to a spot where they again wrenched themselves through another tiny opening in a ventilation shaft. Eventually, this series of shafts and hatches emptied them onto the courthouse roof. But they weren't free just yet. They scaled the slanted roof toward the original courthouse (right over the sheriff's quarters), entered a trap door into the attic, shimmied down a ladder near the clock tower, walked past the courtrooms and down the steps, unlocked the front doors, and disappeared into the darkness of a sleeping Salisbury, free to do as they pleased. When they were done, they simply retraced their footwork, and climbed back into their bunks, sharing their ill-gotten gains with their cellmates. By the time a jailer or deputy came around to do checks first thing in the morning, every single inmate was accounted for. It was brilliant—prison as an alibi—and they almost got away with it.

Cigarette butts and a pair of overalls were found in the courthouse

---

9 $583 in 1955 is roughly equivalent to $7,000 in 2025.

attic, a discovery which lead folks to wonder: was someone living up there? After a few unsuccessful surveillances, a trap was devised that lead straight back to Jesse Pollitt's prisoners. In the space between the jail and the roof, more than a dozen whiskey bottles were found, some of which came from the Red Men's Hall break-in. Money was found shoved inside toilet paper rolls. The gig was up. The mystery was solved. And the sawed-off bar on that empty cell was finally replaced.

But for Jesse Pollitt, the man in charge of Maryland's most impregnable jail, the whole thing was a terrible mess. First, it hit the national press wires. Then, during a March 1955 session, a grand jury in Wicomico County censured the sheriff for "errors in judgement." *Official Detective* magazine devoted an article to the wild prison break in its July 1955 issue. The *Crisfield Times* wrote an opinion piece that acknowledged the personal embarrassment this caused Sheriff Pollitt yet also praised Salisbury and the sheriff for being open and honest about what had taken place.

It was a bit late for soothing words, though.

More than the embarrassment to Sheriff Pollitt, the breakout marked a stunning end to the gleaming reputation of the penthouse prison, which was now understood to have some very real weaknesses. Unfortunately for the sheriff, more troubles were coming.

In August 1956, a reporter from the *Salisbury Times* visited the jail, as was normal, and saw something curious in the log book: an erasure mark and a fictitious name substitution. When pressed about it, Sheriff Pollitt gave instructions that no one but officials and attorneys were allowed in the jail now. This raised the ire of the journalists who printed a cheeky article: "Nobody knows whether or not the sheriff's jail docket is closed today. ... The docket has had a here-it-is-there-it-isn't status." Even the *Baltimore Sun* entered the fray by rehashing the prison break and the feud with the *Salisbury Times* while also taking a few shots at the aging sheriff and his religious leanings. This earned an excoriating letter to the *Sun's* editor from Richard Pollitt, who defended the character of his father. In November, the *Salisbury Times* printed an article calling for better records to be kept in the sheriff's office, mentioning again the name deletion and fake substitution.

Two days later, as if the sheriff needed more aggravation, three of his deputies, including his chief deputy, Edward Mitchell, were brought up on illegal deer hunting charges by the sheriff of Worcester County.[10]

By this point, Sheriff Jesse Pollitt had had enough of the newspapers. He filed a libel suit for $50,000[11] against the *Salisbury Times* for the November article. When the newspaper reported his libel suit against them, right next to that, and perhaps on purpose, was another article about one of Pollitt's turnkeys. Emerson Dykes of Parsonsburg had been fired after the sheriff exchanged heated words with Dykes, a prisoner's lawyer, and members of the prisoner's family. The ex-jailer swore he'd run as a Republican against Pollitt in the next election. This new article rankled Pollitt even more and he quickly filed another libel lawsuit against the paper—this time for $100,000.[12] However, in late March 1957, the libel suits were dismissed unanimously. One judge said, "After careful reading of both declarations, and I read them many times, I am unable to find anything disparaging or critical of Sheriff Pollitt. Not one word there made me think one whit less of a man we always admire."

The tit-for-tat appeared to be over.

This term had been plagued with disasters and Sheriff Jesse Pollitt decided he was done. He did not seek re-election, leaving the race wide open. Another person who did not run, as he had promised, was Emerson Dykes, the ex-turnkey. He opted for a life raising flowers and was noted especially for his gladioli which were often over six feet tall.

Very soon, there would be a new sheriff in town.

---

10 Edward Mitchell would be a future and unsuccessful candidate for sheriff. The other two deputies were Norman White and William Shockley, a future sheriff of Wicomico County. After three trial postponements, they were all found innocent.

11 $50,000 in 1956 is roughly equivalent to $588,000 in 2025.

12 $100,000 in 1956 is roughly equivalent to $1.2 million in 2025.

– A NEW SHERIFF IN TOWN –
FIRST TERM: 1958 – 1962

When Sheriff Jesse Pollitt decided not to run for re-election in 1958, it left the political field wide open and, in early February 1958, Sam Graham announced he was seeking the position once more. This had him facing off with Pollitt's previous chief deputy, Edward Dempsey Mitchell, who had already announced his intentions to run. (This was the same chief deputy Edward Mitchell who had been caught spotlighting deer near the town of Berlin.) Sam appeared to have the backing of numerous supporters, telling the *Salisbury Times*, "Many friends have urged me to become candidate for sheriff. I'm highly appreciative of their confidence and support."

By this point, the combined social capital of Sam and Dorothy Graham was on the rise. Dorothy, in 1955, was named the vice-principal of the recently constructed Wicomico High School on Long Avenue in Salisbury. She and Sam attended Nelsons Memorial Church in their town of Hebron. In addition to being a Mason, Sam was a member of several organizations like the Eastern Shore Shrine Club, the Hebron Lions Club, the Moose Lodge, the Elks Lodge, and the Brotherhood of Railroad Engineers and Fireman. Given all those associations, Sam was able to garner real support for his campaign.

One of the immediate issues he wanted to address was the transparency of the office. This was a reference to the closing of the jail logs as well as other record keeping issues that occurred under Sheriff Pollitt's watch. Neither Edward Mitchell nor Sam Graham approved of keeping

Wicomico County Sheriff Samuel A. Graham caught in a happier moment.

Image courtesy of the Edward H. Nabb Research Center for Delmarva History and Culture, Salisbury University Mel Toadvine Collection

the logs away from reporters, and both men said they wouldn't handle it the way Pollitt had. "The records and conduct of the office of sheriff under me will be open at all times to public scrutiny," Graham told a *Salisbury Times* reporter on February 3rd, 1958.

Sam defeated Mitchell in the primary and, in November 1958, went on to face his Republican challenger, Henry Thompson, a retired agent from the Federal Alcohol Tax Unit. On Election Day, the faith of Sam's many friends proved well-placed: he won the race for Wicomico County Sheriff with 6,378 votes to his opponent's 4,387. Sam Graham took out a small ad in the paper to thank his supporters and declared, "I pledge to do my best as your sheriff." On that point, few had any doubt.

There was another important victor on Election Day 1958. A young and handsome lawyer named Alfred T. Truitt, Jr. won the office of Wicomico County State's Attorney. He was the son of a former mayor of Salisbury and a 1944 graduate of Wicomico High School. After he turned eighteen on April 5th, 1945, he joined the United States Army Signal Corps where he earned the rank of sergeant. World War II was

Alfred Truitt with his wife, Clara May, and their five children

Image courtesy of the Truitt family

nearing its final stages ... Allied forces were liberating concentration camps and Hitler was on the run, soon to be dead. Alfred Truitt, just barely out of high school, was given the sobering assignment of photographing the Nuremberg Trials. Here he had a front row seat to the vile atrocities committed by the Nazi regime. On October 15th, 1946, Alfred was sent to photograph Hermann Göring after he committed suicide by cyanide capsule in his prison cell. Another historic photograph taken by his camera lens, as he would later tell his family, was one of General Patton right before the car accident in which he was paralyzed. Patton later died from those injuries. The entire experience deeply effected Alfred and it was there that he first fell in love with the law.

He returned stateside and enrolled at Western Maryland College, but his studies were interrupted when he and another student pulled a prank and found themselves in hot water with the school's administration. Alfred and a buddy formulated a harebrained plot to put a cow in the bell tower, which must have been a hilarious sight, especially when the college president arrived. However, neither Alfred nor his friend had a plan to get the cow down, which forced the college to dismantle portions of the bell tower in order to return the poor bovine to greener pastures. (This was a story he would tell again and again over the course of his life, entertaining all within earshot.) Eventually, he was allowed to finish his studies and then turned his eyes towards the University of Maryland School of Law, graduating in 1953. By that point, Alfred Truitt had married a gorgeous debutante named Clara May from a well-heeled Philadelphia family. She had attended a boarding school with Grace Kelly and the von Trapps, according to family lore. The couple was married in 1950, and soon Alfred and Clara May had a house full of children. Between 1952 and 1959, they had three girls and two boys.

Alfred Truitt, who was known to his family and friends as Sonny, was dedicated to public service. He could have entered private practice and fattened his bank accounts, but he chose the life of a civil servant. Right out of law school, he ran for the Maryland House of Delegates but lost. That didn't dampen his spirits, though. Like Sam, he wanted to work for the people of the county and so he ran for the position of Wicomico County State's Attorney as a Democrat. Alfred won in a landslide, earning 4,600 more votes than his Republican opponent. Despite the twenty-year age gap between the two men—Sam was 52 and Alfred was 31—they formed a meaningful friendship and were often found together at the Truitt family's kitchen table, laughing and sharing stories, which is easy to imagine given Alfred's natural knack for storytelling.

On Wednesday, December 10th, 1958, Samuel Adams Graham took his oath of office, administered by Circuit Court Clerk Joseph W. T. Smith, the same man who had sworn him in as chief deputy nearly ten years prior. Bald and stout, wearing a dark suit with a striped tie and white pocket square, he took his oath in a ceremony held in the sheriff's office in the courthouse. The outgoing sheriff, Jesse Pollitt, had agreed to stay on for a short while, likely to help smooth the transition. Under

Sam, there were four or five full-time deputies and several part-time deputies. Within a week, Sheriff Graham was at a ceremony to lay a cornerstone for the Westside Community Center in Bivalve with Mayor Jeremiah Valliant of Salisbury, Maryland State Senator Mary L. Nock,[1] and Wicomico State's Attorney Alfred Truitt. It was official: he was now a figurehead in local politics.

Life as sheriff got off to an interesting start for Big Sam. Within days of his swearing in, he was involved in a sensational case out of New Jersey. Two White eighteen-year-olds, who were wanted for questioning in the murder of a New Jersey prosecutor, stole a car, which led to a high speed chase that ended in a shoot-out in Wicomico County. A Salisbury city officer was shot in the face and a Maryland State trooper was shot in the leg; luckily, both survived. One of the suspects was also injured. The lead photograph in the paper was Sheriff Graham, dark suit and big hat, holding one of the young suspects by the arm. The very next day, Sheriff Graham found himself in the home of Willie Ross, a 53-year-old Black grocery store owner who had been shot dead by his wife, a 33-year-old mother of four children. Graham found ten gallons of bootleg whiskey in the home and told the papers he would not release the names of witnesses in the case. He only added that the children were safe in the custody of friends.

Then he had to contend with the red tape of the office. When Pollitt had been sheriff, he had three extra personal vehicles that he loaned to the department in return for the county's payment of gas mileage. Graham went before the county commissioners to ask for help. The county made an offer to purchase Pollitt's cars, but he flatly declined. However, as Christmas Eve 1958 approached, Pollitt, perhaps warmed by the holiday spirit, decided to sell the cars to the county for the sheriff's department to use. Now Graham's deputies could hit the road again.

---

1 Mary Layfield Nock spent nearly thirty years in Maryland state politics. Born in Quantico, she was the first woman State Senator from the Eastern Shore and served as the President pro tempore. Nock, a champion of public education and women's rights, once infamously voted against allowing baseball to be played on Sundays.

*Dorothy H. Graham
1963 Wicomico High School
yearbook photo*

Image courtesy of the
Edward H. Nabb Research Center
for Delmarva History and Culture,
Salisbury University

All this in the first two weeks on the job!

In the spring, his home life and work life overlapped in a grotesque incident. A group of seniors from Wicomico High School, where his wife, Dorothy, was vice-principal, went entirely too far for a prank. Eleven boys dug up a grave with the macabre notion to place the skull on the desk of their teacher. The grave belonged to a Black woman buried in 1893. Somewhere along the way, they decided against the idea and left the skull in the city park where it was subsequently found. They were charged with delinquency and Judge Rex A. Taylor, whose wife also worked at Wicomico High School as an English teacher, ordered them to rebury the skull. Each of them were given probation and had to pay $20[2] toward the expenses. Sheriff Sam Graham, along with a funeral director, watched as the teenagers reburied the skull and other bones in a new casket and a new vault. Witnessing the somber event, Graham said the boys were "quiet and serious minded as they dug away the dirt." Given her reputation as a straight-laced and rule-following disciplinarian, one can only imagine the conversations between Sam and Dorothy over that series of events.

Before his first year as sheriff was out, there was an attempted

---

2 $20 in 1959 is roughly equivalent to $220 in 2025.

jailbreak. On July 4th, 1959, two inmates were thinking about their own independence. A seventeen-year-old juvenile and a 21-year-old man were being held on charges of safecracking. At 9:30 p.m., they rushed Deputy Roscoe Purnell and made it just outside the main jail door before the deputy pulled his gun and shot one of the men in the arm. Of the incident, Graham said Deputy Purnell "did a good job and saved us a whole lot of trouble." Although the break was averted, Graham knew the penthouse prison was in need of repair; more than two decades had passed since the Wicomico County Jail had opened. For example, the tracks on which the cell doors sat and slid were worn and nearly inoperable. Graham approached the county commissioners about getting the doors fixed and they approved his request to the tune of nearly $800.[3]

There were a few other incidents at the penthouse prison during his first term. One prisoner, a man from North Carolina who was being held on assault with intent to kill charges after an altercation with a Maryland State Trooper, was found hanging by a noose fashioned from his shirt. He was revived, after which Graham had the man sent to Crownsville State Hospital, the all-Black psychiatric facility in Anne Arundel County. Months later, another prisoner—a trustee who was serving a four-month sentence for petty larceny because he stole $25[4] from a Main Street gas station—was found inside the car of an appliance store owner. The trustee had been given permission by Sheriff Graham to walk down to the pharmacy to have a prescription filled. Due to being found where he certainly wasn't supposed to be, the prisoner got six-months in the Maryland House of Correction for auto tampering. (The trustee system only worked when the trustee could be trusted.)

In January 1961, Sheriff Graham announced a personnel change in the penthouse prison. Deputy Purnell, the man who had shot a prisoner in the arm during the botched Independence Day escape, was retiring. Deputy J. Merril Shockley took his place. Perhaps it was time for a fresh

---

3 $800 in 1959 is roughly equivalent to $8,800 in 2025.

4 $25 in 1962 is roughly equivalent to $265 in 2025.

set of eyes in the jail. Months prior, in November 1960, a prisoner cut his wrist with a razor blade and was immediately sent to Peninsula General Hospital where he remained under guard until he was transferred to Spring Grove State Hospital, a psychiatric hospital in Catonsville and the second oldest in the country. The prisoner had used a single-edged razor blade to cut himself and this was a point of serious concern for the sheriff because he knew that his prisoners were issued double-edged razor blades for shaving. Graham said he did not know how the prisoner got his hands on non-issued razor blades. Contraband was making its way into the penthouse prison, a problem with dire consequences.

In April 1959, Sheriff Graham had bristled at a report by the Maryland Board of Corrections. A state inspector had found that the Wicomico jail was "found to be in disorder. There were magazines strewn about the cells, food litter and soiled torn blankets and mattresses." The inspector's report also suggested a fresh coat of paint and a deep cleaning as well as more guards and finding outside work for the prisoners to do. This did not sit well with Sheriff Graham who recalled that a recent grand jury took a tour of his jail and they had found it in "generally excellent condition, clean and sanitary." He did, however, acknowledge that there were magazines on the floor, which the inspector had pointed out to him during the visit. "There may have been a few ... The prisoners are more orderly when they have something to read. I think our jail is clean and it's open to anybody that wants to come up to look around. If they can make any specific recommendations, I will—and I'm sure the County Commissioners will—do all we can to straighten any bad condition they find," he said. This would not be the last time Sheriff Graham tangled with a Baltimore inspector about his jail and it would not be the last time he was in the newspaper refuting negative claims.

The suggestion that the sheriff find outside work for the prisoners did come to fruition. Maryland allowed county sheriffs to compel prisoners to work on labor details under the pretense that using a prisoner in this way would offset the cost to maintain him and, as an added bonus, the work would rehabilitate the prisoner, keep him from the temptations associated with idleness, and make him more apt to be able to return to society as a proper functioning citizen. This created a cheap and readily available work force that was extraordinarily valuable. At that time in Maryland, prison labor and the goods manufactured by inmates was worth $3.3 million[5]. In addition to working on road crews, prisoners made furniture for public schools and hospitals, made license plates and street signs, canned vegetables and fruits, sewed clothing, and made mattresses for state psychiatric facilities.

Prisoners compelled into labor tidied up the golfing greens at Winters Quarter Country Club in Pocomoke; they fought forest fires and cleaned up after hurricanes. The men from the Poplar Hill Correctional Camp in Quantico were used to clear buildings and debris for the laying of Route 50 through downtown Salisbury: one editorial said that because of the use of prisoner labor, parking downtown was "almost a pleasure." Around 1960, Sheriff Graham decided to use prisoners being held on lesser crimes like gambling, vagrancy, drunkenness, and petty theft for labor details in the county. Those prisoners would be paid fifty cents[6] a day. Sam emphasized that his labor details were made up of volunteers only. If an inmate didn't want to work, then he could stay in his cell.

Graham's work as sheriff did not go unnoticed. He was nominated to be the new president of the Maryland State Sheriffs' Association. Although he lost to the sheriff of Prince George's County, he became the organization's second vice president. Months later, Sam Graham hosted a meeting for the organization at the Howard Johnson restaurant in Salisbury, where his good friend and Wicomico County State's Attorney Alfred Truitt gave a speech. In front of fifty or so sheriffs and deputies from around the state, Truitt praised Graham's efforts to build a real crime fighting force. His well-dressed deputies in their painted

---

5 $3.3 million in 1958 is roughly equivalent to $36.7 million in 2025.

6 $0.50 in 1959 is roughly equivalent to $5.50 in 2025.

cars—two standards started by Pollitt—had possibly caused a 10-15% decrease in crime with their recent patrols. Truitt said this was especially true in relation to bootlegging, "an old Eastern Shore occupation." Sheriff Graham was sending his deputies to Pikesville for training at the Maryland State Police barracks. To the citizens of Wicomico County, Sheriff Sam Graham was building a modern day police force.

Despite the landmark decision of *Brown v. Board of Education*, segregation remained an integral part of everyday life in America: schools, restaurants, bathrooms, public transportation, prisons, and law enforcement. Sheriff Sam Graham took a step towards integration when he hired the first Black deputy in Wicomico County's history. Harrison Parsons was sworn into office by Circuit Court Clerk Joseph W. T. Smith on Friday, February 5th, 1960. He had worked for more than forty years at the Eastern Shore Public Service Company. Nicknamed "Smoke," Parsons was a solidly built man at six feet tall and more than 250 pounds. He patrolled transmission lines on foot and reported any problems he saw; he was said to have walked more miles than any other man in the company. Married with six children (one daughter and five sons), he was a man of his community. In 1959, he was working as a school crossing guard. Once, when a couple of folks were hauled into court for not stopping for him as he helped the children cross the street, Parsons told the judge, "If they couldn't see me, as big as I am, they should better have an eye examination." And the judge agreed. With the Wicomico County Sheriff's Department, his main duties were to work in the Black neighborhoods of Salisbury as well as Salisbury High School and its athletic events. However, the funds to pay for Parsons and a proposed second Black deputy came from the Salisbury High School and its PTA instead of being funded by the county like the other deputies. Sadly, Harrison Parsons passed away seven and half months later after an illness. He was seventy-two. His obituary noted that he was Wicomico County's first Black sheriff's deputy.

Graham's first term was going well. His deputies busted a

safe-cracking ring operating up and down Route 13 in Salisbury. They even busted an unruly band of children who were breaking into the dog pound and freeing the imprisoned canines. "No Trespassing" signs had to be posted, causing Sheriff Graham to lament (and joke) to the newspaper, "This is not the first time the kids have been around here, but now they're getting out of hand. Nine dogs have been released this week. ... We're asking parents of that section to keep kids away from the pound—or we'll start impounding some children."

Politically, he was riding a wave of good news for Democrats. During the 1960 presidential campaign, he and Alfred Truitt, along with Truitt's wife, Clara May, attended a swanky dinner for John F. Kennedy, Jr. in Pikesville, Maryland on Friday, September 16th, 1960. Influential Democrats across the state snapped up their $100-a-plate[7] tickets. Kennedy focused several of his remarks on Soviet premier Nikita Khrushchev, saying that he hoped Democrats, Republicans, and Independents would stand firm together against his regime. He also issued a stern warning to the Soviet leader that he should not meddle in the American election. The next morning, on the front page of the *Salisbury Times* was a photo of Sam Graham, Alfred Truitt, and Clara May Truitt next to another photograph of Maryland State Senator Mary Nock shaking JFK's hand. Less than two months later, Kennedy beat Richard Nixon.

Sam and Alfred surely celebrated then.

---

7 $100 in 1960 is roughly equivalent to $1,100 in 2025.

PART II

– THE EVOLUTION OF A HURRICANE –

In the summertime, a television meteorologist will draw your attention to a rather indiscernible cluster of clouds in the Atlantic Ocean. *This little disturbance*, the meteorologist says, *is something we ought to keep an eye on*, yet you hardly know what you are looking at. The disturbance looks like any other puffs of white and gray in the heavenly, top-down view of our planet. And so you forget. So does your neighbor. Our attention goes elsewhere. It must.

But that little disturbance does not dissipate. As it moves deeper into the vastness of the Atlantic, it feasts on warm water and hot air. It grows, taking a slow, meandering path ... each step incrementally more violent than the last. The low growls of thunder rumble into longer and longer distances. Alone in the darkness. Blotting out the sun and moon and stars. Its edges lash out. The center holds tight, wrapping itself around a fortress-like wall of dense thunder clouds and blinding bands of rain. Wild. Dangerous. No longer a minor disturbance, this tropical storm is gaining definition and strength at an astonishing rate.

Now, that television meteorologist is back to tell you *uh-oh*. While we weren't looking, the tropical storm gorged on a banquet of the worst possible atmospheric and oceanic conditions and it is now a powerful hurricane poised to smash into the coast. This mighty tempest will be the ruination of everything in its path. It will rip homes apart and break out storefronts. It will cause a deluge of destruction and damage. And it will take innocent lives.

The storm is such a force that it must be named, and with that naming comes an intimacy. We become as familiar with it as we do our friends and lovers. We say its name over and over; we hear it all around us. We read its name in newspaper headlines and on crawling television banners. It is a unwelcome guest we did not invite but have now conjured and cannot postpone. The terror resides in knowing that what is to come exists on a scale of imagination you cannot comprehend.

Here is your warning, the meteorologist says. *This will be unpredictable. If you live close, you must prepare or you must leave because when the storm hits, there may be no one to save you.*

Then, just as predicted, the hurricane slams into the coastline with a wild ferocity. We watch, helpless, hopeless, as every awful possibility is realized. We aim for survival. That small, nameless disturbance had grown while we were not paying attention, and now it commands us as an audience to its horrors. The storm rages and we hang on. People we loved are gone; places of our memories vanish beneath its fury. The hurricane will not last forever, but it will last long enough. And we know that when it is over, we will rename it with words like "beast" and "monster" and "killer."

The task at hand becomes one of salvage, rebuilding, healing. And, of course, eventually preparing for another ...

– "A STORY OF A SERIES OF MOST UNFORTUNATE CIRCUMSTANCES" –

A CROWNSVILLE STATE HOSPITAL REPORT ON JOSEPH J. BARTHOLOMEY, JR.

The story of this hurricane begins with two star-crossed teenagers. Dolores Miller was just eighteen when she married nineteen-year-old Joseph Bartholomey on Friday, June 14th, 1940. Dolores was the oldest of four children in her working class, Baltimore Catholic family and had, at best, an 8th grade education. Her new husband was one of five children also born to a blue collar, Baltimore Catholic family. Joseph's father was a fireman who worked out of the Number 1 Truck Company on Gay Street for two decades. Joseph had a 10th grade education but had taken an apprenticeship with a printer when he was sixteen. Unlike most men his age, Joseph never served in the military because of a severe burn he sustained in his younger years.

A few years into their marriage, they had a little girl, Shirley. This part of their married life, Dolores would later say, was happy or at least held happier memories. On Tuesday, March 18th, 1947, their son, Joseph James Bartholomey, Jr., was born at Sinai Hospital in Baltimore, Maryland. At the time of his birth, Dolores and Joseph Sr., along with their daughter, Shirley, were living in an apartment with Michael and Leona Bartholomey, Joseph's brother and wife, on Guilford Avenue in Baltimore. It was a typical city neighborhood filled with brick row houses and concrete sidewalks; an elevated streetcar scuttled by the iconic House of Welsh restaurant at 301 Guilford Avenue. A few blocks east lies the historic Green Mount Cemetery where John Wilkes Booth, John Hopkins, Maryland Governor Albert Ritchie, and even Napoleon Bonaparte's sister-in-law are all buried. Jimmy, as Dolores called him, was born without any physical problems or major illnesses, but she noted he was slow to walk and to talk. As he grew up, she saw that Jimmy was friendly yet destructive, overactive and quiet. He was terrified of the dark and often wet the bed in the middle of the night. By day, he bit his fingernails and struggled to get along with other kids.

The turbulence in the marriage of Dolores and Joseph seemed inevitable. Dolores was a nervous person, at times unstable, and Joseph had a roving eye and a penchant for alcohol. The contentiousness was so great, according to Dolores, that she nearly lost Jimmy in the sixth month of her pregnancy. The arguments were insufferable and relentless and happened in front of their two children as well as Leona and Michael Bartholomey.

After three years of cramped living, Joseph and Dolores moved their family into a place on Port Street, a narrow, one-way street densely packed with block after block of row houses. Not long after, Leona and Michael Bartholomey moved out of the Guilford Avenue apartment and rented the row house next door to Dolores and Joseph. They had no children of their own, but living so close afforded Leona and Michael a chance to see Shirley and Jimmy more often.

Sometime in 1951, Dolores said she awoke to find a $50[1] bill on the table with a letter saying simply, "I can't stand you. I'm leaving." Dolores knew that he'd met a young woman, a co-worker at the Glenn L. Martin Aircraft Company Plant, and she had begged her husband not to leave. She even offered to look the other way if he'd just stay until the kids were old enough. *I cannot raise them myself,* she pleaded. It was among the truest things she ever said.

Their separation had a shattering effect on the family. Dolores was

---

1 $50 in 1951 is roughly equivalent to $615 in 2025.

struggling as a waitress, working for $28[2] a week in Wilhelm's Tavern in Middle River, roughly ten miles or so from the Port Street homes of the Bartholomeys. Financial support from her ex-husband was sporadic: she said she'd receive weekly checks and then suddenly nothing for months. After Joseph left, the children asked for their father and she told them he would be back. Dolores later recounted how Shirley and Jimmy would wait by the window each week; sometimes he came, sometimes he didn't. Shirley remembered it that way, too. Their divorce was final in 1952.

From all accounts, both familial and legal, Jimmy took the splintering of his family particularly hard. Perhaps his pain began with living with two parents who always argued and then that pain was sealed into his young heart with the final fracture of his father leaving them. He continued to wet the bed at night and began to act out and in ways that didn't seem to make sense.

One day, he had been playing outside and came running into the house. He was visibly upset. Dolores asked him what was wrong.

"Mom, I see the devil in the sky." Tears were streaming down his face.

"Jimmy, there is no devil. There is no one after you."

But he could not be consoled. He continued to cry and refused to go back outside to play. That night, when Dolores put him to bed, Jimmy was still in a frightened state.

"What are you scared of?"

Jimmy whispered, "The devil is after me."

Dolores, not knowing what to do, left the lights on. After that, she always kept a light on for him.

• • •

After the divorce, Joseph rebounded romantically. He married a woman named Marie Betts. Jimmy lashed out, calling her "a stupid girl" and "a crybaby." This marriage was short-lived and Joseph

---

2 $28 is 1952 is roughly equivalent to $340 in 2025.

separated from her only to move back in with Leona and Michael at their row house on Port Street. His second divorce was final in 1954. Joseph went to court to inquire about gaining custody of his children, but the court denied his request because he was a single man living in a room in his brother's home. Briefly, Joseph considered sending Jimmy to the Maryland Training School for Boys because of his tendency toward unruliness, but Jimmy, at seven, was too young for admittance.

That same year, Jimmy received his first Holy Communion. He must have looked as innocent as a lamb in a fresh, white suit with his brown hair slicked down, framing his hazel eyes. When they got home from church, Dolores took Jimmy upstairs to change out of his suit. Dolores recalled that as they lay in bed, he became uncooperative as she began to wrangle him out of his clothes. And then Jimmy balled up his little fist and struck her in the face.

At one point, also likely in 1954, Jimmy went to live for a short time with Leona and Michael Bartholomey. His difficult behavior put such a strain on their marriage that they separated for a short time. They reconciled once Jimmy was out of their home.

In 1955, Dolores's already difficult life became even more complicated when she became pregnant by a married man. This was as bad a scenario as she could have found herself in during the conservative 1950s of America: a young, uneducated, divorced mother of two children now pregnant as the result of an extramarital affair. It was enough to render her "unfit" in the eyes of society. As her pregnancy waxed on, Dolores was no longer able to work and no longer able to take care of Shirley and Jimmy. The kids needed to go to school. They needed food in their bellies. They needed to go to church. All this with a third one on the way. In her desperation, she turned again to Leona and Michael Bartholomey for help. She asked them to take her children.

Well, it was more like Dolores nudged Shirley to ask Leona if they would take care of her and her brother. This is how Leona recalled the situation. Dolores asked through Shirley, a twelve-year-old child.

Although the request was made in a strange way, the logic made sense. They were Jimmy's godparents and they had been fairly consistent figures in Shirley and Jimmy's lives.

The arrangement wasn't meant to be forever, Dolores pleaded, just until she could get her life together enough to provide a proper home for all three of her children. Leona agreed but had one main condition: Dolores needed to give her legal custody so that she could raise the children as she saw fit. Leona also reached out to Joseph, who supported the transition. Her marriage had already been disrupted once by this so Leona likely needed to feel fully in control in order to take the children in again, especially Jimmy. Dolores wanted her children to be raised Catholic and knew Michael and Leona would bring them up in that faith. It was a sad decision but one made with as much empathy and common sense as Dolores could muster.

On November 23rd, 1955, legal guardianship of Jimmy and Shirley was awarded to Leona and Michael. For the next six months, life for the Bartholomeys in their home on Port Street wasn't as even-keeled as perhaps Leona had hoped when she accepted custody of her niece and nephew. Joseph Bartholomey shared a room with his eight-year-old son, but he was rarely home at night. There were heated disagreements like when Joseph brought a young woman into the home and Leona took exception to it. She told him that he'd have to find somewhere else to live. The living arrangement came to an abrupt end when, one night, Leona and Michael went to see a movie and left Joseph to watch the children. Upon their return, they found that Joseph had taken a bed, a desk, some other bits of furniture and moved out, leaving his children behind.

Joseph found living quarters in Victory Villa, a neighborhood built during World War II for the workers at Glenn L. Martin Aircraft Company Plant in Middle River, Maryland. He wanted his kids to come live with him, but it did not go as Joseph had hoped. His job demanded long hours and he was absent more than he was home. Shirley was unhappy and begged to return to Dolores. He relented. Jimmy was unsupervised for much of the time, which caused the neighbors to complain. However, instead of sending Jimmy back to his mother and sister, Joseph made a startling and cruel decision. He took his nine-year-old son to a boarding house and abandoned him into the custody of strangers.

From September 1956 to March 1957, Jimmy lived with other young boys at the boarding house operated by Ms. Redman on W. 37th Street in the Hampden area of North Baltimore. Records of the time show that a 67-year-old unmarried woman named Bertha F. Redman[3] lived at 902 W. 37th Street; she was possibly trained as a nurse. The house was part of a single unit duplex built in 1920 on the corner of W. 37th Street and Elm Avenue with tight living quarters and a small kitchen. This would have been sufficient for a single, older woman, but adding in a group of young boys would have made those spaces feel incredibly cramped. Jimmy would later say the people who ran the place beat him and the other boys. For more than six months, save for three visits from his father, Jimmy had no contact with his family … not a word from the people who loved him. Dolores later said that, during those six months, she had no idea where her son was. Thanksgiving and Christmas came and went; the new year might as well have rung in without a sound.

Jimmy's abandonment at the Redman boarding house came at a time when he was extraordinarily vulnerable. By this point in his young life, he had already bounced around between different living situations and caregivers and he was struggling. His father had discarded him. His mother wasn't coming for him. He was still wetting the bed. He said he was physically abused. The months at Ms. Redman's had to be a dark and lonely time for him.

Sweet rescue came on his tenth birthday. On March 18th, 1957, Jimmy left Ms. Redman's boarding house with only the clothes on his back and went to live with his maternal grandparents, Eleanor and Charles Miller.

---

3 There are alternate spellings associated with this woman. Her obituary shows her last name as "Redmond"; however, "Redman" seems to be used more consistently in phone books and other documents.

Ms. Redman had the last word, though: she kept Jimmy's clothing because Joseph Sr. owed her $30[4] and he didn't have the money. For Jimmy, this was the first time he had seen his family in seven months.

Eleanor and Charles Miller were a middle-aged couple living in a small, red brick bungalow at 798 Wise Avenue in the Edgemere area east of Baltimore. Their home on Wise Avenue, unlike Mrs. Redman's boarding house, was located on a triangular lot on a nice residential street where trees lined the road and each home had its own yard. One social worker described it as "neat, clean and comfortably furnished." Eleanor, fifty-four, used to work at Epstein's Department Store and had made $48 a week plus commissions while Charles, fifty-eight, was unemployed and sick with cancer. When he had been able to work, he, like Joseph Bartholomey, Sr., had been a worker at Glenn L. Martin Aircraft Company Plant earning $67[5] a week. While Joseph worked as a lithographer, Charles's job is unknown.

Eleanor contacted the Juvenile Bureau to let them know Jimmy was now in her care and that she intended to keep him, regardless of the financial concerns. Joseph Sr. had promised to pay $10 a week, but Eleanor said he only ever mustered up $20.[6] Dolores occasionally stopped by to bring clothing for Jimmy, but not much more as she continued to battle her own set of problems. In 1956, she had given birth to a baby boy and named him Ethan Lyle Bartholomey.[7]

Dolores's living situation was a little complicated. She and the new baby, along with her daughter, Shirley, were living in a row house at 2425 East Hoffman Street. The house belonged to Eleanor Miller's mother, who was Dolores's maternal grandmother. While Dolores worked, her grandmother watched over Ethan and Shirley.

---

4 $30 in 1957 is roughly equivalent to $340 in 2025.

5 $48 and $67 in 1957 are roughly equivalent to $540 and $760, respectively, in 2025.

6 $10 and $20 in 1957 are roughly equivalent to $110 and $230, respectively, in 2025.

7 Name changed.

The Millers enrolled Jimmy at Edgemere Elementary School where he liked to shoot marbles and play baseball. They took him to Catholic Mass every Sunday. On July 18th, 1957, Eleanor Miller was awarded custody of her grandson. She stated in a social worker's report that Jimmy was "stubborn but not hard to get along with" and that he was often kind and generous to others, yet he seemed to be highly nervous and had showed little interest or feeling for his mother and father. Because their home was small, Jimmy didn't have a room of his own; instead, he slept on a rollaway cot in their living room. At night, he continued to wet himself.

In 1957, Joseph Bartholomey Sr. married again, this time to a young woman named Betty Lou Marsh from Baltimore. Betty dropped out of school after the ninth grade and went to work. At eighteen, she married, but it only lasted nine months. Both the bride and groom had domineering mothers and the stress of it all caused her to have a nervous breakdown. Betty, the young divorcee, recovered and soon met her matrimonial match.

The marriage of Betty and Joseph Sr. appeared to be the most stable either had known—they would be married forty years—and soon they were expecting a child of their own. Eleven-year-old Jimmy left the Millers home in Edgemere in June 1958 and moved into an apartment with his father and new stepmother. They enrolled him in Middlesex Elementary School in the Essex area of Baltimore. Not long after he had been enrolled, the school called his maternal grandfather, Charles Miller, because Jimmy was misbehaving in class and causing general disruptions in the building. The elementary school sent Jimmy for a psychiatric evaluation; Joseph and Betty accompanied him for that visit.

At home, Jimmy remained unsettled and Betty felt her pregnancy only served to agitate him further. When she gave birth to their daughter in July 1958, she was frustrated by Jimmy's boisterousness. She would later say he was constantly "making a racket" and trying to aggravate her at every turn. Joseph was working two jobs to provide for his family and he wasn't able to spend a lot of time with Jimmy. This little girl was Betty's first and her nerves were straining under the pressure of being a new mother. Neither parent seemed to know how to handle Jimmy's constant antics and his apparent jealousy of his newborn half-sister. The conversation returned once more to the question of what to do about Jimmy Bartholomey.

They reached out to the Children's Aid Society to see about placing him at the Esther Loring Richards Children's Center, an inpatient mental facility for children with serious emotional issues, but Dolores was said to have refused to participate, resisting any attempts to treat Jimmy psychologically. Back to the drawing board, Betty and Joseph approached Leona and Michael Bartholomey again about taking Jimmy in. The couple, still childless, agreed. *Again.* And just like all the other times before, it would not stick. He ended up leaving his aunt and uncle to go live with his mother who, after three months, called the juvenile authorities in Baltimore. Jimmy was charged with delinquency and placed on probation. Now, he was running with gangs of boys in the streets and hot-wiring cars. He hooked school and would run to his mother's house or his father's house only to be returned to whatever relative was housing him at that particular time. This cycle was endless.

Now that Dolores had involved the courts, a judge called a hearing to determine where and with whom twelve-year-old Jimmy should live. Present at this hearing in October 1959 was Dolores Bartholomey, Joseph and Betty Bartholomey, Leona and Michael Bartholomey, and Eleanor and Charles Miller. Seven adults, four homes, and one troubled twelve-year-old boy. The judge asked Leona if they were in a position to take him.

"Well, I think so," Leona said. "I'd love to have him again if there wasn't any interference."

The interference to which Leona referred was Dolores and Joseph. They were constantly fighting and it got to Jimmy. All the bouncing around he did ... Leona felt sorry for him because he never had a stable home. It was always this home or that apartment. This family member or that one. This school or the next. Each time he moved, he started out fine, but he always regressed into a problem child that needed to be somewhere else with some other custodial figure.

"I love him," Leona told the judge. "I love him and I want to take him. I never had any children of my own, and I want to make a home for him."

The judge turned to Jimmy, "Who would you rather live with?"

"I want to live with my uncle and aunt."

And so the judge ordered Jimmy be placed with Leona and Michael Bartholomey. *Again.* They enrolled him at a Catholic school, Fourteen Holy Martyrs on South Mount Street in Baltimore. The sisters reported to Leona that he was doing well those first weeks. *A model student, a good kid,* they said. One sister even told Leona, "We have made him a charge boy, a safety on the street to guide the children back and forth."

Leona and Michael surely let out a sigh of relief. They were proud of him and heartened to hear of his positive progress ... until the phone rang one day. Jimmy was bullying the other children. He was disruptive in the classroom. Jimmy, the sisters said, had to leave the school. Leona and Michael then enrolled him at Arbutus Junior High School, just southwest of Baltimore. Jimmy seemed to acknowledge his behavior was the reason for the change in schools: "Aunt Leona, I am really going to try to do good. I will really try." This was a rare admission from Jimmy, one that probably pained his aunt who was doing all she could for him.

He was still wetting the bed at night and it pained Leona to see it, but she was determined to help. She told him, "Jimmy, we will try to conquer this thing." She set alarms in the night to wake them, one alarm for him and one for herself. She even took him to see a doctor. Jimmy's bedwetting, the doctor said, was a response to his emotional problems. Given his life's constant upheaval, his abandonment, and his family's dysfunction, that diagnosis likely made sense to Leona and she told the doctor, "We will do anything we can to help him, just tell us what." After several visits with the doctor, a prescription medication for Jimmy, and tranquilizers for Leona and Michael, Jimmy finally broke free of the constant bedwetting. He was twelve years old. Leona and Michael were proud of him; they saw Jimmy was proud of himself.

While that was one triumph, Jimmy sabotaged himself in school. He was causing trouble on the bus and was kicked off. Then it fell to Leona to drive him to school. The Bartholomeys had a neighbor whose daughter was a traffic cop and sometimes she'd give Jimmy a ride and drop him off a few blocks from Leona and Michael's home. That came to an end when the school approached the cop, saying that he was being disciplined by the school and would have to get home on his own. This upset Jimmy who then threatened the traffic cop by saying *he was going to get her.*

Anger gathered in him. Resentment and loneliness took root. He would not be calmed or comforted. He would never be tamed. One night, while Leona was in bed, she heard shuffling in her room. When she turned on the bedside lamp, she saw Jimmy on the floor, crawling towards her on all fours.

She snapped at him, "What in the hell are you doing on the floor, boy?"

"I was just trying to scare you, Aunt Leona."

She sent him back to his room. Unnerved, Leona was wide awake for the rest of the night. And probably many of the nights that followed.

• • •

Despite still being on probation from his mother's charges of delinquency in 1959 and despite the best efforts of Leona and Michael Bartholomey, Jimmy continued down a destructive and delinquent path. He continued to hook class regularly, hang out in the streets, run away, hot-wire cars, even stealing one. All this meant he had violated his probation and he had left no recourse for the courts. A judge remanded Jimmy Bartholomey into the custody of the Maryland Training School for Boys in Loch Raven, Maryland. It was a reformatory school, later made famous in the 1990s by another son of Baltimore: John Waters. His movie *Cry-Baby* featured a young Johnny Depp in the starring role of Wade "Cry Baby" Walker, a teenage bad boy who finds himself wrongfully accused of a crime and sent to the Maryland Training School for Boys where he nearly gets his impressive pompadour shaved off and leads the other teenaged prisoners in a catchy song pleading with the jailer to let them go free. But there would be no Hollywood musical numbers or campy scripts for Jimmy Bartholomey during his stay at this iniquitous institution.

No, Jimmy Bartholomey was in real trouble this time.

The Maryland Training School for Boys was a violent, punitive, soul-breaking place … home to a number of sadistic adults and ruthless, streetwise teens. It was not a place where broken boys would go and get better. It was not a haven of rehabilitation or a refuge where they could learn from their mistakes. No. This was a place of sanctioned cruelty and like many others before him and after, Jimmy went inside the doors of the Maryland Training School for Boys as a petty thief with a devil-may-care attitude, but he would emerge changed … and not for the better.

– DELINQUENTS IN A HOUSE OF REFUGE –

In January 1849, the mayor of Baltimore urged the building of the House of Refuge for young delinquents. A scourge had befallen the citizens of Maryland: young men were losing their moral and religious compasses and turning to lives of crime. Gangs of boys roamed Lexington market, stealing purses and picking pockets. Thieving and vagrancy were problems. Two young boys stole watches while four other boys were found sleeping in bacon carts. Arson, too, as one seven-old-boy tried to burn down a barn. To stop the wave, city officials proposed the House of Refuge, a place where delinquent boys and young men could be made to change their nefarious ways. Wayward children, especially boys, were seen as antagonistic and prone to troublemaking and crime; this was a problem—a danger—to society. Finding a way to rehabilitate and recast them as proper, responsible citizens was imperative ... or else those broken boys might grow up to become dangerous men.

Within two days of its opening in October 1851, three boys who had been arrested were sent to the House of Refuge. The youngest was ten. Month after month, the newspapers reported on various misfits, pickpockets, thieves, ne'er-do-wells, truants, and pitiful souls who were sent to the House of Refuge. By 1910, the name was changed to the Maryland School for Boys and within two years, a new facility opened in Loch Raven, Maryland with a slight variation to the name—the Maryland Training School for Boys.

The Maryland Training School for Boys, possibly circa 1924
Image courtesy of the Hagley Museum and Library
Dallin Aerial Photography Collection

Documented escapes and reports of abuse at the reformatory school emerged at least as early as 1919. In one case, the superintendent of the school repeatedly whipped bare skin of a seventeen-year-old with a leather strap three inches wide and three feet long. Then, he made the teenager stand still for nearly four hours before letting him go; afterwards, the teenager became mentally unwell and had to be transferred to Spring Grove State Hospital. Other boys reported being abused at Maryland Training School for Boys, too. One father came forward to say his son had his underwear taken from him. Boys were made to work outside, regardless of the weather conditions. They were placed into solitary confinement as punishment for running away. Another father wrote a letter to the *Baltimore Sun* and said his son was also whipped by that same superintendent. He begged for the thrashings to stop.

They did not.

Boys continued to be whipped as late as 1941. They continued to be battered and tormented. But they weren't alone: the young Black boys at the Boys Village at Cheltenham reformatory school were abused too. They were beaten with rubber hoses. They were exploited, being made to work for pennies[1] a day. The school was notorious for deplorable conditions and tuberculosis outbreaks. One social worker who visited the school in February 1943 wrote that the Black boys at Cheltenham were "locked in damp basement cells without adequate clothing and little to no food" and that the officers of the school beat them into unconsciousness and even death. One line in that report inspired pure terror: "gruesome atrocities reminiscent of the middle ages were committed with alarming regularity."[2]

For the young delinquent boys of Baltimore, there was no respite. There was no refuge at all.

• • •

In the summer of 1951, three teachers from the Maryland Training School for Boys came forward with allegations of abuse and cruelty as well as administrative inaction. What they and others witnessed and knew to be true was nothing short of horrific: regular beatings, inhumane punishments, sexual assault, even the death of a seventeen-year-old boy. Together, these three whistleblowers recounted a chilling narrative, which was published in the evening edition of the *Baltimore Sun* on June 29th, 1951.

One teacher spoke of a young boy who was stripped to his underwear and made to walk across the campus with only a towel during a particularly cold winter's day. Children as young as eight years old were

---

1 A penny in 1919 is roughly equivalent to less than two dimes in 2025.

2 In recent years, the graves of at least 230 young Black boys have been re-discovered in the woods near the reformatory school where they died. The boys, as young as 13, were buried and forgotten; some only had a cinderblock for a headstone.

Here is an exterior view of some of the MTSB buildings.
Image courtesy of the Baltimore Museum of Industry
BG&E Print and Negative Collection

regularly beaten by staff. The instructors encouraged the older boys, who were given militaristic titles like "lieutenant" and "sergeant" to "work over" their younger counterparts. Boys were held in lockup cells for up to three weeks wearing just their underwear. One winter, a runaway boy was caught and thrown into the icy Gunpowder Falls River as punishment. Broken noses. Broken legs. A boy was set on fire. Some boys had their heads shoved into toilets; others were forced to eat cigarettes. One of the worst examples was a story of sexual assault: a teacher instructed a few of the older boys rub turpentine into the genitals of a younger boy.

The abuse wasn't only physical. Boys, as young as eight and nine, were denied visitation with their families but made to work on coal piles, filling bucket after bucket for the school's boilers. The administration heavily censored their mail, which meant the boys could be disconnected from their families. The superintendent of the training school, Elbert L. Fletcher, reportedly told one boy that his mother no longer cared for him.

In the newspaper, Superintendent Fletcher responded to the allegations by saying he welcomed an investigation but he felt the three teachers had overstepped; he painted them as being bad at their jobs and called them "disgruntled employees" who had lowered themselves professionally by coming forward. But Elbert L. Fletcher had seen the abuse firsthand. One boy had been made to stand in front of Fletcher, strip down, and let the superintendent count each of the twenty-seven bruises on his body. Of the young boy who had turpentine rubbed into his genitals, Fletcher brushed it off by saying it was just paint applied to the boy's testicles. However, the *Sun* reporter discovered an internal document, which was signed and dated by a school official, acknowledging the use of turpentine on the young boy's genitals. Fletcher was aware of what was happening in his institution, but took a handwringing stance of *I'm doing the best I can with what I have*. He denied most of the claims, yet he did acknowledge that violence did happen: "In an institution like this, a man's a fool to say force is never used." Yet he saw the bruises on the boys. He knew of the sexual assault on the young boy. He *knew* and he did nothing.

The teachers feared that bringing these boys—angry, defiant, and already at risk—into a ill-run facility where they were further abused was only going to make them worse. When the boys had downtime, the teachers overheard them sharing advice on how to pick locks, hot wire cars, and crack safes. The boys fought with each other, sometimes at the encouragement of staff. Adding to the volatility was the overcrowding. The Maryland Training School for Boys was designed for 200 but currently held 400.

More staff members came forward with similar accounts. One former staff member relayed a story about a seventeen-year-old boy who was injured in a fight with another boy. When she worked at the school, she lived in the staff housing on the grounds. That night, another MTSB employee brought the injured teenager to her cottage. She immediately knew the situation was dire and told the other staff member that the boy needed medical attention. The answer: "No, give him an aspirin and he'll be alright." The teenager died at two in the morning. Another former staff member told the *Sun* that she felt the school was nothing more than "a breeding place for crime"; three of her former charges were already in prison for serious crimes.

In August 1951, a grand jury in Baltimore County heard the claims of the whistleblowers but rejected outright their allegations that the school had been overly abusive. They refused to bring a single indictment against anyone at the Maryland Training School for Boys. The grand jury did acknowledge that boys had been beaten, perhaps even severely, but felt these were isolated incidents mostly instigated by the boys themselves; brutality was not the standard, they decided, and beatings were kept at "an almost irreducible minimum" by the administration. The final note was an excuse: the school was doing all it could with what little it had, said the grand jury.

More allegations surfaced and those, too, were ignored. One account said Superintendent Elbert Fletcher himself had grabbed a boy by his hair and shook him. The reformatory school remained overcrowded and poorly managed as it burgeoned in an atmosphere of violence and suffering. Despite the noble efforts of those whistleblowers, absolutely nothing changed. These boys would be perpetually lost.

• • •

Nine years later, on November 21st, 1960, thirteen-year-old Jimmy Bartholomey, slim and short, entered the Maryland Training School for Boys for the first time. Superintendent Elbert L. Fletcher was still in charge of the sprawling complex of administrative buildings, staff cottages, and student dormitories where, for the next eight months, Jimmy would learn what life was like for the boys at this reform school.

He said the older boys beat him. He was also possibly sexually assaulted there. He told two versions of the sexual encounter. In one telling, he said a woman at MTSB had sex with him; in another, he said that he was hitchhiking when a woman picked him up and had sex with him. He seemed reluctant to talk about it, even later in his life. There is no way to know what exactly happened, but if either of those two scenarios are true, then Jimmy's account of his first sexual experience is unequivocally sexual assault.

On December 27th, 1960, a little over one month into his stay at MTSB, a psychologist evaluated Jimmy and gave him a series of tests. One was the Wechsler Intelligence Scale for Children. Originally developed in 1949 and still used today in a revised format, the purpose of the test was to gain insight on a child's intellectual abilities. Jimmy had a full scale IQ of 90 and his verbal score was 97. Both of these placed him within normal limits. However, his performance score was 83, which could suggest that he had difficulties interpreting nonverbal cues, nuance, and spatial relationships between people, himself, and objects. The psychologist noted that Jimmy was "unpredictable in his performance and does not seem to be functioning at his optional[3] capacity." Today, an examiner might see this as a nonverbal learning disability and modern studies in this arena have associated links between these types of low performance scores with antisocial personality disorder. (This would have been a prescient indication of what was to come for him.)

Other tests given to Jimmy included the Machover's Projective Drawings, which asks the subject to draw things like a house or a person, and a Rorschach Psychodiagnostics, which has the subject look at various blots. These two tests were used heavily in the 1960s to gauge intelligence and personality traits, and while they remain in the toolkit today, they are not considered to be the gold standard they once were. As the field of psychology has evolved, so too have the tests and interpretations. For example, one psychologist at MTSB observed that Jimmy wrote "awkwardly with his left hand" and then noted this "might be an indication of emotional blocking ... ." This would not be an assessment

---

3 It is likely that the writer of the report meant to say "optimal" instead of "optional."

made by mental health professionals today as simply being left-handed does not equate to being emotionally stunted.

In the notes from his examinations, Jimmy was described as "ungovernable" and "a master manipulator" and "threatened and distrustful of authoritarian figures." The MTSB psychologist wrote that Jimmy "seems afraid to like anyone, and when he starts liking someone he is sure that he will be hurt by them and separated from them." He was afraid of being abandoned, yet he would abandon those with whom he had developed a close relationship. One can imagine Jimmy may have felt it would be better for him to leave before the other person had a chance to abandon him first. The psychologist's findings did not inspire hope: "When seen for testing (the examiner had not yet seen his folder), [Jimmy] seemed very guarded, evasive and unpredictable, which was later understandable on reading his history. ... His folder contains the most comprehensive history and is the best presentment of a case the examiner has noted during his stay at MTS [sic]."

The final note on Jimmy's 1960 psychological evaluation was foreboding. If Jimmy didn't rehabilitate and if the therapeutic recommendations weren't followed, then Jimmy's stay, the psychologist said, "will be only a temporary respite to an urgent problem." And like many of his fellow MTSB peers, he would find himself behind these same brick walls again.

While Jimmy was at the school, the Supreme Court of Maryland ruled in February 1961 that the state could no longer keep the Maryland Training School for Boys segregated. The ruling stemmed from a 1959 case of a young Black boy who wanted to go to MTSB rather than the Boys Village at Cheltenham. Calls to integrate all the reformatory schools began in March 1961. Meanwhile, the cottages at both of these facilities—the all-Black Boys Village at Cheltenham and the all-White MTSB—were undergoing renovations, which meant that the boys were forced to double up their living and sleeping quarters in already stressed and overpopulated institutions. Officials at both schools noted that the "pressure" was rising in each case.

Jimmy Bartholomey's eight-month stay at MTSB did not rehabilitate him. He turned fourteen inside the institution where he said he was beaten. Intimidated. Possibly sexually assaulted by a woman who worked there. There was no relief. There was no cure. He did not get better. He was released into the custody of Leona and Michael Bartholomey once again in July 1961. He stayed until September. Then he was off to Betty and Joseph who now had two children. The old cycle was starting anew. Here. There. Somewhere else. Once, he ran away from Dolores and when she found him, he and a bunch of other boys were sniffing glue. The odds of Jimmy's recidivism were increasing with each passing day.

• • •

On October 17th, 1961, Betty called the police because Jimmy had run away. They had argued the day before and he had not gone to school. The police eventually found him at Leona and Michael Bartholomey's home. Jimmy's uncle returned him to his exasperated parents. When the police spoke to the vice principal of his junior high school, they discovered Jimmy had brought a .38 caliber revolver to school and had kept it in his locker. The gun belonged to Jimmy's paternal grandfather, the Baltimore firefighter. When Betty asked Jimmy about the gun, he told her some boys had threatened him so he had it for protection. Joseph Sr. had typically taken a hands-off approach to discipline but this time was different. Perhaps it was a growing frustration with his young teenage son. Perhaps he lost his cool. Maybe sparing the rod had spoiled the child, as the Bible said. Either way, this time, he beat Jimmy himself.

Less than a week later, on October 23rd, 1961, the police picked him up again—this time for petty larceny. Betty had sent him to the Mars Super Market and among his actual purchases was a shoplifted item valued at $0.36.[4] Jimmy had enough money to cover the item, but instead, he pocketed it. The manager wanted to press charges and this angered

---

4 $0.36 in 1961 is roughly equivalent to $4 in 2025.

Jimmy who vowed he "would get even" with the man. Betty learned all this when the police called her to say they had him in custody.

Joseph and Betty continued to take Jimmy to his appointments with his case worker. The November 1961 notes state that Jimmy was "hypersensitive about his size" and that he "trys [sic] to be bigger." He said he'd kill himself if he stayed short. That Thanksgiving of 1961, Dolores asked for Jimmy to spend the holiday with her. When he returned to Joseph and Betty, they said he came home acting "silly and nasty."

The incident with the gun at school and the theft at the store landed Jimmy back in Juvenile Court with charges of possession of a deadly weapon, running away, and petty larceny. A probation officer was sent to Joseph and Betty Bartholomey's home on December 5th, 1961. The probation officer took stock of the Bartholomey home, located in the Middlesex section of Baltimore County. As a stay-at-home mother, Betty excelled; the children were clean and well-fed and the infant boy played quietly in his playpen. Betty described Jimmy as both "emotionally unstable" and "very kind." On one hand, he steals and threatens and lashes out, but he was also devoted to his younger half-siblings who adored him in return. Betty felt that contact with Dolores, Jimmy's mother, caused him to become "spiteful." The friction between Betty and Dolores was evident. Betty told the probation officer that Dolores lived in a "mixed neighborhood in Baltimore City" and that she felt Dolores led a questionable lifestyle. Whenever Jimmy ran away to be with Dolores, she would always call someone to come get him, Betty said. Dolores didn't seem to want him, a feeling Jimmy was sensing too. Betty admitted to the probation officer that she found it necessary to slap Jimmy "to make him have respect for his father and for her." Joseph Bartholomey Sr., Betty reported, rarely punished his children and allowed them to do as they please. Matters of discipline always fell on her. Although Betty stated she slapped Jimmy to make him behave, his psychiatric records would later state that these were "severe beatings imposed upon him" by his stepmother. The truth about the severity of these incidents remains unclear except to say that Betty did admit to laying her hands on Jimmy. Joseph Sr. took a backseat in matters of discipline, yet Betty was quick to point out that he was very good about playing with the children and providing for his family, bringing in $96.00[5] per week and paying all their bills. In the probation officer's notes of that visit, she wrote that Jimmy came into the room and had a "rather flip and smart-alecky attitude." Physically, she described him as a "small boy for his age, freckles and a rather impudent, elfish little face." (The probation officer's use of the word "impudent" suggests her own bias in the situation.) Jimmy said, with a shrug of his shoulders, that he didn't know why he did the things he did. He said he loved his father and stepmother and wanted to be with them. He even said he loved Betty, but he found it hard to express such feelings.

Two days after the probation officer's visit, the Juvenile Court sentenced Jimmy to a year of probation. It didn't matter, though. He ran away and was sent back to the Maryland Training School for Boys on January 19th, 1962, but only for a few days. This detention was short because Jimmy was headed to the Maryland Children's Center for psychiatric evaluation.

• • •

The Maryland Children's Center was a two-story brick building located on Westland Avenue in Arbutus, Maryland. It opened in November 1959 and cost the state just over half a million dollars[6] to build. The 56-bed facility was designed to be an "institution for the detention and study of children adjudged delinquent by the courts," according to a February 1959 *Baltimore Sun* article. Its origin can be traced to February 1958, when a bill passed in the Maryland legislature to establish a diagnostic center to examine troubled youngsters deemed to

---

5 $96 in 1961 is roughly equivalent to $1,000 in 2025.

6 $500,000 in 1959 is roughly equivalent to $5.5 million in 2025.

be unmanageable. That bill was signed into law by the governor shortly after. Although the Maryland Children's Center was not segregated by race—Maryland was slowly working toward the integration of juvenile facilities—girls would not be sent there.

Two of the early cases admitted to the Maryland Children's Center included a fourteen-year-old Black boy who had fatally stabbed another teen during an argument over a newspaper, and a fifteen-year-old White boy who had painted swastikas on houses and wrote "Jews Go Home" on a bedsheet and hung it from a railing at his school. In October 1961, a fifteen-year-old White boy was admitted to the MCC after going on a shooting spree at his high school in Havre de Grace. The teenager walked into his principal's office, pulled out a .32 caliber gun, fired four shots, and then headed off to the library where he opened fire again. Miraculously, no one was harmed in this school shooting.

Jimmy Bartholomey, fourteen-years-old, entered the Maryland Children's Center on January 22nd, 1962. He did not adjust well. Jimmy lashed out at the hospital staff, hurling insults and threatening them with physical harm. Sarcastic. Rebellious. He hid from the counselors at shower time. When the staff spoke to him, he made cow and pig noises at them while tugging at his ears. Within the first week, he ran away. Twice. The first time, he and another boy—his only friend—escaped together, but their adventure was cut short when Jimmy fell and cut his arm. His friend waited for him and the waiting is what got them busted. Jimmy blamed himself for them getting caught, but he needed medical attention. The laceration on his right forearm required stitches. The second time he ran away, he was apprehended by the Ferndale Police who said he had stolen a car. Other attempts to run away were not successful.

He was listed as being in ninth grade; however, testing at the Maryland Children's Center put his equivalencies at roughly sixth grade. Jimmy was reading at a fifth grade level and his language skills were on par with a fourth grader. In general, his grades had been poor. Betty said she had tried to push him to study more, but it was a winless proposition. At the Center, Jimmy refused to cooperate with the school program and was noted as being disrespectful to the teachers. They saw he had difficulty expressing himself and stuttered when he was excited.

Just like at MTSB, he was given a series of tests. An Otis Test of Mental Abilities scored his IQ at 77, placing him at below average intelligence, but his full scale IQ score on another Wechsler Intelligence Scale for Children was 93, which is in line with his earlier results from MTSB. There was no performance score—the one that indicated he struggled with nonverbal cues—noted in the MCC record. An achievement test showed he was lagging academically. Other subjective tests, like the Rorschach and drawing tests, which are still in use today in updated editions, gave the examiners an impression of an immature and emotionally impoverished young teen who was "desperately trying to find someone whom he can trust and someone who will somehow help him develop a sense of belongingness."

The examiners noted that he seemed to want affection and security but remained bitter and angry: "It was almost as if he had a definitive need to be wanted and liked but he was afraid to let himself go." (This echoed the same point raised by the MTSB psychologist.) In one meeting with an MCC doctor, Jimmy spoke of accepting responsibility for his actions. This was positive and he smiled at Jimmy. But Jimmy saw the smile and changed course. His expression darkened, clouded over by belligerence. Jimmy appeared to refuse the very things he wanted most—attention, affection, tenderness. His hostility was a mask for his fear.

While he was at MCC, he complained about having nightmares and often awoke at 2:00 a.m. and walked around. He said he had a feeling that someone was calling his name. This pacing in the middle of the night was something Dolores had also noticed during the times he lived with her. "These rooms here can drive you crazy; they make some creaking noises," Jimmy said. But this didn't only happen in the middle of the night. Jimmy told an examiner that this sensation of having his name called was fairly normal. "It happens anytime; it feels like I am nuts, like I am crazy or something. ... If you walk in the night later than the time that you are supposed to be out you think somebody is following you." These admissions speak to a level of paranoia beginning to exist in his mind. When the examiner probed more on this, Jimmy said it feels like he is going crazy but knows he isn't. And then he smiled.

Jimmy's psychologists wrote that he had an uncanny ability to sense a riff between adults and then worked to capitalize on that. This was a reference to Jimmy being the root cause of the temporary split between Leona and Michael Bartholomey and harkened back to the MTSB report that called him a "master manipulator." His respect for authority appeared nonexistent.

At the Maryland Children's Center, the staff knew the older boys had an established hierarchy. Newly admitted boys would hang back while figuring out the players and the pecking order. Not Jimmy. He bragged about stealing cars and guns and the staff saw this as an effort to muscle his way into the top tier of "wise guys" in his unit. He would pull pranks on other boys, which resulted in the opposite effect. At times, perhaps when he was not seeking to be the center of attention, he could be found engaged in quieter activities like chess, reading, and watching television.

He did open up to the staff a few times. He told them his family was "lousy." He said he liked his father and worried about him often because Joseph had had a heart attack. Of his stepmother, Betty, Jimmy said she had blackened his eyes and bloodied his nose: "We just did not get along." Dolores didn't want him, but he wasn't able to articulate why he felt that way. When asked about his hopes and dreams, Jimmy said he had a few. He wanted to be six feet tall. He wanted to be a professional baseball player or a printer like his father. He told one examiner that if he had three wishes for anything in the world, the very first thing he'd ask for would be a German Shepherd dog like the police have. This was an interesting point for the examiners who noted this "tendency to transfer affection to animals reflects his tremendous need for acceptance and affection as well as signals his difficulty in establishing good interpersonal or satisfactory relationships with people."

With one examiner, Jimmy bragged about stealing a gun—the incident in which he took his grandfather's gun to school. He told another story about how he ran away one time and refused to give the police his name for three days until he was taken to court and was recognized by a probation officer. "If you steal something and you don't get caught, you're lucky," Jimmy said to the examiner. So the examiner posed a thought experiment to Jimmy: say there is money in a desk in this building and no one would find out if you took it, would you take the money? Jimmy thought about it and replied, "It all depends if I am mad or not at this place." When asked why he steals things, Jimmy offered, "I just do them because I want to do them; then later on I change my mind." He didn't seem to have a great deal of insight into his own motivations.

On Valentine's Day 1962, the Maryland Children's Center issued a letter to the Juvenile Court recommending Jimmy be removed from his parents and placed back at the Maryland Training School for Boys with continued psychiatric observation. The letter said MCC regarded Jimmy as "an immature youngster who exhibits poor control of impulses and inadequately suppressed rage." His diagnosis was severe adjustment reaction of adolescence, meaning that the events of his young life had lead him to have significant emotional and behavioral problems. His was a maladaptive reaction to the difficult life he had led thus far and it impaired his ability to function in his day-to-day life.

Understanding this diagnosis is critical to understanding Jimmy and what was to come for him. Today, mental health professionals refer to the *DSM-5* or the *Diagnostic and Statistical Manual of Mental Disorders*, which is in its fifth edition, when working with patients with mental health concerns. The 1962 diagnosis of severe adjustment reaction of adolescence would now be classified as conduct disorder, which is characterized by the *DSM-5* as a significant and reoccuring pattern in a young person's behavior that involves the consistent violation of the rights of others and rule-breaking. Additionally, this behavior causes setbacks and impairment to the person's overall ability to function in society. Conduct disorder has four categories of behavior per the *DSM-5*:

- Lying and being deceitful (including theft)
- An aggressive and bullying nature (including towards animals)
- Breaking social rules (including running away as well as missing school and curfews)
- Purposefully damaging and destroying the property of others

Based on the documentation available, the diagnosis, both then and now, appears to fit Jimmy and his pattern of behavior. There was nothing in his immediate environment to stem the tide of this diagnosis. His family situation was nothing but upheaval; his reform school was a notoriously abusive facility; and outside of those, there was no supervision or care, nothing to tether him to the right side of things. The last line of the Maryland Children's Center committee's evaluation report would prove to be startling in hindsight: "The need is for strict external controls with the hope that he can be further observed by a psychiatrist, since it is possible for him to present more pronounced psychiatric symptoms in the future."

Two days later, on the recommendation of the Maryland Children's Center staff, Jimmy Bartholomey was once again committed to the Maryland Training School for Boys.

• • •

On February 16th, 1962, Jimmy Bartholomey returned to MTSB where, a month later, he turned fifteen. He wasn't exactly blossoming into a teenaged heartthrob or a six-foot-tall muscled baseball player. Instead, he was a self-conscious, gangly teenager with brown hair and hazel eyes, weighing in at a whopping 95 pounds at 5'1" with pale skin and scars on his chin, his left wrist, and the back of right hand. He was awkward and shifty, often found singing softly to himself. He attended school for half a day at the ninth grade level; on Sundays, he participated in Catholic services. Jimmy also worked in the machine shop, an outdoor detail, a hospital detail, and as a messenger boy. The latter job was a position of trust and status, which indicates he must have had periods of good behavior. A case worker noted this in his file: "[Jimmy] did quite well behavior-wise for a long period of time while he was working on hospital detail. He maintained 'Honor' status for several months." But it did not last. Jimmy lost his privileged status when he got into an altercation with a supervisor and ran away from the Maryland Training School for Boys in August 1962. Joseph and Betty had been visiting him one to four times a month until he ran away.

The staff noted that superficial contact with him was usually positive and friendly, however, any attempts to probe deeper led to him shutting down completely, sometimes aggressively. Considering the violence occurring at MTSB, perhaps Jimmy had reason to close himself off to the staff. Decades later, lawsuits would emerge as men reported being sexually abused as boys at the school as early as 1962; when they reported the incidents, they were ignored. A MTSB psychiatrist evaluated Jimmy on September 11th, 1962 and wrote, "The prognosis is an individual that has been so deprived and who presents a severe character disorder as he does is necessarily poor; under the special circumstances that he is in it is even worse. I can't adventure at this point any suggestions."

Jimmy summarized his perspective: "I do what I want to do when I want to."

He presented a posture that was impenetrable. Jimmy was walled off, hardening himself against the world. Just before Christmas 1962, he was released from the Maryland Training School for Boys. Any hopes for a positive reintegration would be dashed against the rocks in less than six months.

– PRISON BREAKS AND SWEET POTATO PIES –
SECOND TERM: 1962 – 1966

Sheriff Samuel A. Graham announced he was running for a second term and no one stepped up to challenge him. In November 1962, he garnered 8,433 votes from the people of Wicomico County. Interestingly, there were two write-in votes cast against him, one of whom was the wife of the *Salisbury Advertiser's* editor. Alfred T. Truitt, Jr. also won his race for State's Attorney by another wide margin over his Republican opponent.

Mere weeks after his re-election, Sheriff Graham was hit with another brouhaha involving his wife's high school. This time, instead of skeletal remains, it was a football game. Wicomico High School held its homecoming game on Wednesday, November 28th, 1962 against rival Cambridge. Sheriff Graham, who was present, assigned six deputies to maintain order because a rumor was swirling that the goal posts might be torn down. During the game, a Cambridge football player was hurt and the Cambridge football coach approached a deputy to take him to the hospital. An ambulance was not readily available so the deputy said they'd transport him by car. The coach refused and again asked for an ambulance. His request went unanswered, and according to the coach, the deputy walked away. The player was loaded into a car and taken to Peninsula General Hospital. Despite that, Cambridge won for the first time in eleven years, thumping Wicomico 33-0, and that's when tempers

A photographer captures the tempers flaring at the football game. Sheriff Graham is pictured on the right with his finger pointed.

Image courtesy of the Edward H. Nabb Research Center for Delmarva History and Culture, Salisbury University, Mel Toadvine Collection

flared. Cambridge students attempted to take down the goal posts, which prompted Wicomico students to form a perimeter around them. Sheriff Graham was caught in the mayhem yelling and pointing fingers at the Cambridge students. (One goal post was damaged.) Eventually, the Cambridge folks left and the Wicomico fans went home to nurse their wounded pride.

But the fight wasn't over just yet. The injured football player was the son of the former mayor of Cambridge and town dentist, Dr. Russell P. Smith, Jr. The young man, although listed in "satisfactory condition," had a suspected head injury and was held overnight in the hospital for observation. The next morning, an incensed Dr. Smith called Sheriff

Graham, demanding to know the name of the deputy who refused to help his son. Dr. Smith said the deputy's answer was to "get him there to the hospital as best you can."

Sheriff Graham refuted this version of events, saying that his deputy offered a car because an ambulance wasn't available. Dr. Smith said it didn't happen that way. This enraged the otherwise mild-mannered sheriff who yelled into the phone, "Don't call me a liar!" and hung up on Dr. Smith. When a *Salisbury Times* reporter asked Graham about this testy phone call, he said, "When I told Dr. Smith that I didn't know which deputy had talked with him at the game, he told me I was lying. I figured that we had ended the conversation so I hung up the telephone." Big Sam could tolerate many things, but being called a liar was not one.

And if this gridiron battle was to be a prognosticator of his new term, then it foretold of disorder, injury, and frustration for Sheriff Graham.

• • •

August 1963 was a busy month for breakouts in the penthouse prison. On August 6th, 1963, a seventeen-year-old simply walked away from a deputy. The juvenile was serving a three-day sentence for stealing a salesman's sample case. He was believed to be with a fourteen-year-old girl and had headed off to Ocean City, Maryland. Two days later, a twenty-year-old who was being held on charges of auto theft, breaking and entering, and petty larceny got away from custody by mixing in with a prison crew headed for a road detail. Once he was among the crew, he went down the unattended elevator and out the door. Both escapees were found quickly: the seventeen-year-old was indeed with the fourteen-year-old girl, but they were in Leesburg, Virginia instead of Ocean City, and the twenty-year-old was captured in the Wicomico Theater.

Sixteen days later, on August 24th, that same twenty-year-old and another inmate, who was being held on a murder charge, made their escape from Graham's jail. The men sawed the bars off their cell with hacksaws; at around 2:20 a.m., they called out for the lone, on-duty deputy. When Deputy J. Merril Shockley approached them, they clubbed him with a piece of steel bar and dragged him into a detention cell. They took his keys and fled the jail in a white Buick convertible.

Sheriff Graham, living next door, heard strange sounds and went to investigate only to find Deputy Shockley a bloody mess. He had lacerations all over his scalp. The escapees had been gone for forty-five minutes. In their cell, the sheriff found that two ¾ inch bars had been removed, leaving an opening measuring about 10" by 12" wide. After a quick manhunt, the escapees were found the next day.

The sheriff learned the men had paid $20[1] to a couple of teenagers who smuggled in four hacksaw blades. One of the teens had shoved the contraband into his sock. Here again was an example of illicit items making their way into the penthouse prison. This should have raised alarm bells for everyone in the jail, especially Sheriff Graham, yet security measures did not appear to tighten. As for the teenaged smugglers, they were charged and sentenced to no more than five years at the Maryland Institution for Men in Hagerstown, Maryland.

Five months after the hacksaw escape, in February 1964, Sheriff Graham had to contend with two more break-outs that were entirely preventable. One prisoner, who was also wanted by North Carolina authorities for escape, had a seizure and was sent to Peninsula General Hospital. No one had assigned a guard to him so the prisoner quickly removed his leg shackles and walked out of the hospital. He was later found on a bus in Delmar. The next day, the Salisbury city police officers arrested a man who reportedly had stolen goods from a gas station. But when the Maryland State Police heard of the arrest, they were baffled because they had already arrested that same man several weeks earlier and he was supposed to be in the county jail. Had he escaped without notice? After a bit of head-scratching and conversations, the answer was made clear. The man's attorney, Vaughn E. Richardson, and the sheriff

---

1 $20 in 1963 is roughly equivalent to $200 in 2025.

had had a conversation about the prisoner leaving town if he could raise the fare. This conversation was overheard by a turnkey so when a call came into the jail about releasing the prisoner, that turnkey let him go.

Then on July 12th, 1964, three brothers, all juveniles, somehow managed to slip by Deputy J. Merril Shockley and hop into the elevator, which had been left unlocked by mistake. The boys hailed a taxi and made it as far as a trailer park on the north end of Route 13 in Salisbury. They were found and returned to the jail.

Not even three months later, early in the morning on October 6th, 1964, three more prisoners tried again, although this time they were thwarted by Sheriff Graham. One man was in the jail awaiting trial on burglary charges; the other two were there on breaking and entering and larceny charges. Once again, poor Deputy J. Merril Shockley was the target, the same deputy that Graham had found bloody and beaten in August 1963. This time, the inmates beat him with the wooden handle of a plunger and stabbed him with a broken comb; they grabbed his keys and his pocketknife. Just then, a trustee walked in with a cup of coffee for Deputy Shockley and saw what was happening. The prisoners asked the trustee about operating the elevator, but the trustee told them the electricity to the elevator was turned off at night. This wasn't true, but it stalled the three men. As the prisoners focused their attention on cracking the jail's safe, the trustee alerted the sheriff in his quarters next door. Dorothy Graham called for the Salisbury police as her husband rushed into the jail.

The scene erupted into a bloody and violent brawl between the lawmen and the prisoners. When the fight was over, the three inmates were back in their cells and the deputy and sheriff were sent to the hospital. Shockley had lacerations to his forehead and right eye as well as stab wounds to his abdomen and Graham had been stabbed in his chest and abdomen. Both men had long hospital stays for their injuries: Shockley was released after two weeks, but Graham stayed another week longer because his surgical incisions broke open, requiring extra medical care.

The same night that Sheriff Graham was released from the hospital, a massive prison riot broke out at the Maryland House of Correction in Jessup involving 800 prisoners. They took guards hostage; other guards locked themselves in open jail cells for safety. The riot was put down with assistance of local fire companies and a hundred law enforcement officers. Being in prison, whether as jailer or prisoner, was not for the faint of heart.

Before the unruly month of October 1964 came to a close, Deputy John Walston and Deputy John Kellam were accidentally locked *inside* a cell with those same three prisoners who had viciously attacked Shockley and Graham. They had been taking inmates to the shower area so that they could search the cells when a mechanism on the doors failed and locked them in. Fortunately, the prisoners remained calm and compliant while a mechanic was called to get the deputies out. For the attack on Deputy Shockley and Sheriff Graham, two of the three men later received fifteen-year sentences while the third received a twelve-year sentence.

Whether Sheriff Sam Graham could admit or not, his jail wasn't safe or secure. He and at least one of his deputies had the scars to prove it. Contraband was being smuggled in. Prisoners were escaping the penthouse prison. Prisoners were escaping custody. In January 1966, a man arrested for fighting at the Silver Dollar Tavern in Fruitland was taken to the hospital; when the deputy turned his back, the man walked away. A month later, a trustee went missing, but was found in a stolen truck in Washington, D.C. The trustee system mostly worked, but it did fail … like the time another trustee was allowed to go home early only to be promptly arrested for assaulting his wife. And reminiscent of little Rick Pollitt strolling into the prison to quiz the inmates about their life choices when his grandfather was the sheriff, similar visits happened under Graham's watch, too. Alfred Truitt's office was on the second floor of the courthouse and frequently his eldest child, Christine, would drop by after school. She and her friends would swing by Reed's Drug Store for an afternoon snack and then walk over to the courthouse. After seeing her father, she and her friends, who were in middle school at the time, sometimes went upstairs to the jail. They could see the inmates sitting in their cells. Again, by modern day standards, this is unthinkable and boggles the mind as to why the sheriffs did not see this as a problem. But apparently, in the 1950s and 1960s, getting into (or out of) the penthouse prison was so easy a kid could do it.

• • •

Every spring, at the opening of the new court session, Sheriff Graham invited the members of both the grand jury and the petit jury to a marvelous luncheon at the jail. When a *Salisbury Times* reporter asked about the political optics of such an event, the sheriff offered a small grin and said, "Well, it doesn't do any harm." Should there be any naysayers or grumpy political sentiments about his luncheons, the sheriff reminded the reporter they were paid for by him personally, not the county.

The bi-annual luncheons were a sought-after affair. Once the indictments were turned in, the grand jury was invited to a feast in the sheriff's quarters where card tables where set up all over the apartment. Everyone from the jurors and judges to clerks and probation officers mingled and chatted as the luncheon began, which, of course, was the main event. Even the newspaper editor noted that while the socializing aspect was important, "the meal is the thing." The food was prepared by the jail's cook, a Black woman named Emily Furr who had been employed there since 1949. Her renowned luncheon spreads included generous portions of ham and turkey, savory gelatin salads, fruit and nut molds, hot breads, pickles and olives, coffee, and homemade sweet potato pie. Of that sweet potato pie, one reporter wrote that it "had no equal on the Eastern Shore" while the editor declared that Emily Furr "serves up the best sweet potato pie you'll ever eat." She declined to discuss her recipe, only offering up that she used "canned potatoes (bent cans purchased at a reduced price from a local cannery)." The following week, the petit jury was invited for their turn at the sheriff's tables.

The luncheon was a tradition started by Sheriff Jesse Pollitt, but he had only fed the grand juries. Graham listened to the rumblings in the courthouse and quickly picked up that the petit juries were also looking to be invited to a luncheon. After all, why should the grand jury be so special? Even members of the press would sneak into Emily Furr's kitchen to steal bites while she was cooking; her sweet potato pies were an obvious target for sticky fingers. The jury members were served by women who worked in the courthouse. These ladies were welcome to eat at the luncheon too, but if they wanted a plate, then they had to pay for it.

As for the prisoners, their usual fare was not on par with these jury luncheons, as one might imagine, but that changed when the holidays rolled around. That's when the prisoners got a chance to sample Emily Furr's finer delicacies. On Thursday, November 24th, 1966, Sheriff Graham strolled into the prison kitchen. He was there to check on the meal she was cooking for the twenty-eight inmates. The sheriff and the cook had a mutual admiration for one another. Their fond regard may have started with good food, but it appeared to blossom into respect and kindness. Sheriff Graham was a man who loved to eat and Emily Furr knew just what he liked and enjoyed making it for him. He often took guests to the jailhouse kitchen just to introduce them to her. That Thanksgiving, as Big Sam peeked in the oven to cast a hungry eye on the 22-and-a-half pound bird roasting to perfection, Emily Furr gave him the rundown on the meal to come for the inmates: roasted turkey, homemade mashed potatoes, peas, cranberry sauce, and of course, her famous sweet potato pie. *There would be enough for seconds*, she told him.

Is it possible that Sheriff Graham snuck out of her kitchen with a piece of that pie? Only Emily Furr would know ... and if he had, well, she probably cut that slice herself.

· · ·

Sheriff Graham announced his own bid for re-election on May 4th, 1966. Despite the prison breaks and inmate incidents, he had a solid resumé on which to lean. He had successfully lobbied for more money for his department for cars, uniforms, raises, and extra staff, including another turnkey to improve overnight coverage in the jail. Graham had also increased the civil services his deputies provided to seven days a week. And his 1964 stabbing had elicited sympathy from the public. One man even wrote a letter to the editor of the *Daily Times*[2] saying, "Sheriff Graham and his deputies get few pats on the back and on occasion last year they were stabbed in the stomach. These men risk their lives for the citizens of Wicomico County. They are as underpaid and underpriced as any other group of peace officers." The *Daily Times* often remarked on Graham's jail as being clean and orderly. This was certainly evident when the bi-annual jury luncheons were occurring as many people who attended those would meander about the top floor, often right into the jail itself. (What the prisoners thought of citizens taking tours of their lockup can only be guessed. Perhaps it was akin to being an animal on display in a zoo.) Then there was the issue of those same prisoners being used as road work crews, a measure many in the public saw in a positive light.

Before the month was over, Sheriff Graham found himself running in the Democratic primary against two men: John L. Gordy, a painting contractor, and Oliver "Bob" Simpson, owner of a gas station. John Gordy, in addition to being a painter, was also a special, non-paid deputy[3] under Graham. Once Gordy announced his bid, it is unclear if he

---

2 On Friday, December 11th, 1964, the *Salisbury Times* changed its name to the *Daily Times* to reflect that its readership extended well beyond Salisbury, serving many communities across Delmarva.

3 These special, non-paid deputies were men who had been deputized, at various times for various reasons, with full law enforcement powers. They did not directly work for the sheriff's department as part- or full-time men. In 1967, one special, non-paid deputy would cause Graham great embarrassment when he shot at two men at a Christmas party.

continued in that capacity, especially given the tone of his political ads aimed directly at the sheriff. In one ad, he challenged Graham to have a Q&A with him on television or radio; in others, the tag lines were "We need a change - now!" and "Vote for a full time man!" Meanwhile, Bob Simpson quickly discovered that running for a public office meant one's private life became public as well. In the same article that announced his candidacy for county sheriff, Simpson had to apologize for two prior convictions: one for a 1960 possession of an untaxed alcoholic beverage for which he paid $500[4] and took a one-year suspended sentence, and another in 1962 for disorderly conduct which was suspended after a $10[5] court fee. Simpson took his lumps and told the paper, "These things are mistakes that are behind me. I'm sorry they happened. That was a long time ago." But perhaps not long enough as he only got 385 votes in the primary to Gordy's 1,390; Sheriff Graham took the primary in a landslide with 5,174 votes.

In the general election, Graham faced off against a familiar rival, former Wicomico County chief deputy Edward Dempsey Mitchell who had lost the 1958 Democratic primary for sheriff. Mitchell had worked for the sheriff's department from 1951 to 1958, presumably leaving after he lost the election to Graham. Now, Mitchell was running as a Republican and in his announcement for his candidacy in July 1966, he did not hold back: "The sheriff's office will not be a haven for political favors if I am elected. It will be open to all of the people of Wicomico County, with honest and equal service to all." As the campaigning progressed, Mitchell sought to differentiate himself from Graham, even going so far as to stylize himself in a white cowboy hat in his political ads above the slogan: "The Good Guy in the White Hat." His ads were the most direct hits that Graham had faced since his election in 1958. Mitchell posed blistering open-ended questions like "If you need assistance, would you like a Sheriff that will give you immediate help instead

---

4 $500 in 1960 is roughly equivalent to $5,400 in 2025.

5 $10 in 1962 is roughly equivalent to $100 in 2025.

of referring you to the Maryland State Police or Salisbury Police?" and "Would you like a dedicated Sheriff who is sincerely interested in law enforcement, not building a political machine?"

Sheriff Graham did not fight back in his newspaper ads. He was a busy county sheriff, after all. In September 1966, he was in the paper discussing a literal shotgun wedding in which the bride's father opened fire at the reception. The shotgun blast struck the bride, the groom, and the groom's brother—all survived. The father fled the scene and Sheriff Graham announced to the *Daily Times* that the search was on. (He was later brought up on assault charges.) Graham continued his work as the county's top lawman. He had requested and was granted an increase in payment to physicians who examined prisoners suspected of being mentally ill. Evening patrols had been beefed up. His political ads were simple and concise: "Sheriff Graham earnestly asks for your vote and support on November 8th. His qualifications, accomplishments and record in office merit your consideration." And that was it. That was all he had to say.

Election day was Tuesday, November 8th, 1966 and Republicans saw big wins all across the nation. In California, Hollywood movie star and former Democrat, Ronald Reagan won his gubernatorial race with 57% of the votes. For the office of Maryland's governor, Spiro Agnew, the son of a Greek immigrant, won an interesting three-way race. Locally, Republicans gained control of the Wicomico County Council while Democrats saw the votes swing in their favor for other offices. Among them were Alfred Truitt for Wicomico County State's Attorney and Samuel Graham for Wicomico County Sheriff. Graham defeated Edward D. Mitchell by more than 3,000 votes.

With this victory, Sam Graham headed into what would be his third—and final term—as the sheriff of Wicomico County.

– CROWNSVILLE STATE HOSPITAL –
"MARYLAND'S SHAME"

After his release from the Maryland Training School for Boys in December 1962, Jimmy went to stay with Dolores who was living with her grandmother and her other two children, Shirley and Ethan. The five of them were at 221 N. Madeira Street, a narrow lane with compact row houses on each side, located a few blocks from the historic Patterson Park in Baltimore. Like the many times before, this was a turbulent arrangement. He roamed the streets of Baltimore, fighting and selling drugs and stealing cars. In April 1963, Jimmy, now sixteen-years-old, was tried by the Criminal Court of Baltimore City for auto theft and given two years probation.

Jimmy was spiraling. His family could see it and they were frightened. There was one Easter when Jimmy was living with Dolores and his half-brother, Ethan. In an effort to get him to join the festivities, Dolores said to him, "Come on, help me dye some eggs."

"Mom, aren't you scared of me? Don't you know I'm crazy?"

"Jimmy, please don't say that."

He ran out the back door and paced in the yard. There was something in his hands. A knife? Dolores couldn't quite make out what it was. She watched as Jimmy stared at her through the window. Menacing. Dolores, now terrified, locked the back door and called her brother. When her brother arrived, he went out to the porch and called to his nephew, imploring him to calm down and come back inside. Jimmy responded by throwing the knife at him. It missed. Eventually, he was able to settle Jimmy down and get him back in the house.

The escalation of his behaviors was troubling for everyone in the family and no one seemed to know how to manage it anymore. He was no longer stealing candy bars and back-talking; now, he was older, more streetwise, more dangerous.

In early May 1963, Jimmy grabbed a butcher knife and threatened to kill his great-grandmother. When the police arrived, they arrested Jimmy and took him to a jail in Baltimore. Dolores told authorities her son had been acting abnormally for weeks; he even threatened to throw himself out of a second story window. Because of this episode, Jimmy was committed to Crownsville State Hospital on May 4th, 1963.

If there was a place to rival or outdo the nightmarish conditions of the Maryland Training School for Boys, this was it.

• • •

Crownsville State Hospital was originally called the Hospital for the Negro Insane of Maryland[1] and it was established by a bill passed in the Maryland Legislature in 1910. In the spring of 1911, the state purchased a 566-acre farm near Crownsville, Maryland, several miles northwest of the state capital of Annapolis. Almost immediately, Black men from other Maryland hospitals like Spring Grove State Hospital in Catonsville and Montevue Hospital in Frederick were sent here. When they arrived at the Hospital for the Negro Insane of Maryland, they were not greeted by a hospital. There were no medical or psychiatric facilities. Instead, the newly-purchased farm had a large wooden building, possibly an old curing house for willow or tobacco, and this is where the men were kept. They slept on cots with rolled-up mattresses, side by side, in a room with wooden walls and a lofted ceiling. There was a long

---

1 The history of Crownsville State Hospital is thoroughly researched and expertly presented in *Madness: Race and Insanity in a Jim Crow Asylum* by Antonia Hylton, published in 2024 by Legacy Lit, Hachette Book Group.

Crownsville State Hospital, circa April 2024.
On the left is the administrative building.

Image courtesy of the author

table with benches on each side where they ate their meals. Lanterns hung from the tall rafters; if they were to look up, they would see the exposed lengths of timber beams. In short, the patients were living in a barn.

Every day, these men worked the fields of the farm, producing fruits and vegetables for themselves and for sale. They were put to the task of building the hospital and its patient wings. They harvested willow to send to Spring Grove in Catonsville and Springfield Hospital Center in Sykesville, Maryland, where those patients would use the slender reeds to make baskets. They even built a railroad spur near the hospital. But these men received no wages. They were patients who could not say no or go home. They were Black men whose free and constant labor, always overseen by White administrators and managers, was going to the good of the State, a set-up that harkens back to that darkest of institutions: slavery. There was no mention of therapy other than the work itself ... hard labor alone was to be their remedy.

On March 8th, 1912, a fire destroyed their barn. The men had just sat down to eat their dinner around 6:00 p.m. when the blaze began. All seventy patients made it out including a paralyzed man who was pulled from his cot and heroically carried to safety by another patient. The building was gone in a matter of minutes. One patient, who had given himself the name "Golden Prophet," said the fire was punishment for keeping him against his will. The actual cause of the fire is unknown.

Crownsville State Hospital, as it was renamed not long after the 1912 fire, became a massive complex of three- and four-story red brick buildings designed to house up to 250 patients. The farming continued as evidenced by the barns scattered across the emerald lawns and open fields of the campus.

Life at the hospital was brutal for the Black men, women, and children who were admitted there. Few were discharged. They were more likely to die inside the massive brick walls of the asylum. This was especially true in the days when the hospital was a tuberculosis colony. Children with epilepsy were left at Crownsville because their families were often unable to care for their special needs. There was a myriad of reasons why a patient might find themselves in Crownsville and it wasn't always a mental or psychiatric one. Orphaned. Unwanted. Alcoholic. Homeless. Syphilitic. Those muted by trauma. Many of these patients never saw their families again. Jails, almshouses, and asylums from all over the state of Maryland sent their Black inmates to Crownsville.

But this was not a place where they would go to get better. They endured horrific treatments like lobotomies and both electroshock and insulin shock therapy. Some patients were injected with malaria. They were put into tubs of hot and cold water for up to twenty-four hours at a time. Other patients had holes drilled into their skulls which were filled with oxygen or helium, a practice called pneumoencephalography. This very likely happened to a young Black girl named Lucile Elsie Pleasant who was admitted to Crownsville in 1950 due to her epilepsy and other mental disabilities. Her mother, Henrietta Lacks, came to visit her daughter regularly until her death in 1951. Then, Elsie Lacks, as she was known, languished away at Crownsville where she died in 1955 at the age of fifteen. Her mother's legacy was tied to a different Maryland hospital. The immortal HeLa cells that transformed cancer research came from Henrietta Lacks when a doctor at Johns Hopkins Hospital took samples of her cervical tumor. No one asked Henrietta's consent to have her tissue multiplied for generations to come; no one asked Elsie or her family for consent to drill into her skull either.

These "treatments" were more like science experiments performed on people who had absolutely no agency over their own bodies. They could not say no. They could not leave. They *had* to endure. And when they died, their bodies were buried in nameless graves on the hospital grounds.

• • •

In early January 1949, the *Baltimore Sun* ran a series of articles about the state of Maryland's five mental hospitals. The exposé, "Maryland's Shame," was written by Pulitzer Prize-winning journalist Howard M. Norton. His months-long investigation was published alongside photographs of men, women, and children in all manner of filth, exploitation, and degradation.

Norton's reporting explained that the five hospitals—Spring Grove State Hospital in Catonsville, Springfield Hospital Center in Sykesville, Rosewood Center in Owings Mills, Eastern Shore State Hospital in Cambridge, and Crownsville State Hospital near Annapolis—had a combined patient capacity of 6,000 yet they held more than 9,000 people. The overcrowding led to unimaginably unsanitary conditions: children smeared in fecal matter, thin mattresses so covered in dirt and urine that flies collected in droves, persistent stenches of body odors, and hoards of patients fighting over broken toilets. Some hospitals ran out of beds, cots, and chairs, forcing patients to sleep on the concrete floors.

Each facility was woefully understaffed, which meant that patients, including violent ones, were escaping and that patients who could have been treated and made better were overlooked entirely. In Springfield, where there was just one nurse for the 3,000 patients living there, he saw a woman tied to a stair banister. These people were among the most vulnerable in the state and yet the majority were not receiving any psychiatric treatment or even basic medical care.

Maryland's shame, indeed.

Norton's commentary on Crownsville was bleak. There were more than 1,800 Black men, women, and children packed into a facility that only had room for a thousand and, for them, there were eight doctors, a single nurse, and 110 attendants. "The Dumping Ground," as Norton called it, had patients sleeping in damp, dark basements and sweltering attic spaces. Children slept two to a bed. They had no toys to play with and there were no educational opportunities provided for them like there was for the White children at Rosewood.

Because Crownsville was racially segregated—one of only three of its kind in the entire country—all the attendants and medical staff were White. This was a requirement. The starting pay for attendants was a paltry $1,380[2] per year, which did not attract the best sort of employees. One attendant, Norton reported, had been "turned over to the police for allegedly raping a girl inmate." In much of the exposé, the patients are referred to as "inmates" (like prison inmates). Although the word choice is unfortunate as it implies criminality to a group of people who were in need of therapy and medical care, there are similarities. They could not leave. Those who were able-bodied (or "borderline cases") worked for nothing while others received the benefit of their labor. The rest spent their hours in an endless idle state of nothingness and boredom. They were fed poorly. Maryland was spending roughly $0.49 per patient per day on food in the five hospitals which was less than what was spent on prisoners who received anywhere from $0.54 to $0.60 per

---

2 $1,380 in 1949 is roughly equivalent to $18,600 in 2025.

inmate per day.³ They received little medical or therapeutic care. They slept in tight, uncomfortable quarters that reeked of body odors. They rarely, if ever, saw their families. And the patients, just like the prisoners, had very little hope of rescue or release.

After the expose, Governor William Preston Lane's office and the *Baltimore Sun* received a deluge of correspondence from people across the state and beyond. Some of the letter writers were shocked and appalled by what they had read; others independently confirmed Howard Norton's reporting by giving their firsthand accounts of things they witnessed in the five hospitals. But every writer echoed the same refrain: what was Maryland going to do about this? The answer was as expected: not much at all. The year after Norton's exposé, every psychiatric hospital in the state saw its budget cut by nearly a quarter.

If there was a hell on earth, then Crownsville State Hospital was as good a candidate as any other. This is where Jimmy would spend two years as a teenager.

• • •

Sixteen-year-old Jimmy Bartholomey arrived at Crownsville State Hospital on May 4th, 1963. The spring sunshine cast a hearty warmth over the sprawling green lawns, touching everything from the ancient willow trees that peppered the lush campus to the cows and pigs in the pastures. The winding paths and roads revealed a maze of facility buildings, cottages, and barns resting on more than 1,700 acres, of which about 530 were still being used as fields for agricultural purposes. Cows grazed in preparation for their time in the dairy. The capable patients of Crownsville did the farming, the planting, the raising, and the butchering. The beauty of that May day may have even lessened the imposing feeling of the brick buildings with their barred windows and flat facades. The administration building, with its four, tall white columns

---

3 $0.49 and $0.60 in 1949 is roughly equivalent to $7 and $8 in 2025.

and second floor balcony, gave a slight air of a distinguished mansion and in the sunlit perfection of the day, it may have even looked inviting.

Yet, this was Crownsville State Hospital and it was many things but welcoming was not one of them.

On January 7th, 1963, four months prior to Jimmy's arrival, Crownsville State Hospital finally integrated the patient population. The medical staff had included Black employees since at least 1949. Feelings of resentment and animosity among the families of White patients were well-known; they bristled at the notion of having their loved one at Crownsville, long noted for its Black-only patient population. The racist overtures played out in the community and in the newspapers, and while the immediate fervor was hot, it eventually fizzled out. Black or White, the nearly two thousand patients at Crownsville fared no better than patients at any other psychiatric hospital in Maryland.

Jimmy Bartholomey was Patient #25257. "Pugnacious and homicidal": this was how he was summarized in his patient notes. One examiner wrote that Jimmy did not respond well to hospital policies, but then again, records note that he saw authority as something to be resisted and resented, not respected. So, hospital policies be damned. The staff did seem to understand that he posed a high risk of escaping and running away. (And he would.)

That same month Jimmy was admitted to Crownsville, Dolores Bartholomey suffered a nervous breakdown and signed herself into Crownsville, too. This only complicated things for Jimmy. The staff did their best to keep them apart because, according to his hospital notes, any time Dolores came around, Jimmy became agitated and hostile. She stayed about two weeks and left.

Within two months of his commitment to Crownsville State Hospital, Jimmy eloped for two days on July 2nd, 1963. The term "elope" was frequently used by the hospital and newspapers alike to refer to an escape. (Perhaps it sounds less dangerous to have a psychiatric patient "elope" rather than "escape.") The second time he eloped was a few days later, on July 8th and he was gone for over three weeks. His sister, Shirley, brought him back because he was fighting. His next elopement occurred on August 27th and was twenty days long before he was returned to Crownsville by the police. His fourth elopement, on October 21st, lasted just a single day. The staff noted that each time he eloped, he went to see his mother.

Elopements from Crownsville were common and had even resulted in patient death. For example, just a month and a half before Jimmy (and Dolores) were committed to Crownsville, a patient had eloped. The 32-year-old woman was found dead the next day, face down in a wooded area about a thousand feet from her building. She had only been at the hospital for five days. On February 10th, 1964, a 34-year-old male patient eloped and was found dead forty-six days later by a Boy Scout near the Severn River. Another man escaped in June 1964 and vanished from sight. Other patients eloped but either came back or were returned by the police or their families.

While Jimmy was there, the treatment of patients remained questionable. Several children were purposefully injected with hepatitis. A patient who had been living at Crownsville since 1950 had given birth. She had been raped by one of the staff members, a person who was supposed to care for her. The patient's mother filed a $200,000[4] suit against the administration during the summer of 1963. Some patients were given intense doses of thorazine to make them compliant. Sexual activity and sexual assaults were commonplace at Crownsville State Hospital. One child, under the age of ten, said he was molested in a bathroom. Some female patients were rumored to have sex for cigarettes. A condom dispenser near the canteen was routinely empty.[5]

Crownsville State Hospital wasn't a good place for Jimmy. He

---

4 $200,000 in 1950 is roughly equivalent to $2.6 million in 2025.

5 In Antonia Hylton's book, she draws attention to CSH staff members who were kind and did all they could to help the patients under their watch. It is unfortunate that their good deeds are unreported in most materials.

stopped taking classes, effectively ending his meager education at the 11th grade. He got into fights. He was caught stealing. He broke into the soda machines. In early March 1964, he was caught drinking. The one bright spot was that his relationships with his family seemed to improve slightly, including a two-day visit (not an elopement) to see his family where he somehow managed to secure a job as a printer's assistant. But when his sister called about extending the visit, the hospital denied her request. A few weeks later, on April 29th, 1964, seventeen-year-old Jimmy was discharged from Crownsville State Hospital. He had been there for almost a year.

He went to live with Dolores. *Again.* This time, she was living at 6816 Eastbrook Avenue in Dundalk, east of downtown Baltimore. This blue collar neighborhood was spacious compared to the row house on North Madeira. The house on Eastbrook Avenue was a duplex and connected to four other duplex units, each with a small front yard and narrow backyard. Nearby, the open air Eastpoint Mall catered to every shopper's desire with stores like Hutzler's and Hess Shoes. While this quaint neighborhood was more pleasant than a mental hospital, Jimmy's darkness remained.

One day, Dolores recalled that while she was standing in the kitchen talking to Jimmy, he turned to her and said, "Mom, someday I am going to have to kill someone."

She responded with alarm. "Jimmy, please don't ever say that! What makes you say things like this?"

"I just know I have to, then I know I am going to be alright."

Another day, while Dolores was sitting in a chair, Jimmy approached her with a knife in his hand. Dolores froze. He took the blade of the knife and ran it up and down her arm. The fear in Dolores's throat finally let loose. "Jimmy, if you want to do it, just go ahead!"

He stopped and looked at her. Then he laughed.

To no one's surprise, Jimmy got into trouble. *Again.* On August 25th, 1964, Jimmy and a friend were drinking and decided to break into a house. He stole some jewelry which he attempted to hide in Dolores's home, but she found it and turned him into the police. (Apparently, he had been doing this for some time, breaking and entering into homes; this was just the first time he had been caught.) He was arrested and jailed for two days before a judge placed him on probation and ordered that he be returned to Crownsville State Hospital. *Again*. He'd only been gone four months.

On August 27th, 1964, seventeen-year-old Jimmy Bartholomey was sent back to Crownsville. Upon his intake, the examiner noted that he was "untidy" and "unkempt," but that he was also "friendly and cooperative." The diagnostic impression, the examiner wrote, was adjustment reaction of adolescence and transient personality disturbance situation, which were in the same diagnostic ballpark as his diagnosis from the Maryland Children's Center. However, these terms are no longer used, and modern mental health experts would likely use conduct disorder to describe what was going on with Jimmy. He was a young person routinely behaving in a way that violated social norms and rules in serious ways like stealing cars and a gun, breaking into homes, and bullying others and constantly running away. He generally lacked feelings of remorse for his actions. By today's definitions, if a child with conduct disorder continues these behaviors into adulthood, then that diagnosis would likely be replaced with antisocial personality disorder.

Jimmy admitted to the staff he had been breaking into homes regularly without being caught. They noted he was "slightly depressed" and was "quiet most of the time." Jimmy was oriented to reality and denied having any hallucinations. He could remember and recall information but the examiners felt that "his judgement ... was impaired and so was his insight."

Impaired judgement was a theme for Crownsville State Hospital during this time. The superintendent, Dr. Charles Ward, found himself in legal trouble: driving on a revoked license, owing child support, and writing bad checks. Although the staff at CSH generally liked Dr. Ward, they were concerned about his drug use, specifically amphetamines, as both his behavior and driving were seen as erratic. In September 1964, the state commissioner of mental health asked him to resign. Ward flatly refused to leave Crownsville, an act that launched a seven-month long court battle he ultimately lost.

Meanwhile, for Jimmy, there was a brief moment of possible rescue in March 1965, the same month he turned eighteen. The acting superintendent of Crownsville wrote a letter to a judge in the Circuit Court of Baltimore County requesting his advice on possibly placing Jimmy with his sister, Shirley, who was now twenty-one and living in Tacoma, Washington with her husband, who was in the Army. There was no hope that Jimmy could live with Dolores or Joseph and Betty. The new arrangement appeared to be headed for a green light, pending airfare for Jimmy, but at the last moment, it fell apart when Shirley and her military man split up.

So he was stuck at Crownsville, but he had turned eighteen. Little Jimmy was gone. No more small-time escapades. No more nicknames. Only a handful of people would remember the boy he had once been. He was legally an adult now and his actions as a man would have calamitous consequences. When his crimes hit the newspapers in the years to come, no one called him Jimmy Bartholomey. The storm now had a real name and the world would come to know him as Joseph J. Bartholomey, Jr.

On June 17th, 1965, Joseph eloped from Crownsville State Hospital again and headed for the Eastern Shore of Maryland. He met a 23-year-old woman in a bar in Ocean City and lived with her for a short time. Then he got a job working for Maryland Cup Company but was fired because he could not, or would not, follow orders and slacked off. He bummed money from friends and his family. His summer on the lam ended when he was taken back to Crownsville on August 20th, 1965.

True to form, ten days later, he was gone *again*. This time, he made a key and escaped from the Meyer Building on the Crownsville campus with three other patients. They had walked about half a mile from the institution when they saw a Chevy sitting in a driveway. Joseph saw the key was in the ignition so he got in the driver's seat. The foursome headed to Ocean City. Each of them knew different people in Ocean City and Joseph was trying to get back to that 23-year-old woman from the bar.

As reasonably expected, their attempt at freedom went awry. Two of the young men returned to Crownsville. Joseph and a patient named Michael stayed behind. Michael was speeding and the police gave chase. He took a sharp turn onto a dead end road, but when he tried to back out, the cops were behind them and he hit the police car. Then, Joseph and Michael tried to run, but they were caught and jailed.

By this point, Joseph's crimes were piling up on themselves: he had stolen cars, used and sold drugs, committed larceny, escaped from multiple state institutions, violated his probations, issued numerous threats including one to kill his own great-grandmother, admitted to several instances of breaking and entering into homes, and now he had assaulted a police officer. After this eventful elopement, Crownsville State Hospital immediately discharged him.

Charged with assault with intent to kill and auto larceny, Joseph was now in the hands of the Worcester County Circuit Court, which ordered him to be admitted to yet another psychiatric institution. The court needed an answer to a critical question: was Joseph Bartholomey mentally competent to stand trial for the assault and theft charges?

– CLIFTON T. PERKINS STATE HOSPITAL –

IMPRESSION: SOCIOPATHIC PERSONALITY, ANTISOCIAL REACTION

Thursday, September 2nd, 1965 was a warm, sunny day for Marylanders. The sweltering heat of the summer was beginning to recede into milder temperatures. On this picturesque day, with a blue sky and white puffy clouds overhead, Joseph Bartholomey was admitted to Clifton T. Perkins State Hospital, Maryland's maximum security psychiatric facility. The hospital was located in Jessup, a small town southwest of Baltimore that was also home to the Maryland House of Correction, a violent prison known by its equally violent nickname, "The Cut."

Clifton T. Perkins State Hospital sat on 45-acres of green grass surrounded by tall trees and railway lines on Dorsey Run Road. The Maryland House of Correction was about a mile away on the east side of the railroad tracks. The hospital traces its roots back to 1959 when Governor J. Millard Tawes signed a bill for the establishment of a maximum security psychiatric hospital. One newspaper stated that the new facility was reserved for "mental patients who constitute a menace to society." The original hospital was a two-story brick building with six wings and by mid-January 1960, there were already thirty patients at the facility, which was designed to hold up to 250 patients. Those patients came from Crownsville and Spring Grove. And just like the penthouse prison in Salisbury, this hospital was also hailed as a modern marvel.

One national expert called it "almost singular" in its efforts to maintain maximum security while allowing the patients an unusual level of freedom and comfort. The hospital's namesake was Dr. Clifton T. Perkins, who had been the head of Maryland's department of mental hygiene. Months after his death in November 1959, there was a push in Annapolis to have the brand new hospital named in his honor. The decision was made official in April 1960.

That same month, on April 12th, 1960, three patients escaped from Clifton T. Perkins State Hospital, casting doubt on the "maximum security" part of its billing. The men forced open a door and then scaled a fourteen-foot wall with a pole, but they were captured within hours by Maryland State Police after they stole a car and ended up in a fight with the cops. (An event that sounds right out of Joseph's playbook.) This was the first escape from the hospital, which had just opened in January.

Clifton T. Perkins State Hospital was a place for the worst of the worst cases. Take, for example, Mack Wilson Fierst. He was considered a very dangerous man who had once been charged with murder among other crimes; the *Baltimore Sun* described him as "a vicious, deliberate, cold-blooded, extremely dangerous 'beast' who would murder anyone who would stand in his way." His behavior was certainly striking: in a move straight out of a Hollywood thriller, for thirteen years he had managed to successfully fake paralysis in his right arm as well as muteness, communicating through "grunts and pantomime," according to the newspapers. Fierst escaped from CTPSH in April 1961 by sawing away the grill on his window using a hacksaw likely left behind by a worker. He jumped from the second story window and ran, igniting a thirteen-state alarm that even involved the FBI before being captured ten days later in Washington, D.C. (In the late 1980s, he'd be arrested again—this time for running cocaine.) Another infamous CTPSH inmate was Reginald Oates, who sexually assaulted and killed four children in Baltimore's Gwynns Falls Leakin Park. His crime spree came to an end when he was detained by cops staking out the park after receiving reports of missing children. Police knew they had their killer: in his possession was a paper bag containing body parts. When the bodies of the missing children were found, the detective saw the horrific mutilations he had performed: one was missing his hands, another his head, and some were missing their genitals. Reginald Oates, an eighteen-year-old, unemployed, Bible-reading janitor, was determined to be incompetent and was sent to Clifton T. Perkins for the remainder of his natural life.

This hospital was not designed for the meek and mild.

• • •

Dolores filled out the history questionnaire for Joseph when he arrived at Clifton T. Perkins State Hospital. Her handwriting was blocky and unsophisticated; the printed letters were an odd combination of both upper case and lower case. She listed her son's occupation as "laborer" for the Maryland Cup Company; by this time, Dolores had worked there for several years as well. In a question about his sexual behaviors, Dolores wrote that Joseph "would be seen fooling with himself in public." Later, Joseph would deny this behavior, saying he had only masturbated once or twice in his life and he remained generally tight-lipped about his sexual experiences. She wrote that he drank alcohol and "at one time there was reason to think he took pep pills." This note is a bit odd since she had previously complained about him selling drugs and catching him sniffing glue. On the topic of religion, Dolores noted they were Catholic and that Joseph would go to church, but said he "has been seen to look at the Lord's picture and curse at him." There is a tinge of a mother's desperation when she writes that her son "did not want to be loved, very disobedient … seems to be getting into deeper trouble … always felt as though he was never wanted and everyone was against him." She said she was told he once tried to strangle himself in jail, but she did not indicate when or where that might have happened.

The form asked for an evaluation of the mother and father. Dolores wrote of herself: warm, kind, understanding, and good provider. Of her ex-husband, she wrote that he had no interest in his first children, meaning Shirley and Joseph as opposed to the children he had with Betty. In another spot, she wrote that Joseph Sr. drank heavily—something Shirley also recalled—and that he had walked out on the family when the children were young. On a question about the onset of the current trouble, Dolores wrote "seen a change when father left his family." Reading between the lines, Dolores had some unresolved resentment towards Joseph's father.

The nursing staff evaluated the new patient. He was just a hair over 5'7" and 126 pounds. Eighteen years old. Scars on both arms and wrists and a small laceration on his upper lip just below the left nostril. Freckles on his chest. No tattoos. Left-handed. No tonsils. Mild temperature of 100°. No medications other than Fostex cream, perhaps for acne or some similar skin issue. No history of seizures. Negative for syphilis.

Joseph's history with women is sparse and hard to discern. In his Perkins file, his mother is listed as his first point of contact, but a young woman named Carol Smith[1] from Pasadena, Maryland is listed as the alternative. In a conversation with a social worker at Perkins, Joseph did not mention Carol and only gave his mother as his primary contact. He also did not mention her during interviews with the psychiatric staff. During one conversation, Joseph said he had been with three or four girls since his first sexual encounter at thirteen with an older woman at the Maryland Training School for Boys. He told the doctor he wasn't engaged and didn't go steady with anyone. Yet, shockingly, in another conversation with a Perkins social worker, he said he had gotten married when he was sixteen and had lived with her for three weeks until her parents discovered what they had done and had the marriage annulled. Was this a reference to Carol Smith? A teenage marriage is suspicious given that he was at Crownsville for most of his sixteenth year, but with Joseph Bartholomey just about anything was possible including

---

1 Name changed.

wholesale fabrication. He told the Perkins social worker that he still corresponded with her and was interested in her while also relating the story of the 23-year-old woman in Ocean City who was his reason for eloping from Crownsville.

On November 18th, 1965, Joseph was given a battery of psychological tests, one of which was the Wechsler Adult Intelligence Scale. (He had been administered the child's version twice before.) On this test, his full scale IQ score was 95 and his verbal was 101—average results showing a consistency from his youth into adulthood. However, his performance IQ was 88 and fell in the low average range again. This was similar to low performance score five years prior at MTSB, and again, this could indicate he might have had a nonverbal learning disability.

Joseph was assigned to Ward 3 at Clifton T. Perkins State Hospital. Over the course of several weeks, he was interviewed by social workers, nursing staff, and psychiatric doctors. With one social worker, he appeared "marginally friendly and cooperative and participated well" in their discussions. He acknowledged he had committed the crimes but did not express any remorse or regret over them. He didn't think he was insane and denied having hallucinations or delusions. He ate, slept, and maintained good hygiene. The social worker noted Joseph was "a nonchalant individual." But on Ward 3, Joseph's initial friendliness wore off quickly. He used profanity and argued with other patients and hospital staff. When he was moved to Ward 4, he cursed at the attendants. He was loud which agitated the other patients.

A duality emerged again in the psychiatric notes. It was something that his family noticed and then other social workers and mental health professionals had started to see as well. Joseph, in one-on-one settings, could be friendly. One doctor wrote that Joseph was "cooperative and attentive and a good rapport could be established with him ... [he was a] rather attractive young boy who tries to create a good impression and usually is successful in doing so." But if he had an audience, Joseph could turn on the bad boy persona and he liked to be seen as a rebel, as unbreakable. He wanted the attention and the notoriety. When he attended group therapy, he pushed his chair away from the others and lobbed complaints and insults into the center of the group. But if his disruptive efforts went unnoticed, he quieted down and inched closer to the group. In a ringleader role, Joseph threatened to start a riot with three other patients after a dispute with the hospital staff. For this, he was moved to yet another ward.

For the three months Joseph was at Clifton T. Perkins State Hospital, from September 2nd, 1965 through early December 1965, no one from his family came to visit him, although Dolores and Shirley said they wrote letters to him. The staff sent letters to his family but received no response. One examiner saw the internal turmoil his family caused him: "... his early years prior to his parents [sic] divorce were filled with much overt hostility and very little love and attention. The continuing changes in living arrangements made him feel unwanted and insecure. The fact that his mother kept and raised his younger, illegitimate half-brother, not him, has caused the patient much confusion and resentment. ... In light of his past and present behavior, and his lack of insight, judgement, and uncontrolled impulses, I believe his anti-social behavior will continue."

Dolores sensed the resentment Joseph felt toward Ethan; Joseph fought with him, and in turn, Ethan appeared to be afraid of his half-brother. The psychiatrists noted his family history as being a large part of Joseph's problems. One doctor wrote: "The patient is the product of a pathological family and has suffered a continuous traumatic experience since this very early childhood." Joseph also seemed to acknowledge this when he told a Perkins social worker, "I never got too settled because I knew it would be just a matter of time before they'd move me again, I really didn't care though."

His diagnosis was sociopathic personality, antisocial reaction. Today, mental health professionals would use a diagnosis of antisocial personality disorder. It describes the person's consistent inability to conform to the norms, rules, and laws of society. They understand right from wrong but that does not dissuade them from doing what they want to do. The *DSM-5* describes antisocial personality disorder as a consistent pattern of behavior, exhibited from childhood into adulthood, in which the person continually violates and disregards the rights of other people. Antisocial personality disorder behaviors include, but are not limited to the following:

- Will not conform to societal rules, laws, or norms and does so repeatedly, even to the point of arrest
- Lying, being deceitful, manipulative, even to the point of conning others for personal gain
- Being impulsive and not taking responsibility
- An aggressive and bullying nature, even to the point of physically assaulting others, which also includes not taking into consideration potential harm to self and other people
- A lack of guilt, shame, remorse, and conscience, especially when others have been harmed and hurt by their actions

Further, to diagnose a person with antisocial personality disorder, the person must also be a legal adult, have exhibited these traits before the age of fifteen, and show that this is their consistent behavioral pattern, not sporadic or episodic within the confines of another diagnosis.

At Clifton T. Perkins State Hospital, Joseph denied having delusions or hallucinations or hearing voices. Instead, he understood what he had done wrong and why he was in the hospital; his take on recent events was that everyone was just blowing it out of proportion. What he had done wasn't really a big deal, Joseph intimated, and he resented being hospitalized. The prognosis wasn't cheery. Joseph's criminal endeavors combined with this antisocial behavior would continue and likely escalate if he did not receive constant supervision and immediate rehabilitation while in protective custody.

On November 22nd, 1965, Joseph appeared before a medical conference of eleven staff member to determine if he was competent to stand trial in Worcester County. In that meeting, Joseph never denied his involvement in the crimes for which he was arrested. Rather, he simply shrugged it off. Indifferent and aloof. As if the entire meeting was a waste of his time. The medical conference went like this:

"What kind of punishment would you think to be suitable for you?"

"I think I've been locked up long enough. I mean, it was an accident, that we hit the cop. It wasn't on purpose. Of course, we did steal the car."

"What about stealing the car? Is that something you should be punished for?"

"I think I've done enough time already."

"How long has this been since this actually happened?"

Joseph answered, "Three months."

"You think three months being confined is enough punishment for stealing a car?"

"I've been confined for two straight years."

"Oh but this was before the car stealing, wasn't it?"

Joseph replied, "Yes."

"You think that time should be applied to your punishment for stealing the car three months ago?"

"No, but I think three months is enough."

When asked about his future plans, Joseph said he didn't know what he was going to do. They probed further and Joseph replied, "I did want to be a ball player. A guy who used to play on the Los Angeles Dodgers told me I might be able to play. That's shot down the drain. I don't know what I'm going to do now." That last statement was certainly true.

The Clifton T. Perkins State Hospital medical committee, based on their findings during his three-month stay in their facility, determined that he was responsible at the time of the crime and therefore Joseph J. Bartholomey, Jr. was competent to stand trial.

– CRIME ON THE RISE –
THIRD TERM: 1966–1967

On December 8th, 1966, Sheriff Samuel Graham was sworn in for his third term and he immediately got back to the task of running the county's sheriff department and jail. On that same day, he proposed to the Wicomico County Council the hiring of four more men for night patrol and expressed the need for two more cars. Presently, he had six full-time men and six cars and sometimes only a single deputy might be on patrol. Sheriff Graham also sought to break the county into patrol quadrants in the hopes that crime might be deterred as his deputies got to know their areas and were seen regularly by the folks there. The council was in agreement and, a week later, they authorized the sheriff to hire two more men instead of four. Crime rates were on the rise, a fact acknowledged by both lawmen and the public. Wicomico County had grown by nearly 24% from 1950 to 1960; it was now home to approximately 50,000 people or more. And, as if to drive home the point about an increase in crime, during the meeting in which the additional deputies were authorized, a thief broke into Wicomico County Councilman George F. Burnett's business and stole $22[1] from a register. It was the third theft at his business in a matter of weeks.

The burgeoning crime rates were felt in county jail as the inmate population swelled. Normally, the penthouse prison held, on average, thirty-five inmates, but by early January 1967, that number was fifty-one.[2]

---

1 $22 in 1966 is roughly equivalent to $215 in 2025.

2 It may have felt more crowded, but the jail had a total capacity for eighty people.

"Look at that book," Sheriff Graham told a *Daily Times* reporter. "I can't ever remember when we had so many up here in jail charged this many serious crimes." And they were serious, as the reporter noted: "Fifteen prisoners are awaiting grand jury action on breaking and entering charges. Three are charged with murder. Two are being held on charges of receiving stolen goods. One is accused of armed robbery. Two others are charged with assault with a deadly weapon. Another is charged with assault and robbery." This already took into account six men accused of major theft who had already been released on bond and the early release of five prisoners during Christmas, although one man decided to stay in the county jail when he heard what the inmates were having for Christmas Dinner. (Another nod to Emily Furr's culinary reputation and her Christmas turkeys and sweet potato pies.)

One of the men hired to do the night patrols was a 42-year-old military veteran from Fort Dodge, Iowa named Delbert E. Fowler. Everyone called him Bud. At seventeen, he enlisted in the United States Navy at Great Lakes, Illinois just thirty-seven days after the bombing of Pearl Harbor. Growing up a poor kid in Iowa, he was no stranger to hard work and the military had much to offer him. Bud served as a mechanic at the U.S. Naval Air Station in Corpus Christi, Texas and was transferred to Kingsville Field in Texas and then to Norfolk, Virginia where he was deployed on the aircraft carrier USS *Coral Sea*. He did not see combat and remained stateside for the war. Bud was later transferred to the Naval Auxiliary Air Station on Chincoteague Island, Virginia. During his time there, he met a young woman from Salisbury named Elizabeth "Libby" Mills at a March of Dimes Dance at the Salisbury Armory on January 30th, 1945. They were married six weeks later and quickly had two sons. When his time in the Navy was up, Bud re-enlisted in 1950, but this time with the Army where he made the rank of sergeant. He was stationed in Japan and Germany as well as several military bases across the United States. While he was in Germany, Bud earned his GED and was handed a diploma. His wife and two boys often followed

Delbert "Bud" Fowler was a career military man who was hired as a full-time Wicomico County Sheriff's Deputy in 1967.

Image courtesy of the author

him, and eventually the entire Fowler family landed back in Salisbury. They moved into their old house at 707 Madison Street; Libby's father had built the house for them when Bud was between enlistments with the Navy and Army. The home was small and modest but they made a comfortable life for themselves. Their sons enrolled at Wicomico High School, where Dorothy Graham remained a formidable figurehead.

On his first day of military retirement in 1964, Bud went to work at a chicken processing plant as a mechanic. His father-in-law—a successful and affluent car salesman in Fruitland—likely disapproved of this job just as he had long disapproved of Bud. Perhaps he felt that line of work was beneath his daughter's expectations or, perhaps more correctly, beneath his expectations for his daughter. His feelings about his son-in-law were as clear as they were unfortunate: he didn't think Bud was smart and he was left to tolerate his daughter's choice as best he could. But even he had to see that Bud was a hard worker, he wasn't a drinker or womanizer, and he loved his daughter. So, he went to speak with his friend, Sam Graham, about giving his son-in-law a job as a sheriff's deputy. This was a more respectable occupation. And so, on July 1st, 1967, Sheriff Graham hired Bud Fowler to be a night patrol deputy. His salary was $4,548,[3] which was pretty good money considering he was coming from the U.S. Army and a poultry plant. Bud even got himself a nice Cadillac, probably from his father-in-law who tended to ensure his daughter had some high class luxuries in her decidedly middle-class life.

Deputy Fowler enjoyed the work and, coming from his long years in the military, it made sense to him: a uniform, a gun, a chain of command, and a sense of duty, honor, and pride. Because the deputies had to self-furnish their weapons and equipment, Libby purchased him a .357 western frame single shot revolver just like the cowboys used to carry. Or at least the ones in the movies and television shows he loved to watch. Fowler was no slouch in his uniform either. Every button was polished, his shoes gleamed, and his gig line was never out of order. He had purpose and he had a job everyone in his family could be proud of. Deputy Bud Fowler would go on to serve the Wicomico County Sheriff's Department for the next twenty years.

• • •

The night patrols were working, according to Sheriff Graham. He had instituted two two-man patrols to cover the county from 11:00 p.m. to 8:00 a.m. every night and the deputies put fifty miles or more on their cars during their shifts. They kept an eye on businesses and bars and served warrants as required. On several occasions, they foiled burglaries including a safe heist at a Salisbury building supply company. The night patrolmen were working closely with city and state police. Sheriff Graham was obviously pleased with their work, telling the *Daily Times*, "We know we can't break it all up. But our midnight crews have done a good job in eliminating a lot of it."

And they had, but in the spring of 1967, a brutal double homicide stunned Wicomico County. On May 1st, a Salisbury woman was on her way home around 8:30 p.m. when she noticed a cab parked on the side

---

3 $4,548 in 1967-1968 is roughly equivalent to $43,000 in 2025.

Sheriff Sam Graham and his deputies stand on the steps of the courthouse. Graham is in the middle wearing his standard suit and hat. Bud Fowler is on the far right in the front row while William Lewis, father of a future Wicomico County sheriff, stands on the far left in the front row.

Image courtesy of the Edward H. Nabb Research Center for Delmarva History and Culture, Salisbury University, Walter C. Thurston Jr. Photograph Collection

of Kaywood Drive, just east of Salisbury's city limits. She saw the driver slumped over the wheel. When she got home, she phoned Wicomico County Sheriff's Deputy William Shockley to come investigate. He discovered two gunshot victims: the cab driver, Francis "Freddy" Grant Jones, and Joyce Messick, a sixteen-year-old sophomore at Wicomico High School. Freddy had been shot once in the back of his head and was barely clinging to life; Joyce was dead with two small-caliber bullets in the back of her head. Freddy was taken to the hospital where he regained consciousness, but then succumbed to his injury.

The community was aghast. Who would kill a teenage girl and a cab driver in such a cold-blooded manner?

On May 8th, Sheriff Samuel Graham, State's Attorney Alfred Truitt, and two members of the Maryland State Police, Lieutenant Thomas E. Veditz and Sergeant Robert Weir, held a two-hour press conference and ran down their combined efforts up to that point. They did not believe it was a robbery gone wrong since both of their wallets were found in the car. They had questioned a hundred people, three of whom had undergone testing for gunshot residue. All were negative. One person of interest was tracked down in San Francisco and questioned but nothing came of that interview. (Within a year and a half, San Francisco itself would be gripped by an eerily similar string of murders committed by the infamous Zodiac killer.)

One possible lead centered on one of Freddy Jones's last fares: a young man who called from a payphone near E. Main Street around 8:15 p.m. There was even a composite sketch made, but it did not yield any more leads. The case eventually went cold and remains unsolved.[4]

• • •

On April 29th, 1967, a Salisbury man named Horner found himself paying $55[5] to the Peoples Court. His crime? Smuggling (or attempting to smuggle) drugs into the county jail right under the nose of Deputy John Walston.

A woman was being held in the penthouse prison on a bad check charge. While there, Horner brought her a tin of mints. Inside the holes of those mints were narcotic pills. Sheriff Graham reported to the *Daily Times* that when the candy came into the jail, Deputy Walston looked at the tin of mints and thought it appeared to have already been opened.

---

4 In 1983, police arrested a Delmar man living in Florida for the murders based on a confession from his ex-wife. Those charges were dropped and the man was released.

5 $55 in 1967 is roughly equivalent to $525 in 2025.

Sheriff Sam Graham, left, stands next to the Salisbury Chief of Police at an event with WBOC, a Delmarva television station.

Image courtesy of the Edward H. Nabb Research Center for Delmarva History and Culture, Salisbury University, Walter C. Thurston Jr. Photograph Collection

The drugs, once discovered, caused Horner to receive a charge of "delivering and procuring to be delivered a dangerous drug and sedative to a person legally detained in the Wicomico County Jail." More astonishing than the narcotics in the candy was the lack of jail time for Horner. There was only mention of the fine. Sheriff Graham reassured folks that items brought to the jail for prisoners such as packs of cigars and cigarettes and boxes of candy were thoroughly checked and that this charge was the first of its type to be brought forward while he'd been in office. Despite the sheriff's reassurances, illicit items continued to find their way inside those jailhouse walls.

Sheriff Graham's job could be a minefield. Escapes. Contraband. Assaults. Even arson. In the early morning hours of Saturday, November 11th, 1967, the sheriff was rousted from his bed because a prisoner had set a fire inside the jail. A 59-year-old man, whose family had sworn out warrants against him for being disorderly, had taken a plastic bottle of drain cleaner, ignited it, and thrown it from his cell into a nearby box containing more drain cleaner, igniting several of those bottles. The Salisbury Fire Department answered the distress call at 4:22 a.m. and firefighters rushed to the courthouse. The noxious chemicals meant the firemen had to wear gas masks as they brought the minor blaze under control. Graham was surely relieved when he saw that little damage had been done; the worst of it was the dangerous fumes lingering in the air. Two men, including the 59-year-old man who started it, were taken to the hospital because they had inhaled the chemicals. How the man obtained the drain cleaner was never mentioned, but his jailhouse insurrection seemed to prove that his family was right about him.

The penthouse prison wasn't the same kind of place it had once been lauded to be. In the days when it first opened in 1937, it was deemed a modern wonder. Nothing could get in or out. It was safe and secure. Locked up tighter than a snare drum. But this wasn't the case anymore and it really hadn't been for the last dozen or so years. Now it was a ticking time bomb.

– THE CUT –
INMATE #52-768

On Monday, December 13th, 1965, eighteen-year-old Joseph J. Bartholomey, Jr. sat before William Pilchard, a trial magistrate of Snow Hill in Worcester County, Maryland. Without a lawyer, he heard the charges against him and pled guilty. Pilchard sentenced Joseph Bartholomey, a young man already intimately familiar with Maryland's reformatory institutions, to eight months hard time at the House of Correction in Jessup, located near Clifton T. Perkins State Hospital.

Joseph was headed to "The Cut."

• • •

A cloudy sky hung over the Maryland House of Correction on Wednesday, December 15th, 1965—the day Joseph J. Bartholomey, Jr. arrived at the prison. His intake paperwork noted he was now 5'9" and he weighed 130 pounds. (He had had a growth spurt of two inches and four pounds in the previous three months.) His occupation was listed as a "box sealer," perhaps from his brief time at the Maryland Cup Company. His reputation as an escape artist, however, did make it to his intake form: "Committed to Crownsville … He escaped."

Christmas 1965 came and went like any other day on the prison tiers. Joseph greeted the new year of 1966 as he became accustomed to life inside "The Cut." Opened in January 1879, the prison was four stories of red brick, metal gates, and thick bars and it was a hell of a place to be locked up. Drug use. Violent beatings. Sexual assaults. The year before Joseph entered, eight hundred prisoners rioted for three hours. They set fires, ripped out plumbing and flooded the tiers, took guards hostage, and smashed windows and light fixtures. It took a hundred Maryland State Troopers armed with shotguns, dogs, and steel helmets to get the prison under control again. The inmates said they were tired of abusive and cruel guards, poor food, a lack of activities, and the sub-par commissary where they couldn't even get soap or deodorant. They demanded that the prison employees who were improperly handling their accounts to be fired. They even sent letters to the *Baltimore Sun* with their complaints. Nothing changed, though, except for one thing: the warden was replaced.

Joseph did not escape this time, although a few others did. One inmate being held as a suspected murderer escaped the prison three days before Christmas; he wasn't caught for three months. A few days before Joseph's birthday in March 1966, an inmate being held for non-support escaped but was arrested four days later at his father's house, which landed his father in hot water with the authorities. Two more inmates—one being held on auto theft charges and the other for assault—escaped in a state-owned truck; one was found several weeks later, but it is unclear what happened to the second.

On March 18th, 1966, Joseph Bartholomey turned nineteen inside the prison while a public outrage swarmed around the Maryland House of Correction. A week prior, on March 11th, three inmates had brutally beaten and sexually assaulted another inmate. The attack bothered the other inmates so much that they sent correspondences to the State Commissioner of Correction Vernon L. Pepersack. A lawyer also sent a note to Pepersack. The day after Joseph's birthday, Pepersack announced a probe into the beating of that prisoner. He told the *Baltimore Sun* that he had been informed of the assault in which the men forced the beaten man to "engage in unnatural acts." The warden, however, appeared unaware of the probe when he was questioned by a *Sun* reporter, but there was enough evidence to send the case to the state's attorney. This came on the heels of a superintendent resigning at the Poplar Hill Correctional Camp in Quantico, Maryland. Commissioner Pepersack told the newspaper they had been planning to charge that superintendent, though with what remains unknown. Other guards at Maryland correctional institutions were also facing suspensions and dismissals. Vernon L. Pepersack, the corrections commissioner, appeared to be cleaning house.

In July 1966, Reverend Mervin Gray, an ordained minister and a guard at the House of Correction, stepped forward with troubling claims about what exactly was going on inside the walls of "The Cut" where Joseph remained incarcerated. Gray stated that known drug addicts were given access to areas like the infirmary where narcotics were stored and that, inside "The Cut's" walls, one could obtain a bag of heroin for $5.[1] He also spoke about how differently Black guards like himself were treated. White guards saw promotions early in their careers while Black guards with decades of service remained without promotions. For coming forward, he was placed on "indefinite leave with pay" while the warden refuted his claims. After a two-day investigation, Vernon Pepersack told the newspapers Reverend Gray's claims were untrue, which is strange given that just months prior he was placing guards on leave for violating prison rules. For coming forward, Reverend Mervin Gray was suspended and then terminated. Ironically though, during the time in which Gray's allegations were being challenged as untrue by prison officials, two inmates at "The Cut" were found with narcotics. When the prisoners at "The Cut" rioted again in January 1967, several inmates were found to be using barbiturates and syringes.

Reverend Mervin Gray had been right all along about the brutal state of affairs inside that prison.

• • •

---

1 $5 in 1966 is roughly equivalent to $50 in 2025.

By August 19th, 1966, Joseph Bartholomey was out of prison and seeking employment. He was living at 628 Delaware Avenue in Essex, Maryland with his mother, Dolores, and his siblings, Shirley and Ethan. The avenue was lined with house after house that was exactly the same on both sides of the street. They were squat, square, brick duplexes with surprisingly spacious front yards and smaller backyards. His employer was listed as "WMC" on a hospital form in September 1966. Joseph was, miraculously, managing to keep himself out of trouble.

In October 1966, in a move reminiscent of his parents, he, at nineteen-years-old, married eighteen-year-old Carol Smith, the young woman who was named on his Clifton T. Perkins intake form. According to Joseph, she was a "straight" girl from southern Pennsylvania, not one to mess around with drugs or alcohol. Her parents, specifically her mother, had money, but Joseph would later say he was unwilling to accept financial support from her parents. He was employed and seemed to be trying to support himself and his new, young wife. Joseph felt they were "getting along real good." For just the briefest of moments, it must have appeared to those around the young couple that perhaps life was settling down … that maybe Joseph had finally grown up and put those restless ways of his youth behind him. Maybe that stint in the Maryland House of Correction had scared him straight.

But it all fell apart in the spring of 1968. A lot of things did.

Joseph and Carol had been living with his father and stepmother, Joseph Sr. and Betty. They had told his parents that they were married and were accepted into the Bartholomey home. Betty and Joseph Sr. were trying to help them get started as a young couple. But when Carol's parents showed up, their secret was revealed: Joseph and Carol were not actually married. They were living in sin under the Bartholomeys' roof and both sets of parents were furious about their marital charade. Then another secret was ushered into the light of day. Joseph Sr. had helped his son find a job, but then the boss called and said Joseph hadn't been coming to work. Betty had watched him pack a lunch every day and leave the house. Only he wasn't going to work. This angered Betty, and the Bartholomeys told the young couple they had to leave because they were not going to support them any longer.

Joseph, now twenty-one, was regularly doing cocaine. He sent Carol back to her parents in Pennsylvania. It was better that way. Joseph hopped into his 1962 Ford Galaxy Sunliner and sped out of Baltimore. He headed for the Eastern Shore once more. He was a single man alone in the world. No one to nag him. No job. Adrift and unsettled. His old habits itching to be scratched. Drugs. Crime. The wilder girls in Ocean City who liked the bad boys. An uninhibited freedom at the beach. A summer of dropping acid and snorting coke and smoking weed while loafing in the surf and sand with a pretty girl or two as the radio crackles with the latest hits by The Doors, The Rolling Stones, and Simon and Garfunkel ... a summer of having nowhere to be and all day to get there until the hot orange sun sinks below the cool blue horizon. What a dream.

There was but one certainty: terrible things lay ahead for him and those close to him.

Terrible, terrible things.

– ALBERT LEE KELLY –
TWO DIRTY BOOTS AND A GREEN THUMB

On the southeastern edge of Wicomico County is the blink-and-you-miss-it village of Powellville. Today, it comprises four stop signs, a few roads, a smattering of small homes and trailers, and a fire department, but once upon a time, there was real industry here. Some intrepid soul took note of an off-shooting branch of the Pocomoke River and built a mill, possibly as early as 1825 or so. Soon a little village began to build up around that mill and when Wicomico County was created, Powellville was embraced into its fold. By 1875, Elijah Stanton Adkins was running a grist mill and a saw mill; a man named White was the postmaster; and elsewhere in the village was a carriage and cartwright shop, a blacksmith shop, a carpenter shop, and at least two stores. Although there was no railroad station, Powellville appeared to benefit from the stops in nearby Berlin, Pittsville, and New Hope. Two years later, there was even a shoe store in town. For the 125 souls who lived in the village of Powellville and its environs, farming was a principal way of life. And like most tiny hamlets of its era, the boom would eventually bust.

Henry P. Kelly was a tall, slender man who found work in the saw mills of Powellville, turning trunks of cedar and cypress into usable lumber. He and his wife, Annie, had five sons: Howard, Albert, Preston, Milton, and Ralph. The Kellys were a hard-working lot, even the children, and unfortunately, they would see more than their fair share of tragedy in the years ahead.

Albert Lee Kelly was born on October 16th, 1906, and he had a 7th

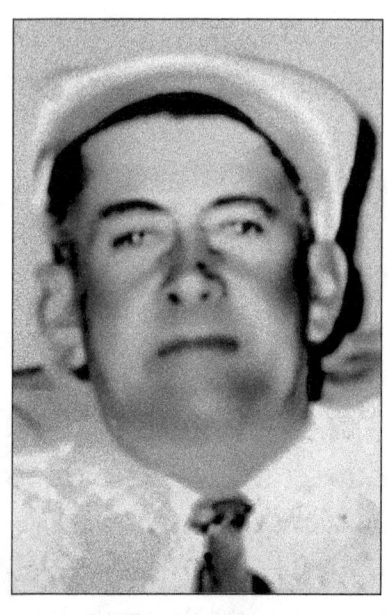

*Albert Lee Kelly
in an undated photograph*

Image courtesy of the Kelley family

grade education. This wasn't uncommon for children of laborers in the early parts of the twentieth century. By 1926, Albert was employed by the H. Lay Phillips Construction Company on Lake Street in Salisbury; within a few years, he met and married Nellie Mae Shockley. For a time, the couple lived in Pittsville and the couple welcomed a son, Alvin, in May 1932. For the Kelly families, life was about to take shocking turn.

On Sunday, August 11th, 1935, Albert's older brother, Howard, was murdered by a Powellville man named Arlie Lewis. Witnesses said the two men had been arguing around midnight and another witness claimed to have seen the men continuing their altercation near a pond in town at around 3:00 a.m. that Sunday morning. Hours later, Arlie Lewis was going around Powellville telling anyone who would listen that he'd killed Howard Kelly. And he had. Howard's lifeless body was pulled from the pond. A terrible gash blotched his face near his left eye. The crime was reported to the Wicomico County Sheriff's Department and two deputies, Marvin Gordy (a future sheriff) and Donald Parks were dispatched to the scene. They arrested Arlie Lewis who confessed to the murder on the ride to jail and then asked the deputies to just shoot him outright.

After a trial in which he was found both sane and guilty of the crime of murder, Arlie Lewis was sentenced to fifteen years in the Maryland Penitentiary. Howard Kelly was thirty-one years old and left behind a wife and two children.

Now there were four Kelly brothers and Albert was the oldest. The 1940 census showed that Albert, Nellie, and their little boy, Alvin, were living with Nellie's father and an elderly lodger. Albert was working as a crane operator for the H. Lay Phillips Construction Company earning an annual income of $1,250; Nellie was listed as a laborer in a shirt factory making about $400 per year.[1] By 1942, Albert's brother, Ralph, was working with him at the Phillips construction company. With black hair and blue eyes, Albert was said to be a good-looking man; one has to wonder if Ralph, the baby of the Kelly family with his blue eyes and brown hair and fair skin, caught some of those head-turning genes.

But bad luck wasn't finished with the brothers just yet. On Saturday, August 28th, 1943, at 11:30 p.m., Ralph and a friend were driving home from Snow Hill when Ralph lost control of the car. It skidded off the road and rolled into a ditch just outside of Powellville. His friend was uninjured but Ralph was likely killed instantly: his skull was crushed and his neck broken. Ralph was just nineteen.

Three Kelly brothers remained.

By at least 1946, possibly earlier, Albert moved his family for the final time to a house at 301 Carey Avenue in Salisbury. He was still working as a crane operator for the construction company, but Nellie was no longer working. Albert's brother, Preston, went into construction work, too. The other remaining brother, Milton, entered the U.S. Army in September 1942 and served in Europe during World War II, which was quite fitting for a man born on the Fourth of July in 1921. He went on to work for UPS.

Life continued for Albert Lee Kelly. Their son, Alvin Lee Kelly,

---

1 $1,250 and $400 in 1940 is roughly equivalent to $29,000 and $9,000 in 2025, respectively.

Albert L. Kelly
in undated photographs, likely the early 1950s

Image courtesy of the Kelley family

graduated from Wicomico High School in 1951, where Dorothy Graham taught World History. His senior year portrait in the yearbook shows a chubby-cheeked young man with dark hair gelled back with clear-framed glasses accentuating his deep-set blue eyes like his father. Small smile. Pug nose. He enjoyed sports, especially baseball. After graduation, Alvin enlisted and served in Korea, and by October 1957, Alvin married a young woman named Margaret Palmer who lived in Baltimore. Children followed quickly: a girl named Bonnie and a boy named Brian. Now Albert and Nellie were proud grandparents.

Margaret Kelly liked her father-in-law. Albert was always kind and friendly to her and she saw how hard he worked for his family. Every night when he came home from his construction job, his dirty boots told the story of his day's labor. Long hours in the rain and sun, in the snow and heat; long hours with the elements on his neck and in his face. They didn't have a lot of money, but Albert Kelly was a rugged, determined man who saw to it that his wife always had what she needed and wanted. Nellie stayed at home as many women of her era did. She would cook chicken dinners with mashed potatoes and gravy when Alvin and Margaret came over; Nellie's recipe for homemade vegetable soup was worthy of envy.

Together, Albert and Nellie had a couple of green thumbs. He loved trees and planted them around his yard. Nellie and Margaret used to take trips to local greenhouses and nurseries to buy flowers and plants, filling up Nellie's red Chevrolet. They would even stop along the road if they saw pretty flowers and dig them up to replant in the yard at home. Maybe they didn't have a lot of money, but their home had beauty to spare. In 1964, Albert and Nellie gave their son and daughter-in-law a portion of their lot on Carey Avenue and Alvin and Margaret built a home where they would spend the rest of their years together. Both yards were full of trees and flowers meticulously planted and maintained. The beautiful magnolia tree in Alvin and Margaret's yard was planted by Albert himself.

When the H. Lay Phillips Construction Company shut down, Albert Kelly found himself without a job for the first time in over four decades. He wasn't ready to retire and they still needed an income so he began looking for work. Although he was sixty-one, he still had his good health and remained physically active and capable. His brother, Milton, told him about a job ... he had heard that the county jail needed a turnkey. And so, likely in February 1968, Albert Kelly was hired as a jailer in the penthouse prison working for Sheriff Sam Graham.[2] He wasn't the only family member to work in the courthouse: when his daughter-in-law, Margaret Kelly, was looking for work, Sheriff Graham got her a job in the assessment office. Their family appreciated the popular lawman.

For Albert Kelly and his family, the new turnkey job was like an answer to a prayer, but sometimes, good fortune is not always what it appears to be.

---

2 News articles state Albert had been working at the jail for about ten months. This is the best discernible timeline.

– A TEMPEST DRAWS NEAR –
SPRING 1968 TO NOVEMBER 1968

Something was different on Delmarva that spring of 1968, almost as if the atmosphere itself was charged with tension and ready to snap. The nation was under stress: the Vietnam War still raged, the feminists and women's liberation supporters were gearing up for demonstrations, and the Civil Rights Movement suffered a mighty loss. On April 4th, 1968, Dr. Martin Luther King, Jr. was assassinated at the Lorraine Motel in Memphis, Tennessee by James Earl Ray, a petty criminal who had a knack for escaping jails and a fondness for racist ideologies. King's brutal murder sent a shock wave through the country: the loss of a brave man who had dedicated his life to service, to God, and to the rights Black Americans were entitled yet routinely denied. Demonstrations and riots broke out across the country. Washington, D.C. and Baltimore were especially hard hit. The turbulence of the time saw a growing list of American political assassinations in that decade: JFK in 1963 and Malcolm X in 1965 and now MLK in 1968.

At Wicomico High School, now integrated, the Black students mourned the loss of Dr. King. Several Black students approached the school's administration to ask that the American flag be lowered to half-staff in honor of his memory. The principal, George Corddry, and his vice-principal, Dorothy Graham, denied their request. The refusal stung and inspired the Black students to protest. Integration at Wicomico High School started in the fall of 1966 and it was a hard and agonizing transition for the Black students who had been assigned to begin the process. They reported that they were shoved in the hallways and told not to speak. White teachers would not call on them in class. They were isolated. They felt the weight of racism every single day. So when the high school administration told them the flag would not be lowered, the Black students chose to protest. They went to the cafeteria and refused to leave or allow other students to enter. The school officials threatened to expel them, but the Black students held fast and in the end, they prevailed.

Several weeks later, on Saturday, May 18th, 1968, Salisbury erupted in violence and anguish after a young Black man named Daniel Kenneth Henry, a 22-year-old deaf and mute man, was shot in the neck and killed after a struggle with two Salisbury city police officers, Detective Jerry R. Mason and Corporal John Guarino. The newspapers reported that police officers spotted a man who was wanted for questioning about a recent burglary. The man ran from the police, but was eventually found and taken to the police department. He was identified as Daniel Kenneth Henry. The police said he confessed to the burglary and other crimes and they placed him under arrest. Suddenly, a struggle broke out in which Henry reportedly went for Corporal Guarino's gun. In the fight, the gun fell to the ground and Henry took off running. Detective Mason picked up the gun and yelled for him to stop. Henry kept running. Mason pulled the trigger, striking him in the back of the neck. In an instant, Daniel Kenneth Henry was dead.

That night, for four hours, there were riots in the streets of Salisbury. A crowd of nearly 300 Black citizens formed outside the courthouse demanding answers. Tempers were flaring. For the Black community, the shooting death of Henry hit too close to home. Martin Luther King, Jr. had just been murdered. The lynching of Matthew Williams was only thirty-seven years past. Black American soldiers who had fought the Nazis abroad returned home to Jim Crow's segregation, remaining second-class citizens in a country they fought to protect. The *Brown v. Board* decision had faced monumental pushback as well as lagging efforts to catch up.

They had lost their neighborhoods to Salisbury's development; roads and sidewalks now ran over where their homes, stores, and cemeteries used to be. Now, a young, deaf and mute Black man was dead. The heartache swelled into frustration that burst into anger and the dam could no longer hold. Cars and store windows were smashed. Fires burned. Screams and cries rang out. The rioting ended when the National Guard arrived to help the local police forces, which had quickly found themselves outnumbered.

Nothing came of the events of May 18th, 1968. The injured were treated at the hospital. The debris was cleaned up. A grand jury declined to indict Detective Jerry Mason on a charge of manslaughter. The NAACP pressed unsuccessfully for Mason's dismissal, citing the Matthew Williams lynching as well as the swift justice administered to a Black man when he killed a White city police officer in September 1958. In that case, Salisbury police officer Henry T. Stephens was taking Johnnie Brown into custody for check forgery and burglary when Brown pulled out a gun and fatally shot Stephens. Brown was immediately captured, tried, and sentenced to die in the gas chamber. In a gut-wrenching twist of fate, ten hours after his slaying, Officer Stephens's wife gave birth to their daughter. Weeks later, in a state of utter heartbreak and unfathomable anguish, she tried to take her own life.

And here is an essential truth: no matter how it comes, no matter who does it or why, murder destroys nearly everything it touches. It is a bell that once tolled can never be unrung. It reverberates through families and neighborhoods, through time and memory. It both breaks us and hardens us. We are left with only pieces of what once was. Hearts shattered. Lives devastated. Upended in chaos, there is no shelter from the storm or safe harbor. There is no closure, only scar tissue.

The Black community felt wronged by the killing of Daniel Henry, but there was nothing to be done about it. Sometimes injustice swallows up all the good around it. Two steps forward, three steps back. On Wednesday, June 5th, 1968, just two months after the slaying of Dr. Martin Luther King, Jr., Robert F. Kennedy was gunned down by Sirhan

Black citizens gather outside the Wicomico County Courthouse (near the entrance to the sheriff's department) after the murder of Daniel Henry. Somewhere in this crowd is prominent Black activist Gloria Richardson.

Image courtesy of the Edward H. Nabb Research Center for Delmarva History and Culture, Salisbury University, Walter C. Thurston Jr. Photograph Collection

Sirhan in Los Angeles, California. Another political assassination. Now the list read: JFK, Malcolm X, MLK, and RFK.

America was spilling the blood of her heroes.

• • •

The late spring and early summer of 1968 saw the arrival of the "June Bugs." This yearly phenomenon, often to the teeth-grinding chagrin of the Delmarva locals, was the pilgrimage of teenagers from Baltimore and other parts of Maryland's Western Shore to Ocean City, Maryland. These teens had spent the cold winter months longing to "go downy ocean, hon."[1] As their high school days came to an end and the summer break began, they packed their best swimsuits and hanging out attire, piled into cars with their friends, made their way over the Chesapeake Bay Bridge with the windows rolled down and the radios up, and cruised down the Eastern Shore highways and byways until, like moths to a flame, they arrived at their beloved Mecca of Ocean City.

Carved by changing tides of the Atlantic and a furious hurricane in August 1933, this resort town has long been regarded as an idolized destination for tourists with its wide expanses of sandy beach, breaking waves, and easy surf-side culture. Those blazing summers saw hormonal and unsupervised teens with access to alcohol and marijuana (and even LSD) testing the limits of their independence. And just as the Western Shore kids were gearing up to get to the beach, the Eastern Shore teens were reporting for duty at their summer jobs as lifeguards and beach rental staff or at the hamburger and ice cream stands. One of the notorious meetups was 9th Street. The girls, with their long hair, bare feet, and trimmed bell bottoms, sported fresh tans courtesy of iodine in their baby oil or suntan lotion. They scanned the boardwalk crowds for cute boys, even bad boys, and they usually found one.

Donna Blair Campbell[2] was a young girl from Baltimore living in Ocean City that summer of 1968 when she met 21-year-old Joseph James Bartholomey, Jr.[3] They began dating and it wasn't long before Donna saw signs of trouble. About a month into their courtship, Donna and her roommate went to a house party hosted by five girls on St. Louis Avenue.[4] During the party, Joseph—for reasons unknown—slit his wrist.

---

1 This phrase translates to "going down to the ocean" with the "hon" being short for "honey." It's an example of the cultural jargon that belongs specifically to Baltimore. People born and raised on the Eastern Shore do not say this.

2 Name changed.

3 Several newspaper accounts mention that Joseph was working in Ocean City that summer. If he was, the details are unknown.

4 It is possible that Donna was living at this house on St. Louis Street. Her testimony at trial was not clear on this point.

The cuts were so bad that he was rushed to a nearby medical clinic on Baltimore Avenue. The party goers feared he wouldn't make the drive to the hospital in Salisbury. Joseph was losing a lot of blood and Donna watched him grow paler. Once they arrived at the clinic, a doctor carried him inside. The situation was grave. The doctor told Donna the blood loss was severe enough to cause Joseph's death.

But he survived. And as love would have it, so did their relationship. Joseph would later say that Donna was the only girl he ever truly loved. (Too bad for Carol Smith, the "wife" he sent back to Pennsylvania.) But like Carol, Donna was an upright kind of young lady. She went to church and didn't do drugs. Joseph, the bad boy, had a thing for good girls. There was a definite connection between them, almost like a Romeo and Juliet pairing ... if Romeo had been an antisocial delinquent drug user and Juliet a nice but awfully naive girl from Baltimore.

By his own admission, Joseph was using drugs: marijuana, cocaine, and LSD—a drug that gained popularity during the 1960s. The counterculture of the time saw it as a way to open gateways in the mind and enhance creativity. Jimi Hendrix, Pink Floyd, and The Beatles were dropping acid. Carey Grant, too. Even the United States government found ways to "use" LSD in covert research operations. Out in California, Charles Manson, a slight and petite man with dark eyes and a past mirroring Joseph's, was luring young, troubled people into his hippie movement with acid and music. That summer of 1968, LSD and other drugs were a regular part of Joseph's life. Was it to escape his childhood traumas or to numb himself from the pain of those days? His peer group was apparently comfortable with the illegal drug scene. And how much did his drug use influence his criminal and violent behavior? One thing is for sure: his drug use would serve the same purpose as pouring gasoline on an open fire.

As the summer began to wind down and Joseph's time at the beach was coming to a close, a new season of trouble awaited him.

• • •

Sheriff Sam Graham had been busy that spring of 1968, too. By the end of May, he had already dealt with several prisoner escapes. The first set happened in mid-February. Two inmates, one from Crisfield and one from Pittsville, were being held on breaking and entering and larceny charges. They took advantage of a mechanical problem. When the jailer was putting the men back into their cells at 10:00 p.m., the lever jammed. When the jailer went to fix it, the two men simply walked out and took the elevator down to the first floor. The Crisfield man was apprehended in Crisfield five days later; the Pittsville man was captured after two months by the FBI in Houston, Texas.

Then, on May 27th, two more prisoners escaped: a seventeen-year-old boy and a 29-year-old who were both being held on breaking and entering and robbery charges. They flooded their cell on purpose. When the jailer came to give them a mop and a bucket, they grabbed the jailer's gun and escaped, breaking the glass on the front door of the courthouse on their way to temporary freedom. A third man, who had been in the penthouse prison for 190 days while he awaited a trial for murder, also tried to escape that night, but Sheriff Graham found him trying to get access to the elevator and was able to wrangle the alleged murderer back into his cell. Both inmates were found very quickly by Salisbury city police officers and returned to the penthouse prison.

The very next day, officers from Salisbury Police Department picked up a drunk man who was lying on the side of the road near Route 50 and Cypress Street. When the police figured out who he was, their records indicated he was supposed to be in Graham's jail, and sure enough, the drunk man was indeed listed on the prison log book as an inmate. He was a frequent guest at the penthouse prison, having spent nearly five and a half months out of the last six in the jail for drunken and disorderly charges. This time, Sheriff Graham had let him out early on good behavior, only he had forgotten to pull his name from the inmate log.

This was the second time in the same month this had happened to the same prisoner.

The incidents in his jail did not appear to cause Sheriff Graham any political hardship. A recent grand jury, no doubt after having feasted on one of Emily Furr's noted luncheons, complimented his sheriff's quarters and jail for being in "excellent condition." He had already been named to the Democratic city campaign committee along with other well-known politicians like State's Attorney Alfred Truitt, Maryland State Senator Mary Nock, and Maryland House Delegate Joseph "Joe" Long, a WWII veteran who would spend twenty-five years in the Maryland state legislature. Sheriff Graham sat as either a member or a chairman of several local charitable organizations like the Shriner's, the United Fund, and the Heart Fund Drive. As the top lawman of the most populated county on Maryland's Eastern Shore, he had a growing sphere of power and influence. He was a political boss. When Baltimore Colts[5] place kicker Lou Michaels was approached by a staff member of the *Daily Times,* Lou asked the newspaper reporter to send his regards to two Salisburians: Bill Riordan, a popular tennis promoter, and Sheriff Samuel Graham. The footballer said he and Sam were old Kentucky Derby associates. Then Lou Michaels added that he thought the larger-than-life sheriff would be a perfect fit for television, specifically a western drama with his ten-gallon cowboy hats and king-sized cigars. (And it wouldn't take much imagination to envision Graham in an episode of *Gunsmoke.*)

The Baltimore Colts kicker wasn't wrong. This is how many of the people of Wicomico County saw Sheriff Samuel Graham. A friendly slap on the back. A strong handshake. A man of the people who often called upon him and sought after his favors. And he granted them. When residents near Delmar reported that vandals were destroying an old cemetery and breaking headstones and monuments, Sheriff Graham assigned his deputies to watch over the cemetery. He was outraged at the defacing of a sacred place: "It looks like a damned meanness to me," he told a

---

5 The Baltimore Colts moved to Indianapolis in 1984.

Daily Times reporter. His deputies kept watch night after night and vandals did not come back.

• • •

The 1968 Presidential election was held on November 5th, 1968 and the winning ticket was the Republican team of Richard M. Nixon and Maryland's Governor, Spiro Agnew. Although they did not carry Maryland, they defeated the Democrats, Hubert Humphrey and Edmund Muskie, as well as the American Independent ticket led by segregationist George Wallace and his running mate, General Curtis LeMay. The race was handily won by Nixon and Agnew, but Wallace and LeMay, perhaps unsurprisingly, carried five states in the Deep South.

Down on Maryland's Eastern Shore, Joseph J. Bartholomey, Jr. was making moves of his own. When the summer ended, he and Donna had moved to Salisbury, living at 308 Gay Street, a narrow, two-story house in a leafy neighborhood half a mile from the courthouse. Still doing cocaine and LSD, he had slipped back into a life of crime and he was running with a rough crowd. One such fellow was Alphonso Graham, who went by the infamous moniker "Al Capone."

On November 9th, Joseph and a young man named Erick Irwin, robbed Voigt's Hobby and Sport Shop and stole more than 20 guns—shotguns, rifles, and handguns—worth $1,914.52 as well as $388.50 in cash. It was a significant score. Erick Thomas Irwin[6] was a local kid who had graduated from Wicomico High School in 1965. There were 406 students in that year's graduating class, including Deputy Bud Fowler's two sons. Erick played in the band—his senior class quote was that he'd be remembered for his "sax appeal"—and participated in the French Club as well as both the junior and senior class plays. His senior year photo reveals a clean-cut teen. A gentle smile that pulls a little more to the right than the left. His hair looping in a single, barreled curl over

---

6 Name changed.

his broad forehead. His eyes looking just off to the side of the camera. Bow tie. Dark jacket. Bright-eyed and ready for success. In 1967, he was accepted into the Jefferson School of Commerce (a business academy) for the 1967-1968 school year. Yet, as it happens with young folks sometimes, his success was self-sabotaged. On May 26th, 1968, Erick was caught up and arrested along with forty-three other people at a house on 36th Street in Ocean City. The police had been watching the house for suspected drug activity; during the raid, they seized marijuana and other drugs. Despite his arrest, Erick graduated from the Jefferson School of Commerce with a general business degree on June 13th, 1968. He wasn't dumb, but he wasn't making smart decisions, either. Although he mostly smoked weed and dropped acid, Erick later admitted to trying heroin.

Three days after the Voigt's heist with Erick Irwin, Joseph and another accomplice named Preston Lee Webster beat and robbed, at gun point, a Salisbury contractor named Albert L. Disharoon at his home on E. Church Street. They took $810.00 in that incident. A week later, Joseph alone robbed Boulevard TV and Radio Service, making off with four televisions worth a total of $399.00. Then, Joseph and Alphonso "Al Capone" Graham made their way to Princess Anne, Maryland in Somerset County where they stole firearms and watches from the Warwick's Hardware worth $2,279.00. In total, Joseph and his cohorts stole roughly $5,791.02 in cash and goods.[7]

How authorities linked Joseph, Erick Irwin, Preston Webster, and Alphonso "Al Capone" Graham to the series of robberies is unknown. Equally unclear is how they all knew each other, but Joseph is a common denominator in the group. At least three out of the four were living in or around Salisbury at the time of the robberies. Joseph resided at 308 Gay Street with Donna Blair Campbell. Erick Irwin had been living with his parents on Winder Street. Preston Webster gave an address of 310 E. Vine Street. The lone outlier was Alphonso "Al Capone" Graham who was from Dillon, South Carolina with no documented Salisbury

---

[7] $5,791.02 in 1968 is roughly equivalent to $53,000 in 2025.

Joseph J. Bartholomey's mugshot after his November 1968 arrest

© *The* Daily Times – USA TODAY NETWORK via Imagn Images

address. Additionally, Joseph, Donna, and Erick were known to be in Ocean City during that summer of 1968, although there is nothing in Joseph's records to indicate they were acquainted then.

Joseph's crime spree ended on November 21st, 1968 when he was arrested by the Salisbury Police Department. He was charged with breaking and entering and grand larceny for the robberies in Salisbury, assault and armed robbery of Albert L. Disharoon, and possession of narcotics paraphernalia. Preston Webster and Alphonso "Al Capone" Graham were also arrested in November. Erick Irwin was not, however. His involvement with Joseph apparently had not yet been revealed.

Once in custody, Joseph J. Bartholomey, Jr. was given a bail of $14,000.00[8] by Judge Raymond S. Smethurst and placed in a cell in Sheriff Graham's penthouse prison.

---

8 $14,000 in 1968 is roughly equivalent to $129,000 in 2025.

PART III

PART III

– FOOLPROOF –
SUNDAY, DECEMBER 8TH, 1968

Wicomico County Sheriff's Deputy Bud Fowler emerged from his house at 707 Madison Street in Salisbury, where he lived with his wife, Libby. Their sons were no longer at home, both having graduated from Wicomico High School and then enlisting in the Army like their father. Dorothy Graham had been instrumental in helping their youngest son, who struggled academically, make it to his graduation. Their small house on that blue collar street was an empty nest as the holiday season started into its upswing. Advertisements in the newspaper enticed shoppers with gifts and specials just in time for Santa: Sears was offering an AM/FM radio and record player cabinet for just $199.88[1] and B&O Office Supplies was giving customers a free turkey if they purchased a new Underwood 21 typewriter. Just the day before, on Saturday afternoon, more than 15,000 people gathered on the streets of Salisbury to watch the annual Christmas parade while the sun moved in and out of gray clouds. Hours later, a light dusting of snow had fallen on Salisbury, ushering in hopes of a white Christmas.

As Bud closed the door to the warmth of his home, the winter chill bit at his freshly shaven chin. He looked every bit like a lawman. His uniform was pressed and perfect, every crease starched, and his badge was as shiny as his black shoes. Bud was, after all, a military man at heart. He had been with the sheriff's department for about a year and a half and found he liked the work. That evening, he would be on desk duty,

---

[1] $199.88 in 1968 is roughly equivalent to $1,800 in 2025.

DEFENDS JAIL. Sheriff Samuel A. Graham, Wicomico County's sheriff for 11 years, says a recent state jail inspector's report that the county jail is outmoded is nonsense. He claims the jail is secure and if there is an escape, it's the fault of the jailer, not the jail.

Sheriff Graham Resents Outmoded Report On Jail

WORKS LEVER SYSTEM. James Collins, one of the two jailers at the Wicomico County Jail, demonstrates how the cell doors can be opened by a mechanized gear and lever system. The sheriff calls the operation foolproof.

SEARCH PRISONER. Sheriff Graham, with his big cowboy hat and cigar, searches prisoner before he is interned in the Wicomico County Jail.

Front page of the Delmarva Living section of the Daily Times *on Sunday, December 8th, 1968*

© The Daily Times – USA TODAY NETWORK via Imagn Images

answering phones and sorting paperwork. Bud Fowler slid into the driver's seat of his spotless Cadillac and started his mile-long ride to work.

It was Sunday, December 8th, 1968.

Just that morning, his boss had appeared on the main page of "Delmarva Living" section of the *Daily Times* with a tense headline: "Sheriff Graham Resents Outmoded Report on Jail." And indeed, he was blazing mad this time. In late November, while Joseph Bartholomey was running amok and getting arrested, the *Baltimore Sun* published a scathing and unforgiving exposé about the deplorable conditions of Eastern Shore jails. Sheriff Graham and his penthouse prison had not been spared. The seven-article series placed the local sheriffs and jailers in a particularly awful limelight and scorched a fresh path of resentment from the beach to the bay and onto Baltimore.

• • •

The author of the exposé was A. W. Geiselman, Jr., who had been a Naval radio operator during World War II. He rooted for the underdog and being a journalist allowed him to fight for the vulnerable and forgotten by taking on corrupt politicians, dishonest cops, and unscrupulous institutions. This exposé was right up his alley. For the reporting, Geiselman followed Joseph D. Egeberg, Jr., a top inspector for the Maryland Department of Corrections. Standing at six-and-a-half-feet tall, Egeberg was a man accustomed to tough situations: he had served as an Army platoon leader in WWII and received both a Purple Heart and a Bronze Star. He had once worked as a newspaper reporter, too. Geiselman and Egeberg, along with a photographer, traveled to the Eastern Shore and took notes and photographs of what they saw: overcrowding, unsanitary conditions, fire hazards, security problems, inmate treatment and injuries, inadequate food and medical care, a lack of proper funding, unusual juvenile incarceration, controversial bail methods, and the segregation of White and Black prisoners. (On this last point, Geiselman wrote that "jailers said this was voluntary on the part of Negroes.")

In Queen Anne's County, trash littered the floor and inmates slept on metal cots topped with thin mattresses, blackened from overuse. Prisoners in Chestertown used "night buckets" because they had no toilets. The Caroline County jail did not have hot water. The odors eminating from the Pocomoke lockup were so intense that passersby could smell it from the sidewalk. Beyond the filth, inmates in multiple counties suffered from a lack of medical care. In the Worcester County jail, a prisoner being held on a charge of attempted rape had been in solitary confinement for more than two weeks with chemical burns to his eyes after a deputy maced him. That inmate had lost thirty-five pounds in two months. Also being held in solitary confinement in that same Worcester County jail was an eighteen-year-old girl from Baltimore; she had been there for four months after she and some boys broke into a store. She had scrawled a poem on the door of the cell about a girl named Judy whose only crime was drinking beer. Other inmates reported she had tried to kill herself by slitting her wrists. The sheriff of Talbot County noted that "a couple of alcoholics" had died in his jail, but, on what he deemed a positive note, he had made an effort to ensure all the prisoners addressed the jail staff as "sir." According to Geiselman, not one sheriff knew how many prisoners had died in their jails.

Sheriff Graham's penthouse prison did not escape the ire of Geiselman's pen or the discerning eye of Egeberg. The exposé revealed that Eastern Shore counties allotted roughly a dollar a day[2] per prisoner for food, which normally resulted in two meals, each consisting of a sandwich, a cup of soup, and a beverage like hot coffee. Geiselman was quick to draw a contrast between that and the lavish jury luncheons Graham provided, noting that the juries ate "fried codfish, bean soup and hot rolls and iced tea with second and third helpings." There was no mention that Graham himself paid for those, but the article did point

---

2 $1 in 1968 is roughly equivalent to $9 in 2025.

out that at least two county sheriffs (Queen Anne's and Worcester) were allowed to pocket any funds not spent on prisoner meals. In Worcester County, prisoner meals of bread and water were not uncommon.

Egeberg was against having children and teenagers mixed in with the adult populations, stating, "It is criminal to put [a minor] at the mercy of the con-wise inmate ... This is literally a school for crime." Yet, in the penthouse prison, Egeberg and Geiselman found a fifteen-year-old boy in a cell being held without bail on a charge of statutory rape of a thirteen-year-old girl. There were other children and teenagers in jails across the Eastern Shore. Two siblings, eight and nine, were being held in a cell in the Cambridge jail in Dorchester County. In Kent County, the sheriff was holding a ten-year-old behind bars. A fourteen-year-old girl had been placed "in the cage" in Somerset County.

A. W. Geiselman concluded his exposé with a number of prison regulations Joseph Egeberg proposed when he had taken office. It was a common sense list: police would be required to search prisoners upon committal to a lockup to prevent violence against themselves or others; police would be prohibited from carrying firearms inside a jail; prisoners would be checked hourly and never left unattended in a jail; ill or injured prisoners would be given medical attention immediately; female inmates would be accompanied by a female matron when entering and leaving the jail; in the event of an inmate's escape or death, jail staff would notify the Department of Corrections within twenty-four hours; each jail would assign a member of its staff to be responsible for cleanliness and insect/vermin control; and finally, prisoners would be properly fed, either from a restaurant or "whatever arrangement may be desirable." At the time of the November 1968 articles, Egeberg was waiting for the measures to be approved. Additionally, he continued to support the idea that regional jails were a better alternative to these county jails and small town lockups.

When the *Baltimore Sun* exposé was released, the public response began and the reaction was mixed. For example, the *Sun* published an empathetic editorial on November 20th after the third article was published: "It is hard to read Mr. Geiselman's revelations without shock. The question naturally provoked is, what is being done?" The editorial placed the lion's share of the blame on local governments for not putting enough funds forward "to provide civilized conditions for prisoners" and added, "So we get what we pay for, a system which rehabilitates no one but which turns first offenders, teenagers, and other perfectly salvageable humans into hardened criminals. ... We have forgotten our prisons and the people inside them and ask ourselves where the criminals come from."

The writer of that editorial might as well have been speaking of Joseph J. Bartholomey, Jr.

However, other readers of the exposé took an entirely different stance. A Baltimore man wrote this to Geiselman: "Sir, I certainly will be relieved when I don't have to read of the deplorable conditions found in your series of seven articles on the conditions of the Eastern Shore jails." This particular writer pondered if the conditions of the jails, as bad as they might be, might not be better than what the criminals had at home. A further point: the writer said he didn't want prisoners to have "hotel accommodations" or a "nice place to live" as he blamed the prisoners for the conditions inside the jail cells. His parting words were concise: "They are in these jails for punishment so let them be punished."

An eye for an eye.

On the Eastern Shore, the *Daily Times* ran an editorial titled "The Regional Jail" on Sunday, December 1st, 1968 which echoed Joseph Egeberg's position of needing centralized facilities. Where Egeberg had once called the Eastern Shore jails "purely warehousing operations," the *Times* agreed that jails should not just be warehouses and that these facilities should have inmate programs with an aim toward rehabilitation. Considered a "social reformist," Egeberg appeared to strive for a balance between community protection and inmate rehabilitation: "I don't advocate molly-coddling and frills. I advocate a program which can help law enforcement agencies to bring criminal offenders back into the community as useful citizens." A noble idea, for sure, but a hard one to put into place.

Feelings of resentment continued to churn as Eastern Shore sheriffs, prosecutors, and judges felt the sting of the reporter's pen. There was a collective umbrage on this side of the Chesapeake for the Baltimore men and the newspaper. Over in Worcester County, the state's attorney, Jack Sanford, was madder than hell and preparing for a fight with Jospeh Egeberg, declaring he was going to subpoena the inspector and make him appear before a grand jury. For many, the earth had been salted. Then came one of the strongest rebukes of the exposé and it came from none other than Wicomico County Sheriff Samuel Graham.

And so, that morning, Sunday, December 8th, people opened the *Daily Times* newspaper and read his rebuttal under that bold headline: "Sheriff Graham Resents Outmoded Report On Jail." The article, written by reporter Mel Toadvine, was accompanied by a few striking photographs. In one, Graham wore his ten-gallon, white cowboy hat and stared into the camera while holding a telephone receiver to his left ear; in another, he clenched a long, unlit cigar between his teeth as he patted down an inmate whose hands were up against a wall. Toadvine's first line—including the exclamation point—would come to bear a depressing amount of irony: "Sheriff Graham runs a tight jail!"

Graham tore into the *Baltimore Sun's* exposé, challenging several points made by Egeberg and Geiselman. One source of contention was Egeberg's continuing call for building new regional jails in lieu of the smaller lockups. Graham dismissed the notion saying, "That's not such a good idea. It would have to be built in the middle of nowhere. Every time a prisoner had to be taken to trial, someone would have to go out and pick him up. Whenever a lawyer wanted to talk to his client, he would have to drive way out in the county. It won't work."

Graham denied his jail was overcrowded, noting that although it was designed to hold eighty prisoners, he averaged about fifty, but no more than sixty-five. He also maintained that juveniles and women were segregated from the adult men in his jail. This was a direct response to Geiselman and Egeberg finding a fifteen-year-old boy in Graham's jail, but they did not mention if he was found in a juvenile cell or not. On that topic, other county officials publicly acknowledged the need to send juveniles to an age-appropriate place.

Prisoner treatment was not a problem, Graham argued. He pushed back on the notion that he or his deputies mistreated anyone in their care. The inmates were not forced into labor, he said, and those who did participate in labor details were all volunteers. Doing so made them eligible to get time taken off their sentences as well as extra coffee at meal time. During the holidays, inmates had special meals with turkey and all the fixings. His prisoners were able to have visitors and Graham explained to Toadvine that, although the prisoner remained behind bars, they could speak to their visitors through a glass window. Security concerns were minimal, argued Graham: "That jail is foolproof... You can open one cell door or all of them. When the cells are opened, the prisoner comes out into a hall, which is still separated from the jailer by more bars." He added, "We have a tight place ... there's nothing wrong with this jail or the treatment given to the prisoners."

Mel Toadvine's article in the *Daily Times* neatly packaged Sheriff Graham's convincing take on the matter. He sounded firm and resolute in his effort to reassure his constituents that everything was under proper control at the penthouse prison. He trusted in his jail and his staff. He felt it was safe. He felt it was secure. And Sheriff Samuel Graham said so: "This jail is as secure as any and better than most ... If a prisoner breaks from this jail, then it's the fault of the jailer, not the jail."

Yet, despite his protestations to the contrary, Sheriff Graham *knew* this wasn't true. He himself had been stabbed in that penthouse prison and other deputies and jailers had been attacked. Prisoners had been escaping since 1955 when Jesse Pollitt was the sheriff. The lever system was aging and had malfunctioned several times. Contraband like razors, hacksaws, and drugs had been smuggled inside, proving that security checks had failed. And at that very moment, Sheriff Graham was completely unaware of the impending catastrophe brewing in his jail. One of his prisoners had a loaded gun in his possession. It had been smuggled inside two days earlier during a visitation. Perhaps the good old sheriff could not or would not publicly admit the failings of his jail, but they were there. And they would soon cost him everything.

• • •

Deputy Bud Fowler parked his Cadillac and walked into the sheriff's department. The office was located in the basement on the east side of the courthouse. This is where Bud was to spend his shift keeping busy with tasks like dispatching units, handling paperwork, and answering the phone. Above him, on the third floor, the twenty inmates of the county jail were milling about. Earlier that morning, there had been twenty-nine prisoners, but nine had been released by 10:05 a.m. for a variety of reasons: one was a juvenile sent to the Maryland Training School for Boys and six had bailed their way out.

At a quarter to five in the afternoon, the winter sun sank beneath the horizon. As the December sky darkened, the mercury dipped just below the freezing mark. At 5:25 p.m., an officer brought in a man charged with assault. Half an hour later, another inmate was let go on bond. Two teenagers, both sixteen, were taken up to the jail by Deputy Kenneth Hennessey at 7:00 p.m. and they were placed in the juvenile cells, which faced the main door into the jail. These two youths had just come back from the Maryland Training School for Boys and would spend the night in custody. Around 9:15 p.m., Deputy Bud Fowler took a man up to the jail and entered him in the logbook as a "night lodger." This brought the prisoner count to twenty-three in total. Inmates that night included four juveniles (one of whom had been there for 108 days), a man who was being held after coming back from Clifton T. Perkins, a woman who had been there a week for a motor vehicle issue, a man charged with "carnal knowledge," another with vagrancy, and several men arrested for armed robberies, break and entering, disorderly conduct, and assaults. Among them was Joseph James Bartholomey, Jr.

Another man, Ralph Lee Pusey, entered the courthouse and asked to speak with the sheriff. Pusey worked at the Esso gas station at the corner of Route 13 and East Main Street in Salisbury, but he was looking for something different. He wanted to be a deputy and the only way to become one was to talk to the boss. Ralph Pusey and Sheriff Graham began talking downstairs, possibly near where Deputy Bud Fowler was manning the desk, and then they both took the elevator up to the jail. Over coffee, the two men discussed Pusey becoming a deputy.

The moon, which had been full just four days ago, had begun to wane and sat alone in the ink black sky above the courthouse. Calm westerly winds enveloped Salisbury in a frigid embrace. A hush fell over the town ... parents kissed their children goodnight and tucked them safely into bed. The lights would go out on the Christmas trees and the folks of Wicomico County would take refuge by the warmth of their fireplaces, comforted by the ease of the day and thoughts of the holiday season. Then they would say their prayers and drift off to sleep.

No one could have imagined what was coming.

– CHAOS IN THE CHAMBER –
THE MURDERS OF GRAHAM AND KELLY

At 9:30 p.m., jailer Albert Lee Kelly was sitting at his desk just outside the main door to the jail when Ralph Pusey stopped to chat. He had good news to share: Sheriff Graham had agreed to hire him and said he'd deputize him in the morning. (Likely, this would have been a part-time deputy position, not full-time.) The two men talked for a few minutes and then Ralph Pusey wandered down the hall to one of the trustee's cells, yelling out to Albert, "When you're ready to lock the boys up, call me and I'll come back up."

Ten minutes later, Albert was on the phone with Nellie. This nightly phone call was a ritual for the Kellys. Every shift, somewhere between 8:30 p.m. and 10 p.m., Albert Kelly called home to check in before leaving at midnight.

"It's been pretty quiet around here tonight," he remarked to Nellie.

"It seems to me they are keeping more noise than usual."

He laughed and said, "They must be celebrating Christmas early." Their conversation turned from the noisy inmates to the upcoming holiday. "Now, tomorrow, we have to go do some Christmas shopping for the children," he said, meaning their grandchildren, Bonnie and Brian.

As their phone call wound down, Albert asked Nellie if she planned to wait up for him, but Nellie said no. Two weeks prior, she had had an operation and her sister had come to stay with them. Nellie said she was tired and was going to bed. They said their goodbyes and Albert hung up the phone.

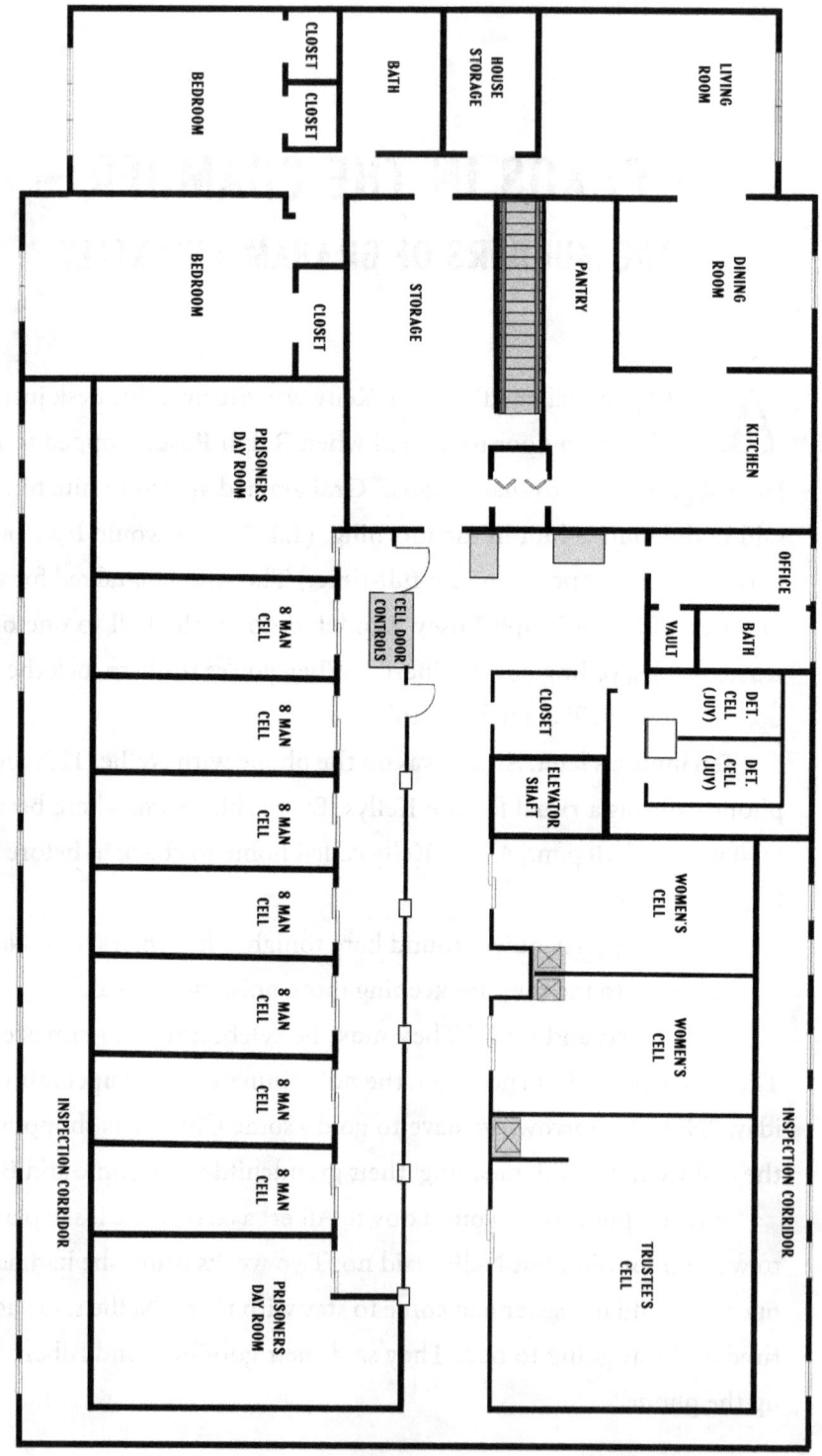

Blueprint of the top floor of the Wicomico County Courthouse

Image courtesy of Patricia Gregorio

Over in the juvenile cell, about twenty-five feet from Albert's desk, sat the two sixteen-year-old boys who had just come back from the Maryland Training School for Boys, brought in by Deputy Hennessey. One of those teenagers was Ralph Anthony Harmon who had found himself in quite a bit of trouble: he and a friend had allegedly stolen a revolver, a rifle, ammunition, and a blank check book from a house on Delaware Avenue and had cashed one of those checks for $50.[1] Also in that same cell with Ralph Harmon (and the other teenager) was nineteen-year-old Vincent Horsey. He was being held on a $10,000.00[2] bond for armed robbery. That evening, Ralph and Vincent were sitting on Vincent's bunk, smoking cigarettes. Theirs would be a front row view to what was coming.

While Albert had been on the phone with Nellie, a 28-year-old trustee named Donald Leon Dashiell sat down at the jailer's desk. He was an air conditioning and refrigeration worker from Mardela Springs serving a thirty-day sentence for assault. This was his first time in the penthouse prison. Sheriff Graham had given him dishwashing duties and had tasked him with serving breakfast to the other inmates. As a trustee, Donald Dashiell was not continuously confined to his cell or the locked day rooms.

Just about 10:00 p.m., Albert told Donald it was time to move the prisoners back into their cells. During the day, inmates were able to spend time in either of the two large day rooms, which had doors capable of locking them in. Donald Dashiell watched as Albert rose from the desk and walked down the hall, toward the large prisoner day room on the far side of the jail. The men went into their cells and Albert locked the prisoners in and came back up the hallway. Then he walked toward the other day room, which was closer to the desk where Donald still sat.

No one knew that a prisoner was readying himself for attack.

As Albert Kelly reached the door of prisoner day room, Joseph

---

1 $50 in 1968 is roughly equivalent to $450 in 2025.

2 $10,000 in 1968 is roughly equivalent to $92,000 in 2025.

Bartholomey yelled, "Open the door!" He pulled the gun on Albert and made his point explicitly clear: *open the door or I'm going to kill you.*

Albert yelled for him to hand over the gun. Joseph refused, aiming the .22 caliber Harrington and Richardson revolver at the jailer. Joseph would not yield. He was never going to yield.

"Go get the sheriff!" Albert yelled back to Donald Dashiell who then looked up and saw the gun in Joseph's hand. "Go get the sheriff and close the door!" He was referring to the main door into the prison, which would have sealed off the prison and everyone inside.

Ralph Harmon and Vincent Horsey, from their vantage point in the juvenile cell, watched as the scene began to unfold right in front of them.

Donald Dashiell immediately sprang from his chair to go get help, closing the main door on his way. He beat furiously upon the door to Graham's apartment.

"What's wrong?" Sheriff Graham asked as he answered the door. Moments earlier, he had been asleep or nearly so in his recliner.

Donald told him about the boy with the gun who was trying to escape.

"What boy?" Graham had to have been in a state of confusion.

"Bartholomey or whatever his name is."

Sheriff Graham and Donald Dashiell raced back to the prison door. Graham tried to get a better look inside the jail through the small window on the door. Donald Dashiell warned him against it. *The boy still has the gun,* he said. Ralph Harmon in the juvenile cell heard Dashiell's warning.

"Is Kelly in there?"

"Yes, sir."

Sheriff Graham knew the situation was grave. He turned to his trustee, "Go downstairs and get some help." He knew there would be a deputy at the desk and that deputy would be armed.

Donald Dashiell ran for the elevator and got inside. Just as the doors started to close, he heard gunshots. Donald pushed the elevator doors open again and peeked out. He saw Albert Kelly falling to the floor, his body pushing the main prison door open. Sheriff Graham was caught behind the door. A chilling realization washed over Donald: Joseph had shot the jailer. Twice. Once in the back of his head on the right side and again in his back near his left shoulder. Donald slid the elevator doors shut and headed for the basement. As he descended, he heard more shots ring out in the jail above.

Just as Joseph grabbed Albert's set of keys, Ralph Pusey, who had heard the commotion, came running up the hallway.

"Shoot him, Ralph!" Graham yelled. But it was no use. Ralph was unarmed.

Chaos electrified the prison.

Joseph was at the main door between the prison and the hallway. He saw Ralph Pusey coming and fired a shot at him, but the shot went wild. Ralph jumped toward the elevator and pushed the door open just a bit. He realized the elevator wasn't there—Ralph Pusey had not seen Donald Dashiell take it down—and by trying to re-open the door, he accidentally stalled the elevator. Luckily, Donald Dashiell had already made it down.

Sheriff Graham, seeing Joseph inches away from being fully in the hallway, threw his hands against the door, doing his best to shut the door and keep Joseph inside the jail. Joseph resisted. He pushed back. This was now a battle of wills. Both men wanted—needed—to be the victor in this moment. Yet, only one of them had a gun and that made all the difference. Joseph pushed against the door just enough to wedge the gun into the small opening and turned the gun toward the sheriff. Vincent Horsey in the juvenile cell saw the gun emerge and could only watch as Joseph pulled the trigger repeatedly. Seven times. Each bullet ripped into the left side of Samuel Graham's massive body. Into his left armpit. The left side of his chest, twice. Then another down his side into his abdomen. Two of the shots hit his left shin. One entered the top of his left foot.

Big Sam Graham fell to the floor ... his life quickly slipping away from him.

With the door no longer barred, Joseph ran down the back stairs and burst into the second floor courtroom hallway. From there, he made his way to the ground floor and ran toward the front doors of the courthouse. He was so close to freedom. He smashed a window on the door and then Joseph James Bartholomey, Jr., free once more, disappeared into the night.

• • •

Deputy Bud Fowler was sitting at the desk when Donald Dashiell burst into the sheriff's office. The trustee told him that Albert Kelly had been shot and that a prisoner had a gun and was trying to escape. Bud and Donald tried to get back upstairs, but because Ralph Pusey had pushed the door open and stalled the elevator, they were stuck. It took a few seconds to get the elevator working again. When they finally reached the jail, Bud stepped into the hallway and was greeted by a gruesome scene.

Both Albert Kelly and Samuel Graham were lying in pools of blood on the floor. Someone had moved Albert's body into the hallway.[3] Sam was lying just inside the door that lead to the sheriff's apartment. Bud stepped over Albert's body to get to Sam; he knew the jailer was dead. He saw Dorothy Graham, who had emerged from the sheriff's living quarters. Ralph Pusey was still there, too. Bud immediately knelt down beside Sheriff Sam Graham and felt his body. There was nothing. No pulse. No life. He was gone. Bud ushered Dorothy to a chair and then headed down the back staircase in the direction of the escaped prisoner. He heard someone call out his name so he turned around and went back up to the jail.

Someone called for an ambulance. Then, at 10:10 p.m., someone called the Salisbury Police Department and the Maryland State Police barrack. Quickly, law enforcement officers began arriving at the scene, including high-ranking officials like Salisbury Police Chief Leslie J.

---

3 Albert Kelly was shot near the controls inside the jail, however, his body was found in the hallway outside the main door. There is no record of who moved him or when, but it happened just prior to Bud Fowler's arrival on the scene. This is supported by Fowler's testimony at trial.

Payne and Maryland State Police Captain Thomas Veditz. Within five minutes of the initial call, Maryland State Police Corporal Samuel Reed Chaffey, Jr. was at the courthouse. As he approached, he saw the bodies of Albert Kelly and Samuel Graham being put into an ambulance to be taken to Peninsula General Hospital. Dorothy Graham was just behind them. Corporal Chaffey took the elevator up to the jail to begin his investigation into the grisly deaths of two fellow lawmen. Two more members of the Maryland State Police—Detective Sergeant Robert D. Weir, Sr. and Sergeant Robert W. Burkhardt—joined Corporal Chaffey's investigation. These three men—Chaffey, Weir, and Burkhardt—were the investigative team that would handle this double homicide.

Other Wicomico County sheriff's deputies rushed to scene. Deputy William Lewis had been at home with his family when he heard about the shooting at the courthouse. Handsome and fit, Lewis looked like a model deputy, complete with his marked police car sitting in the driveway of their farmhouse in Parsonsburg. As he dashed out the door to head to Salisbury, his son, Michael, took in the moment as best as a child can. Seeing his father race from their home to go help became a memory firmly locked in place for Mike, who would be elected sheriff four decades later. Another deputy, Tommy Lewis, had also been at home that night when he heard the call come out over his police scanner requesting ambulances for two patients. As a teenager, he started hanging around the sheriff's department because he was interested in police work. The deputies were kind to Tommy and showed him the ropes; then, on his 21st birthday, Graham deputized him as a part-time lawman. Ever one to help, Tommy Lewis quickly dressed in his uniform and headed to the jail. By the time he arrived, Albert Kelly and Samuel Graham had already been moved to the hospital.

Now, the search was on for Joseph Bartholomey. Deputy Tommy Lewis had three other deputies assigned to him to begin searching the courthouse from top to bottom to ensure Joseph was not still inside. As they began their hunt, Tommy told his men, "Now we've got to stay together because if we don't, we're going to end up shooting each other." One deputy discovered Albert Kelly's keys in the courthouse yard near a tree. A window had been busted out of the front door. They determined this must have been the escape route.

Soon, word reached the men that both Albert Kelly and Samuel Graham were confirmed dead. That official determination was made at 10:25 p.m., not long after the ambulances reached Peninsula General Hospital. For men like Bud Fowler, William Lewis, and Tommy Lewis, in an instant, they had lost their boss and their friend. Hardly anyone could believe this was real, that all this was actually happening ...

Bud Fowler left around midnight. His wife, Libby, had called into the department to find out what was going on and a deputy explained the horrific situation. Bud walked out of the courthouse and got into his Cadillac. His mind could barely comprehend what had happened that night. He looked down and saw that his uniform was stained with the blood of the dead sheriff ... the man who had given him the job he'd always wanted. And what of Albert Kelly? What would his family do now? There was nothing left to do but drive home.

Tommy Lewis was assigned to man the desk in the basement. He was given strict instructions: answer the phone and say nothing. No one knew exactly what was going on and no one wanted to jeopardize the investigation. One of the deputies called in and because the night was so fraught with tension, Tommy hung up on him. These men were dealing with events so far beyond their comprehension that they simply didn't know what to do. Escapes and fights, sure, but this was something entirely different.

This had been a most implausible night for Tommy. How could such a thing have happened? Although Albert Kelly was still relatively new to the department, Tommy knew him to be a good man. And Sam ... the beloved patriarch of the department. He made that place feel like a family. It was Sam who had given Tommy an opportunity to learn about law enforcement and to make a living for himself and his family. Big Sam, with the kind smile and soft heart, was gone forever. When Dorothy

Graham returned from the hospital, Tommy met her eyes. They just looked at one another and said nothing. That night weighed heavy on Tommy Lewis's mind and it would for years to come.

The murder of Wicomico County Sheriff Samuel Graham ended the deputization of his lawmen. Bud Fowler, William Lewis, Tommy Lewis, and all the other deputies no longer had any law enforcement power. They were civilians once again. Now, they would have to wait for a new sheriff to be named and this choice could only come from one man: Spiro Agnew, the governor of Maryland and now Vice-President Elect of the United States.

• • •

Joseph Bartholomey was running. No more bars; no more cages. The night sky opened wide above him. He was free. The winter air hovered around the freezing mark and it nipped at his face and hands. It poured into his lungs as he ran away from the courthouse, away from the jail, away from the men he had just murdered. Cold-blooded and without mercy. He slipped into the darkness of a sleeping city, one that would awake to the horrific and heartbreaking news of his latest crimes.

Then came a troubling realization: he was hurt and he was bleeding. The pain in his back became more apparent as his adrenaline waned. He stumbled into a washette (a small laundromat) just off the railroad tracks. It was 10:45 p.m. He found a phone inside and called his friend, Erick Thomas Irwin. He needed a ride. And quick.

Erick left his house on Winder Street. His mother was still awake and thought his late night exit was odd. He picked up Joseph and drove him north to Dover, Delaware. They stopped at the Capital City Motel on Route 13. Close to midnight, Joseph checked into Room #22 under the name John Davis. He stuck the gun, now empty of all its ten bullets, inside the air conditioning unit.

What was he going to do now? And just how badly was he injured?

– MANHUNT –

Within minutes of the double homicide, a massive manhunt spanning three states was underway. Police across the Delmarva Peninsula had been notified of Joseph Bartholomey's escape and had begun blocking all roads in and out of Maryland as well as any routes leading off the peninsula, of which there were precious few. Lawmen were stopping cars, surveilling all-night diners and gas stations, searching alleyways and hangouts known to Bartholomey, warning cab drivers, and even contacting the local television stations to give his description. During the search, police cars chased a southbound train out of Salisbury on the possibility that he had hopped aboard. Once the train was stopped, a quick search revealed the prisoner was not there. The newspapers would call this search "one of the biggest manhunts in Maryland in recent years."

Back at the prison, police were looking for clues. They started with the visitor logs and discovered that on Friday, December 6th, just two days before the murders, Joseph had two visitors: his partner in crime, Erick Thomas Irwin, and his girlfriend, Donna Blair Campbell. Had they helped Joseph? Had they brought in the gun? Immediately, officers went to the Irwin residence on Winder Street and interviewed Erick's mother. She said her son had received a phone call around 10:45 p.m. and that he left in a hurry without telling her where he was going. She told police that it was "unusual that he left so late." Now police felt sure that Erick was connected to Joseph and the escape.

At some point in those dark morning hours of Monday, December

9th, Erick Irwin returned home from his trip to Dover. How long he stayed with Joseph and what time he got back to Salisbury are unknown. What is known, however, is that the police were still at the Irwin home. The officers asked him about the call and his recent whereabouts, and to his credit, Erick was honest and forthcoming with the details. He told them the caller was Joseph. He told them he took Joseph to Dover and dropped him off at a motel. Erick did not cover or lie for his friend.

Perhaps at this moment, Erick came to a terrible, gripping realization: his rebellious friend wasn't just a thief, he was now a murderer. Breaking into stores and stealing guns and money was one kind of thing, but this? Two innocent men were dead. Joseph had gone too far this time. As Erick stood in his parents home with the news washing over him, one can only imagine the soul-searching to come next for young Erick Thomas Irwin. He was taken into custody, charged with assisting the escape, and jailed in the penthouse prison.

The penthouse prison turned crime scene.

The crime scene triggered by his friend.

His friend, Joseph Bartholomey—the killer.

• • •

Based on Erick's information, which was as solid a lead as they come, the Maryland State Police investigative team reached out to their northern counterparts: Dover City Police Department and the Delaware State Police. At 7:28 a.m., MSP Detective Sergeant Robert Weir told them that Erick said he had taken Joseph "to a motel which was white in color, north of the donut shop on Route 13, on the left-hand side" in Dover, Delaware. A Delaware State Police sergeant thought about that description and the only motel that matched it was the Capital City Motel. It had a white stucco exterior. The sergeant placed a call to the Dover City Police Department and relayed the information.

Dover City Police went to the Capital City Motel. They tried to contact a manager but failed so they pulled back, opting instead to work on stationing officers around the building. At 8:00 a.m., the motel owner approached one of the men and said that his wife was in the motel but he didn't know exactly where. Immediately, they became concerned that Bartholomey might have taken her hostage. The motel owner wanted to go in, but they would not allow it.

Once the police on the scene were satisfied that the building was fully surrounded, several officers plus the owner went into the motel office. The owner's wife was in the room above the office, unharmed and likely unaware of the situation unfolding outside. The motel owner checked the register and confirmed there was a John Davis signed into Room 22.

The police surrounded Room 22 and called for the occupant to come out.

And he did. Without a fight. "John Davis" a.k.a. Joseph Bartholomey surrendered. He opened the door and put his hands up. Then, with his hands on his head, he turned and backed out of the room. He was taken into custody while police searched the room for any other people and weapons. One officer saw that the front panel of the wall air conditioning unit had been removed. He peered inside and found the gun.

It was 8:20 a.m. Joseph's great escape had lasted ten hours and twenty minutes and had cost two good men their lives.

Immediately after his capture, Delaware police officers took Joseph to Kent General Hospital for an examination. A reporter on the scene noticed a curious detail. Joseph was injured and bloody. One newspaper reported that Joseph's right hand was bloody. The explanation given was that he had allegedly suffered a gunshot wound during the jailbreak; another account said he cut his hand. Another newspaper specifically said that there was a gunshot wound to his back while yet another stated that he had cut his hand and buttocks on broken glass. Joseph declined treatment for whatever his injury or injuries were. The *Evening Journal* out of Wilmington, Delaware noted he "exchanged blood stained clothing for a hospital gown." Had Joseph been shot? Could it have been a ricochet

SUSPECT RETURNED. Joseph James Bartholomey, 21-year-old suspect in the slaying of two Wicomico County lawmen Sunday night, was brought back to Salisbury by state police helicopter Monday afternoon. He is shown being led by City Police Detective Jerry Mason, left, and at right, States Attorney Alfred T. Truitt Jr. Later Bartholomey was carried to the Maryland Penitentiary in Baltimore. Two more people have been arrested in connection with the slayings.

(Times Photo)

Joseph J. Bartholomey, center and all in white, is brought back to Salisbury. To the left is Wicomico County State's Attorney Alfred Truitt. The man in the light-colored coat is Salisbury detective Jerry Mason.

© *The Daily Times – USA TODAY NETWORK via Imagn Images*

from one of the shots he fired inside the jail? What was the source of all this blood? Later, Wicomico County State's Attorney Alfred Truitt would say that he cut himself on the glass of the courthouse front doors as he was making his escape, but somehow, somewhere in all that chaos, Joseph Bartholomey had indeed been shot in the back. This was later confirmed in his medical records. The wound was not life-threatening and no surgery was recorded to have been performed. And no one ever claimed to have shot him. The bullet wound is scarcely mentioned save for a few brief mentions in the newspaper and his medical records. It remains yet another bizarre facet in this case.[1]

Once he was released from the hospital, he was taken to the police station temporarily and then he went before a Dover magistrate where he waived extradition on a "charge of being a fugitive from justice." Shortly after 11:00 a.m., both Joseph and the murder weapon were turned over to Maryland State Police Detective Sergeant Robert Burkhardt. Joseph was flown by helicopter back to the Salisbury barracks of the Maryland State Police. This moment was captured by a *Daily Times* photographer who snapped an image of Joseph, wearing a white suit covering his entire body from his neck to his wrists to his ankles, being led away from the helicopter by Alfred Truitt and Salisbury Police Detective Jerry R. Mason, the same officer who had shot Daniel Henry eight months prior. A doctor was called to the barracks, presumably to examine Joseph again, but nothing further was reported on that. He was then arraigned by Peoples Court Judge Robert Dallas on two counts of murder and sent to the maximum security section of the Maryland Penitentiary in Baltimore.[2]

Joseph, twenty-one and deadly, was back on familiar ground: in Baltimore and in prison. In a way, he was back home.

---

[1] Author's Note: I suspect this bullet wound was a possible ricochet-type artifact that happened during his shooting of Sam Graham. In the autopsy, there are unusual trajectory marks for the bullet wounds to Graham's left leg. I cannot prove this ricochet theory; I only suspect it. There was no report of gunfire or a shootout at the motel nor was there any noted suspicion otherwise.

[2] Now called the Metropolitan Transition Center, it is the oldest prison in Maryland, dating back to 1811.

– THE IMMEDIATE AFTERMATH –

On Monday morning, December 9th, 1968, the headlines for the *Daily Times* were as grim as they come: "Sheriff Graham, Deputy Slain; Jail Escapee Here Recaptured." And given the headlines from the day before, they were not only shocking and despairing, but they were also painfully ironic ... that the sheriff had been murdered in the very jail he claimed was safe on the very day his words were printed in the newspaper.

Underneath the headline was a photograph of Sam wearing a pin-striped suit and a tie with diagonal stripes and a light-colored cowboy hat. The photo was taken as he talked on the phone, his mouth slightly open, as if caught mid-sentence. A lit cigar in his right hand. A likeness frozen in time, never to be seen again. The photograph of Albert Kelly was smaller, grainier. Wearing browline glasses, his smile is small, almost like a man asked to pose and smile when he'd rather not. Next to Kelly was a mug shot of Joseph taken by the Salisbury Police Department when he was arrested in November. His face bears a blank expression with dark eyes staring straight back into the camera.

Folks across the county went into a state of shock and mourning. From Tilghman's grocery store in Mardela Springs to Kolb's country store in Allen, men gathered and lamented the loss of their big, friendly sheriff. The questions were the same: how did this happen? A gun in the jail? These sentiments were echoed by Wicomico County Council President Richard S. Wootten: "I'm shocked. This is tragic. I'm sure the whole county is shocked."

The front page of the Daily Times *on Monday, December 9th, 1968 is heartbreakingly ironic when compared to the headlines from the previous day.*

© The Daily Times – USA TODAY NETWORK via Imagn Images

Flags were ordered flown at half-staff throughout Salisbury and Wicomico County. Sad but glowing tributes flooded in. The mayor of Salisbury, Dallas G. Truitt, said of Sam, "I knew him very well. He was one of the most likable individuals I've ever seen. He was everybody's friend." One woman who worked at the courthouse told a reporter that she was sick to her stomach over the murders. An attorney who was friendly with the beloved sheriff said, "I can't understand anyone shooting Sam Graham. He was not the type to create any antagonism or enmity." Judge William W. Travers, the best man at Sam's wedding, said only, "He treated everyone humanely, particularly his prisoners. ... I'm not over it yet."

Alfred Truitt was deeply shaken by the news. It was one of the rare moments that his family saw him show any kind of emotion at all. Alfred was a good man, but he was as stoic as they come. And perhaps he had good reason to be. His early life had been scarred by tragedies. When he was about four or five years old, he was riding in a horse-drawn buggy with his grandfather, possibly on the way to church. His grandfather pulled over and, without warning, shot himself to death in front of his grandson. The horse took the buggy and Alfred back to the family farm near Pittsville. His grandmother spent the rest of her life at the psychiatric hospital in Cambridge, Maryland. Then came World War II and the Nuremberg Trials ... to his dying day, he could still vividly recall how those concentration camps smelled. The men of his generation were expected to be strong and resilient; they were men, after all. Life had given Alfred Truitt reason enough to maintain a stiff upper lip and an unemotional facade, but the murder of his friend split through that rigidity.

His eldest child, Christine, saw her father with his head in his hands, weeping and crushed. She had never seen him like that. And she couldn't understand why Sheriff Graham, a family friend and avuncular figure to the Truitt family, had been murdered. He had been so kind.

When Alfred's youngest daughter, Maggie, approached him with a copy of the newspaper reporting that grown men were crying over Sam Graham's death, he said he understood.

"I was one of them," he told her. Maggie, only eleven, was stunned to hear her father had cried tears of sorrow. She had never seen him shed a tear. But Maggie knew Sam, the sheriff and her father's friend. To her, he was a giant of a man but sweet as could be, like a teddy bear come to life. If her father had wept, then it had to hurt.

This was going to be a somber time in Wicomico County.

The editor of the *Daily Times*, Dick Moore, wrote an editorial lamenting the assassinations of public figures that year. Too much violence filled his newspaper columns day after day. This was the very reason we need men like Graham, he wrote ... men who risk their lives every time they approach a criminal. Moore said he would miss his friend.

Because Sam Graham was a major political figure as the elected sheriff and head of the Democratic party in Wicomico County, and because he was so well-regarded, a great deal of the reporting and attention began to fall on him in a singular way. Two men had been killed that night, but often, in the days ahead, it would be Sam's name taking center stage. Sometimes Albert Kelly's name was omitted entirely when the events were spoken of or written about. This was salt in a fresh wound for Kelly's family who saw the popular sheriff become the focus in the unfolding tragedy. Albert Kelly was a loved man and his family missed him. Their lives would never be the same.

Of the five Kelly boys, two had been taken by murder and one by car accident. The last two brothers saw their silver years before cancer took them, too.

• • •

Although the news had spread like a wildfire across Wicomico County and the Delmarva Peninsula, reports of the tragic murders appeared in Monday morning newspapers as far away as Kentucky and Texas. This massive and compelling story showed no sign of slowing down as local lawmen continued their investigation.

MSP Corporal Samuel Reed Chaffey went to Peninsula General Hospital early on Monday morning to check in on the autopsies of Albert Kelly and Samuel Graham. There he met with Dr. Peter Boolukas. About twelve hours had passed since the murders. As Dr. Boolukas recovered each bullet, he handed them over to Corporal Chaffey, who then placed each one in a wad of tissue paper and then into a glass vial and topped it with a rubber stopper. These important pieces of evidence stayed with him. And not just *with him*, these bullets remained *on him* at all times to ensure the chain of custody.[1]

---

1 Today the chain of custody would be done differently, but this was a standard practice then, according to law experts of the time.

In less than twenty-four hours, the police had already made significant advances in the case. They had Erick Thomas Irwin in custody. He now sat in a cell in the penthouse prison. They also had his statement about the previous night's event. A warrant had been issued for Donna Blair Campbell who no longer appeared to be at 308 Gay Street. However, at 6:00 p.m.,[2] Baltimore homicide detectives found her at her parents' house on Miles Avenue in the northern part of the city and arrested her. (One newspaper account offered this description: Donna "was wearing knee-high mod boots when she was arrested in her Baltimore home.") The Baltimore homicide detectives took her to the Pine Street police station where she was served with her warrant; her charge was abetting an escape. Maryland State Police brought her back to Salisbury where Donna, like Erick, was placed in a cell in the penthouse prison. And, most important of all, was that Joseph J. Bartholomey, Jr. was in custody at the Maryland Penitentiary.

Having the main suspect and his two accomplices behind bars went a long way towards easing public fears. The police were on the case, and despite the horrific losses of Graham and Kelly, at least they could point to these arrests as positive developments.

TUESDAY, DECEMBER 10TH, 1968

As the sun rose on a bitterly cold Tuesday morning, the story of the slain sheriff and jailer continued to spread. Reports of the crime appeared in newspapers far and wide: from Maine to Florida to California and even as far as Canada and Spain. Such a sensational tale would. (Still does.)

One question reverberating in nearly everyone's mind was how did a loaded gun make its way into the county jail? By now, Erick Irwin and Donna Campbell's jailhouse visit with Joseph had been reported in the

---

2 Sources conflict on the date she was arrested. The *Daily Times* twice reports her arrest was on 12/9 and the *Baltimore Sun* articles say it happened on 12/10.

papers. So who brought it in? How did it get through the jail's security measures? One answer was making its way into the public sphere: the candy box theory. The newspapers began reporting that Donna and Erick had brought the gun into the jail inside of a box of candy, possibly asking a man who was painting one of the cells to pass it along to Joseph. Secretly, of course.

Yet there was one detail missing from the news reports. The gun was a .22 caliber Harrington and Richardson revolver with a long, slender barrel and a black hand grip.[3] It was among the twenty guns stolen by Joseph and Erick in the Voigt's Hobby and Sports Shop robbery on November 9th, 1968. (This fact wouldn't be discovered until later.) Perhaps Donna brought the gun into the jail in a box of candy, but had she received the gun from Erick, the other participant in the Voigt robbery, or had Joseph hidden the gun and given her its location? Who was the guilty party exactly? Were they both equally responsible? Erick would point his finger at Donna who pointed hers right back at him. This point of contention has never been resolved.

The forensic investigative work on the case was underway by the Maryland State Police. Corporal Samuel Chaffey still had bullets from their autopsies in his possession. That Tuesday, he turned them over to Sergeant Robert Burkhardt who was to take them to the crime lab. Burkhardt arranged the vials of bullets as well as the recovered gun in a cigar box and took them to the laboratory at the Maryland State Police Headquarters in Pikesville, Maryland. There, he turned over that cigar box to the ballistics expert around noon. It would be up to that expert to scientifically determine if the bullets retrieved from the bodies of Kelly and Graham were fired from the weapon found in the motel room with Joseph Bartholomey.

What started in a box of candy ended up as a cigar box of evidence.

The deputies of the Wicomico County Sheriff's Department were

---

3 In Erick's criminal indictment, this gun is reported to have a value of $32.65, which would be roughly equivalent to $300 in 2025.

anticipating word on the appointment of their new sheriff. They expected Maryland Governor and Vice President-Elect Spiro Agnew to name a new sheriff any day now, and when that happened, all the men would be re-deputized and return to work. The warrants written but yet not issued under Sam Graham would all have to be redone. For now, the men of the Wicomico County Sheriff's Department mourned and waited. John Walston, who had been Graham's chief deputy, was named as "warden of the jail" by the Wicomico County Council. He appeared before the council and said that he was "willing to do anything necessary under the circumstances." It was made clear to him that he did not have the powers of a sheriff, but it was his duty to regain control of the jail and keep it running. Walston was also understandably reluctant to move his family into the sheriff's residence and the council said that they would not require that of him. Bud Fowler was offered the temporary job of turnkey, but he quickly turned it down.

• • •

That Tuesday evening, the Salisbury City Council opened its meeting with a minute of silent prayer, called for by the president of the council, W. Paul Martin, Jr. He said this moment was "for our sheriff who was so violently removed from our midst Sunday night." More than twenty officials stood and bowed their heads. Then they recited the Lord's Prayer. Unfortunately, Martin forgot to mention Kelly. The council meeting closed in time to allow those present to head to the funeral home.

The viewing for Sheriff Sam Graham was held Tuesday evening at Holloway Funeral Home on Snow Hill Road in Salisbury. Although the time listed was 7:30 p.m. to 9:00 p.m., people began arriving as early as 6:00 p.m. The sun had set and twilight had ushered in the dark of night. The temperature hovered around 20° as hundreds of men and women, bundled snugly in thick winter garments, lined up outside the funeral home, each waiting their turn to pay their respects to the esteemed sheriff.

More than two hundred floral arrangements surrounded Samuel Graham's casket while police officers stood a silent vigil next to him. Mike Meise, a reporter for the *Daily Times*, wrote a poignant article about the viewing with lines like: "At least 1,000 mourners approached the bier where Sam Graham lay, the once-twinkling eyes sealed in eternal sleep." The reporter noted that people came from all over the state and the sea of faces, tear-streaked as they were, revealed a man whose friends knew no color lines as White and Black mourned together. Noted Black educators Charles H. Chipman and his wife, Jeanette, attended his services. Charles, a Howard University graduate, taught for decades in the segregated educational system of Wicomico County and he was so revered that students called him "Professor"; Jeanette, a graduate of Virginia State College,[4] had a fifty-year teaching career that began in the all-Black Salisbury High School as the Home Economics teacher. The Chipman legacy would stand for decades in Wicomico County. Emily Furr, the jail's cook and Sam's friend, was heartbroken. She told reporter Mike Meise, "Nobody ever treated me as good as Mr. Sam." Meise's article noted her as "one of Sam Graham's favorite people." Weeks later, she made the Christmas Day dinner for the inmates, telling the *Daily Times*, "It will be just like he would have wanted it." One can imagine her cooking dinner that Christmas Eve in the jail and thinking of him. When she died thirty years later, her obituary mentioned Sam.

Others were left to their memories. For Tommy Lewis, he remembered the ever-smiling, cigar-smoking, cowboy hat-wearing everyman. Even in the depths of grief, lighter moments with Sam came to mind like the time the sheriff borrowed Tommy's Ford convertible to get a milkshake. Big Sam loved milkshakes, a vice his wasitline constantly endured. The sheriff got a ticket, which he shoved into his desk drawer and promptly forgot. Sometime later, Tommy got a notice in the mail

---

4 It is now Virginia State University.

THE IMMEDIATE AFTERMATH – 191

Scenes from Sam's funeral

Image courtesy of the Edward H. Nabb Research Center for Delmarva History and
Culture, Salisbury University, Mel Toadvine Collection

Sam's men carry him to his grave.

Image courtesy of the Edward H. Nabb Research Center for Delmarva History and Culture, Salisbury University, Mel Toadvine Collection

from the Salisbury Police Department about an unpaid parking ticket. He was utterly confused about it so he went to the Salisbury Police Department to tell them he never got the ticket. The stony sergeant on duty was unmoved and Tommy had no choice but to pay the fine. When he returned to the sheriff's department, Tommy complained to Big Sam. This jogged the memory of the ice-cream-indulging sheriff who then fessed up to being the true owner of that ticket. Tommy and Sam had a great laugh over it.

Mike Meise offered this sentiment: "On the lips of many, quiet eulogies. Not many, though, knew about and could talk about big-hearted Sam, the orphan, and Christmas time. Not many knew how Sam quietly passed out money for the purchase of shoes—always shoes—for needy children. Sam never forgot the days when he was in need of shoes."

And here lies a sad truth: young Sam was no stranger to the hard times life can bring, even onto the shoulders of a child. Joseph, too, knew at an early age that this world could be cruel and unbearable. Yet how different these two men turned out to be ...

WEDNESDAY, DECEMBER 11TH, 1968

The people of Delmarva awoke on Wednesday morning to a brutal cold snap. Temperatures hovered briefly around 12°, causing pipes to freeze and teeth to chatter. On that glacial day, many awaited the funeral of Sheriff Samuel Adams Graham. The courthouse closed its doors from 1:00 p.m. to 3:00 p.m. so that anyone who worked there could attend the service at Holloway Funeral Home. Several of the trustees in the jail upstairs asked if they might be able to go and pay their respects. Their request was granted and they were taken to the funeral home and returned before the official service began.

Inside Holloway Funeral Home, six hundred chairs were set up for mourners to witness the funeral. The overflow rooms were opened as well. Just as the night before, men and women came from all over to say goodbye to a man they all considered a friend and to extend their condolences to his widow, Dorothy. His old friends from his railroad days were there. As were his many deputies including Tommy Lewis, Bud Fowler, William Lewis, and the new warden John Walston. Buddies from his civic organizations attended. Clergymen and doctors. Workers from the Mr. Donut coffee shop and the Ames department store. Wicomico High School students. Judges Thelma Duffy, Rex Taylor, Daniel Prettyman, William Travers, and E. McMaster Duer attended along with the soon-to-be Maryland Governor Marvin Mandel, Maryland State Senator Mary Nock, States Attorney Alfred Truitt, attorney Richard Pollitt, who came with his father, Jesse Pollitt, the former sheriff. Even Joseph D. Egeberg Jr., the man at the center of the prison exposé, was there. The police presence was immense: law enforcement officers from all over Maryland and Delaware held the sheriff in silent prayer. There were representatives from the Washington, D.C. Police, U.S. Park Police, the Maryland Crime Commission, and the Marine Police, and many of these departments sent high-ranking officials. The outpouring of support and love filled the rooms and halls of the funeral home. All these people with heavy hearts, crying eyes, and furrowed brows. No words could express how his loss felt so unreal, so unfathomable ... how could such an upstanding man but cut down so despicably?

Reverend Herbert Gladden from Nelsons Memorial Church presided. He read from Matthew 25:23, a verse about being a good and faithful servant. No one could argue with that. In his eulogy, he said Sam had been a "minister of the law" and reminded those present about the dangers faced by law enforcement: good people can sleep easy because of men like Sam and Albert who are willing to face death itself to keep them safe. Reverend Gladden said that he could summarize Sam Graham in a single word: friendliness. Offering words of comfort, Gladden quoted poet James Whitcomb Riley, "He's not dead, he's just away." Then he closed with a refrain, "Well done, good and faithful servant. ... That sums up our feelings for him."

Sam's deputies, in their pressed uniforms, were his pallbearers. They ushered his casket to the awaiting hearse, which passed by a line of two hundred police officers, an honor for a fallen brother. A dozen Maryland State troopers and Salisbury Police officers directed traffic along the route from the funeral home to Wicomico Memorial Park. Reporter Mike Meise of the *Daily Times* solemnly noted, "Sam Graham had gone this route many times before. But it was the final time today. It may very well turn out to be the biggest funeral ever held hereabouts."

Once the hearse arrived at the graveside, his deputies carried him to his final resting spot, as nearly two dozen police officers stood at attention and gave the slain sheriff one last salute. And then, on that bleak winter afternoon, Samuel Adams Graham was laid to rest.

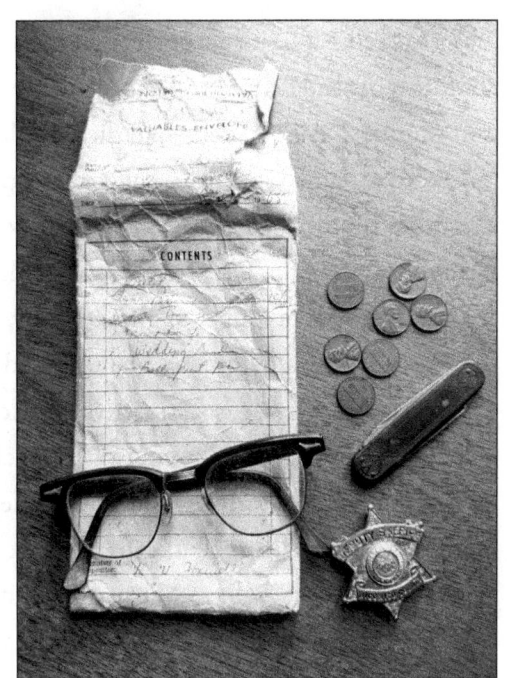

After his autopsy, this envelope was given to Nellie Kelly. It held his glasses, his badge, his wedding ring (not pictured), a small pocketknife, and six pennies.

Image courtesy of the author and the Kelley family

THURSDAY, DECEMBER 12TH, 1968

The courthouse closed its doors again on Thursday, December 12th from 10:00 a.m. until noon for Albert Kelly's funeral. Along with the Kelly family, more than 250 people attended the service including members of the Maryland State Police, Delaware State Police, Salisbury Police, and his own department. High-ranking officers were in attendance. They were there, they said, to honor these men lost in the line of duty.

Just like Sam's service, there were fresh flowers from wall to wall and the Reverend Herbert Gladden of Nelsons Memorial Church presided once again. He opened the service with John 11:25, an oft quoted verse about the resurrection and life and that those who believe in Jesus will live eternally. The reverend spoke of Albert in kind terms—useful, beloved, a man doing a necessary job—and returned again to the same notes of duty for lawmen. "We must have people to keep jails," he preached. "They do not sleep at night so that we may sleep and they are away from their families during the dark so that we may be with our families." Albert Kelly had died while being a faithful servant to his post and his and Sam's deaths were a deeply troubling tragedy. Reverend Gladden then read Psalms 23 and 46 before finally noting that Albert Kelly should be remembered always with love and affection.

Margaret Kelly, his daughter-in-law, sat quietly as the service proceeded. Just days before, she had helped Nellie pick out the casket for Albert. Everything was a strange blur. Reality had been upended. After Albert's autopsy, his belongings were packaged up in a manila envelope and given to his family. Inside was his deputy badge, his wedding ring, his glasses, a small pocketknife, and six pennies. This was all that remained of Albert Kelly, a hardworking man who loved the beauty and harmony of nature ... he had watched as wild daffodils popped up along the backcountry roads while the unmistakable green shoots of day lilies and irises pushed skyward. He knew when to expect the bubblegum pinks and royal purples of the crepe myrtles. His fingers had worked the rich earth and planted trees that still today offer a comforting shade. And now Albert was gone.

Margaret Kelly, tears in her eyes, felt a deep sorrow. She missed him.

Albert's pallbearers were family members while his fellow deputies and other police officers formed two lines where they offered a silent salute as he was carried to his grave. An honor guard stood by in the quiet of the graveyard. A few more words were said and then Albert Lee Kelly was laid to rest at Wicomico Memorial Park. It would be almost twenty-three years before Nellie joined him. She never remarried.

– LINGERINGS OF THE EXPOSÉ –

While the people of Wicomico County were grieving the loss of Sam Graham and Albert Kelly, there was a man over in neighboring Worcester County who was seething with anger and umbrage. Jack Sanford's hackles were up, in spectacular fashion, and someone would have to account for that.

On Monday, December 9th, John "Jack" L. Sanford, Jr., the state's attorney for Worcester County, was still enraged over the *Baltimore Sun's* exposé series. He announced to the local papers that he intended to issue a summons to Joseph D. Egeberg, Jr., the prison inspector, and have him appear before a grand jury. Jack Sanford was ready to rampage, slamming the whole affair as "sensational journalism" filled with "exaggerations and false statements" all for Egeberg's "personal glorification."

The only thing missing was a pitchfork in his hand.

Jack Sanford was a notorious figure in Maryland's Eastern Shore politics. The 59-year-old lawyer had already served fifteen years as a Maryland State Senator as well as several years as the Worcester County State's Attorney. A devout Catholic born in Baltimore, Jack Sanford met and married a young woman from a well-to-do fishing family from Worcester County. He was a smart and devilishly cunning man, two assets that made him an exceptional attorney as well as a controversial figure. One story goes like this: when World War II was on the horizon, Jack feared he would get drafted so he bought a chicken farm because agricultural businesses were important to the war effort and it was enough to earn a deferment. Jack began wearing bib overalls and chewing tobacco, just enough roleplaying to convince a draft board should they ever come around. After the war, he went back to being a lawyer and then had a long run as a state senator. In 1966, he returned to his position as Worcester County State's Attorney and soon he was the unofficial boss of the county, ruthlessly wielding grand jury subpoenas like a blunt weapon.

Jack Sanford's sandblasting of Joseph Egeberg followed Worcester County Circuit Court Judge Daniel Prettyman's questioning of two inmates who were included in the exposé. One was the teenage girl who reportedly scrawled a poem on the cell wall and had possibly tried to kill herself; the other was the man who had chemical burns and lost thirty-five pounds while locked up. When questioned by Judge Prettyman, both of these inmates offered slightly different stories. The young girl said her treatment and the food had been fair. The man blamed his weight loss on a "nervous condition" and said he simply tired of eating bologna and cheese for 110 days straight. He told Judge Prettyman he didn't even know he was talking to an inspector that day.

The following day, a *Daily Times* reporter approached Joseph Egeberg, who was in Salisbury for Graham's funeral, for comment about Sanford's grand jury intentions. "I have nothing to hide," he said. "I'll be glad to answer any questions." Egeberg's was the cool and collected response to Sanford's fiery summoning.

Jack Sanford would have his vengeance, though. The grand jury was scheduled for Monday, February 24th, 1969, in Snow Hill, Maryland. The showdown happened on Sanford's turf and Joseph Egeberg likely predicted how it was going to go: an impassioned Eastern Shore state's attorney with the home field advantage and a courtroom full of his sympathetic Eastern Shore constituents. And that's exactly how it went. Although Egeberg insisted that he was doing his job set forward by guidelines implemented before he took office, the grand jury was harsh in its admonishment of the inspector.

His actions were "inexcusable," they said, and suggested he focus on state-run facilities first before coming to the shore and embarrassing himself with "sensational, but inaccurate reports" ... essentially, the grand jury told him to clean his own house first. Then the grand jury went on to defend the indefensible—the Worcester County jail in Snow Hill. Of this abomination, they said, "It is our belief that the present jail is adequate and the prisoners are receiving adequate and complete meals and are being treated fairly and decently." They reprimanded the *Baltimore Sun*, saying that the exposé was "neither thorough or truthful ... the articles were false and misleading" and "serve no useful purpose to anyone other than the reporter and the paper publishing the same." However, the grand jury report did not specify which articles or portions of those articles were factually wrong, but they wouldn't be stopped: "the grand jury condemns the practice of Mr. Egeberg and recommends that if he has any objections to the operation of the Worcester County jail or any proposed suggested changes in such operation, that he take this up with the proper authorities in Worcester County."

The punitive performance was done. When the *Baltimore Sun* reached out for a comment from Jack Sanford, he was unavailable.

The outrage over the exposé died in the aftermath of the murders of Samuel Graham and Albert Kelly. One day, Graham is defending his jail from the accusations; the very next, the headlines of his death made him appear naive or, at the very least, caught off-guard, something a lawman would never want to be. That the sheriff of Wicomico County had been caught in those opposing headlines certainly proved Egeberg's point, but no one on the Eastern Shore, in the depths of their heartache and anger, wanted to acknowledge that. Rather, it was easier to rage and bluster as Jack Sanford had done and let that stand in the place of a meaningful conversation about what could be and what should be done to keep the officers and jails safe.

Back in Wicomico County, there was about to be a new sheriff in town (again) and security was his priority.

– A NEW SHERIFF IN TOWN, AGAIN –

The day after Christmas 1968, Maryland Governor and United States Vice President-Elect Spiro Agnew made his choice for Sam Graham's replacement. The new sheriff was Eugene McLaughlin Carey.

Heavy set and jowly with a slicked hairline inching its way backwards, 52-year-old Eugene Carey had been a dedicated and decorated military man, having served with both the Army and the Air Force. In 1944, he was wounded on D-Day in Normandy when he stormed Omaha Beach with the 115th Infantry in the 29th Division. He later went on to serve as a first sergeant in charge of a 21-man security detachment for General Eisenhower and his staff at his headquarters in Bushey Park in London. Carey, as well as other servicemen, were sometimes called into Eisenhower's bunker for coffee and warm chats with the general who would ask the men if they had written home recently. During conferences with leaders like Churchill and Patton, Eugene Carey's job was to ensure they were not disturbed. His service and injury earned him a Bronze Star and a Purple Heart.

In the years following the war, Carey had an impressive career: head of the military police in Furamachi, Japan; police superintendent at Langerkopf, Germany; and Chief of Law Enforcement and Security at Olmsted Air Force Base. While in Pennsylvania in 1967, he was the supervisor of a project designed for readiness in the case of a national emergency. Carey retired from the military in November 1968.

The office of the sheriff, while rooted in law enforcement, was and remains a political position, and Agnew's choice was a party one. Eugene

Carey was a Republican and local Republican politicians came out in full force to show their support for the new sheriff. His qualifications were lauded as "tremendous" and one leader solemnly noted that they were fortunate to have a man like Carey in these "troubled times" and that his appointment was "most advantageous" for the good people of the county. And he was a Wicomico man: Carey was born in Fruitland, attended Wicomico High School, and resided in the county after his recent military retirement. One of his sons was serving in Vietnam while the other attended Salisbury State College.[1] The *Daily Times* noted that his salary would be $7,000.00[2] and he could use the apartment next door to the jail. Would he take up residence? "I've never seen it," he told the paper.

This comment revealed one glaring detail: he was not a member of the Wicomico County Sheriff's Department. He wasn't one of them. The deputies, still instinctively loyal to Graham, weren't exactly thrilled with their new boss. They viewed Carey as an outsider and some were irritated that Agnew's choice wasn't a man from their department. Sam Graham made the sheriff's department feel like a family. That was all lost with Carey. Perhaps, as a military man, he came in with a rigid sensibility or perhaps it was a clash of personalities and perspectives. Maybe the men just struggled to get over losing Big Sam. Either way, the already depressed mood at the Wicomico County Sheriff's Department soured even more. One deputy later lamented, "It was never the same after that."

Carey chose not to live in the apartment. He liked his home and he didn't feel the penthouse prison's living quarters were the best environment for his son who was attending college. Also, the kitchen was used to feed the prisoners and he was sure his wife preferred to have the privacy of her own, he told the *Daily Times*. Almost immediately he faced some of the same issues that Sam Graham had once stared down: the

---
[1] The name is now Salisbury University.

[2] $7,000.00 in 1968 is roughly equivalent to $64,000 in 2025.

Eugene McLaughlin Carey is sworn in as the new sheriff of Wicomico County.

Image courtesy of the Edward H. Nabb Research Center for Delmarva History and Culture, Salisbury University, Mel Toadvine Collection

reoccurring idea to consolidate police forces in the county. Another was Joseph Egeberg's prison reports.

In January 1969, weeks after the exposé and the murders, Egeberg provided his report on the penthouse prison. Sheriff Eugene Carey noted that he had already implemented one of the recommendations: a "hotline" or a direct line to local police. This would vastly improve the speed and quality of communication should anything go awry. But the new sheriff didn't stop there. He also had wire mesh installed between the cells to prevent prisoner contact. In mid-February 1969, Sheriff Carey ran an ad for five days in the *Daily Times* announcing a massive crackdown on visitors and visiting hours beginning on February 19th. Only immediate family members were allowed: mothers, fathers, sisters, brothers, spouses, and adult children. One can imagine the sheriff was thinking of Erick and Donna. Sheriff Carey told the *Daily Times* that he had noticed the same individuals coming regularly to visit prisoners and that raised a red flag for him. Other security measures suggested by Joseph Egeberg and adopted by Sheriff Eugene Carey included instituting an isolated control area for the officer moving prisoners and implementing an emergency lighting system with backup batteries.

On paper, Sheriff Eugene Carey was the right man for the job. He had the right background and skill set. He instituted much needed security measures and appeared to run a tighter ship. He tried his best to advocate for his department and his jail. In the spring of 1969, he asked for more deputies and jailers; he got one. He asked for riot gear and mace; he got none. This surely rankled the military man who knew that in order to do a proper job, he'd need the proper tools.

Yet for all his accomplishments and efforts, there remained a disconnection within the department. The deputies didn't seem to hold him in high regard. How had the ex-military man failed to forge a bond with his men? The answer is hard to discern. Years later, one deputy recalled, "You did what you had to do and that was it. You really didn't offer to do any more because you never knew where you stood with him anyway." Carey certainly didn't help his cause any when he fired William "Bill" Shockley, a part-time and well-liked deputy who had been with the department for twenty-three years. Shockley decided to run against Carey in the 1970 election and then Carey fired him for "politicking in uniform."

The military man had a hard two years as sheriff and then it was over. Eugene Carey, the Vice President's handpicked man, lost the 1970 election by almost 900 votes to Bill Shockley. The *Daily Times* remarked that Carey's consolation prize was that since he never moved into the sheriff's living quarters, he was spared the ordeal of having to move out. Sheriff Shockley would hold the job for the next twelve years.

– THE GRAND JURY AND JOSEPH –

On December 19th, 1968, just eleven days after the slayings, a grand jury convened in the Wicomico County Courthouse. It was a cloudy and breezy day ... the bitter cold that reigned over the funerals of Graham and Kelly had broken. Tears had dried; the funerary flowers had lost their petals. Now, there was a shift in focus—what to do with the murderer? A week prior, a *Daily Times* article noted that a grand jury would meet to hear the case against Joseph J. Bartholomey, Jr. and in that same article, it was announced that Richard Pollitt, son of the former sheriff and friend of Sam Graham, was going to be a special prosecutor on the case along with Wicomico County State's Attorney Alfred Truitt leading the way. Now was the time for justice.

A Salisbury businessman had been selected as the jury foreman for the grand jury of sixteen men and seven women. Sam Graham's friend, Judge William Travers would have been on the bench, but he had recently had surgery on his neck, and so, in his place, Judge E. McMaster Duer of Princess Anne, head of the First Judicial Circuit, presided. He called the grand jury session to order, and minutes later, the doors were closed. When they opened again, the grand jury ascended the back stairs to the penthouse prison where Donna Campbell and Erick Irwin remained locked up. It is likely this trip was to allow the grand jury to review the crime scene firsthand.

Alfred Truitt felt confident that he could wrap up the grand jury work in a single day. The evidence was certainly on his side and he had the extra help and support of his special counselor, Richard Pollitt. For

Alfred and Richard, the task ahead must have felt arduous: Sam Graham had been their friend and now they were charged with prosecuting his murderer. And that massive responsibility was theirs alone. They did not call Joseph Bartholomey down from the Maryland Penitentiary in Baltimore; they also left Erick Irwin and Donna Campbell in their cells upstairs. Their testimony was not needed here.

The grand jury, as expected, indicted Joseph James Bartholomey, Jr. for the murders of Sheriff Samuel Graham and jailer Albert Kelly. They also indicted Erick Thomas Irwin and Donna Blair Campbell with being accessories to the murders while Erick alone was indicted for being an accessory to the murders by helping Joseph get out of town. Additionally, Joseph, Erick, and Preston Lee Webster were indicted for their roles in the various robberies. There was no notation about Joseph's other accomplice, "Al Capone."

Judge Duer set bond for Erick Thomas Irwin, Donna Blair Campbell, and Preston Lee Webster at $95,000.00[1] each. Joseph Bartholomey did not get a bond.

• • •

Washington, D.C. was a beehive of activity on Friday, January 3rd as a new Congress was sworn in ahead of Nixon and Agnew's inauguration. In the Senate, Ted Kennedy was named the Majority Whip while the murder trial for RFK's killer would begin in a few days.

Back on the Eastern Shore of Maryland, that same day, Joseph J. Bartholomey, Jr. was flown by helicopter from Baltimore to Salisbury. He emerged in a trench coat, handcuffs, and leg shackles. A dozen cops were placed strategically around the courtroom, but all the attention was on Joseph. He was a celebrity criminal now. His hair was longer as he stood before Judge William Travers, who had recovered from surgery and was back on the bench, and entered his plea of innocence.

---

1 $95,000 in 1968 is roughly equivalent to $875,000 in 2025.

Standing next to Joseph was his temporarily-appointed attorney, K. King Burnett. It was Burnett's job to walk Joseph Bartholomey through his arraignment proceedings. Judge Travers asked Joseph if he had permanent counsel; he said he didn't. His voice did not crack or waver. He conferred in whispers with Burnett throughout the hearing. After each count was read, Burnett made a motion to reserve Joseph Bartholomey's right to plead insanity.

This was the first glimpse into what was to come.

Then Joseph was flown back to Baltimore and placed back into the custody of the Maryland Penitentiary, but not for long.

– LSD AND THORAZINE –

On Friday, January 24th, 1969, three weeks after his arraignment, Joseph Bartholomey was transferred from the Maryland Penitentiary in Baltimore to Clifton T. Perkins State Hospital in Jessup. It had been less than four years since his last admission, but this time, he would only be there for sixty days while the doctors and staff made a formal determination about whether or not he was fit to stand trial for the murders.

Staff psychiatrist Dr. Ian McKay sat down with Joseph upon his arrival at the hospital. The intake form noted his addictions to LSD and methamphetamines; his next of kin listed Carol Bartholomey. (Poor Carol Smith, the young and now deserted woman whom he said was wife but wasn't.) Also listed were his parents, Dolores and Joseph Sr., both of whom were still living in Baltimore. Dr. McKay noted that he seemed somewhat lethargic, but was alert and oriented and ready to talk. As they spoke, Joseph began to weave together a strange and disordered narrative about why he had killed Sam Graham and Albert Kelly and it involved Carol Smith, a pregnancy gone wrong, and drugs.

When Dr. McKay asked Joseph for his account as to why he was back in the hospital, he told the doctor, "The only thing I can remember is I was locked up on about November 19th, 1968 and my wife, she had a baby and it died and I asked the people in the Wicomico County jail if I could go to the funeral. They said no. I tried to get out on bail and they kept raising my bail when I tried to get out. I was separated from my wife and I was living with this girl for six months. She was bringing me dope up to the jail—cocaine in toothpaste. I never squealed in my life—I would never kill anyone in my life."

Dr. McKay pushed Joseph about the night of the murders to see what he could remember, but Joseph's memory seemed to fog over. "I don't know; that's where it stops every night. Did you do it? Why did you do it? How did you do it? Where did you do it?" When Dr. McKay asked him about his previous hospitalizations and incarcerations, Joseph remembered those, saying he'd been locked up "about 300 times" since he was a young boy. He spoke about Ms. Redman's boarding house and told Dr. McKay how the people in charge used to beat him and the other boys. Of his father, Joseph said he used to hate him but he doesn't anymore. "I don't hate anyone," he said. But there was one person who was catching his ire at the moment: his accomplice, Erick Thomas Irwin. Erick had also been admitted to Clifton T. Perkins State Hospital in the weeks after the double murders. Joseph felt Erick had "squealed" on him and he was upset about that.

After the interview, Dr. McKay wrote that Joseph Bartholomey was "pleasant and cooperative and shows no signs of psychosis and little anxiety. He has a sad expression on his face often during the interview."

In addition to his interview with Dr. McKay, Joseph was also given a medical examination on that first day. He was listed as 5'9" and 153 pounds with a low grade temperature and an elevated blood pressure. No tattoos and no birthmarks, but there was a scar on his back where the medical staff made the following notations: "Possibly bullet wound. P[atient] claims [he] was shot - [scar[1]] is small." One additional note says there is a scar on his right lower [hemithorax[2]] posteriorly. The bullet wound is again mentioned in his Clifton T. Perkins discharge summary paperwork two months later: "Healed gun shot wound of right lower hemithorax." Again, Joseph does not state who shot him or when

---

1 In the medical chart, this word is illegible, but it is possibly the word "scar."

2 In the medical chart, this word is also illegible, but my best estimation is that it is the word "hemithorax."

this injury occurs, but the gunshot wound is noted twice in his medical notes at Clifton T. Perkins State Hospital: once upon his admission and again when he was discharged. This bullet wound remains a minor mystery.[3]

That same day, in an interview with a social worker, Joseph said he had been at the hospital for the delivery of his baby, but the infant died during childbirth. This is a different account, which could be an interpretation on the part of the social worker. Either way, the social worker noted that he said he was having memory lapses, but appeared to be coherent and had no problems answering questions.

The staff at CTPSH asked the administration at the Maryland House of Correction for any medical or psychiatric records that may have existed for Joseph at their facility. The response came on February 7th, 1969. They did not have any such records on hand, but they offered a warning: "Your attention is invited to the fact that Bartholomey is considered an escape risk."

During his sixty-day stay, he was interviewed by the doctors. Joseph repeatedly told them he did not remember the events of the night of December 8th, 1968. In one such session with Dr. James Addison, his story remained fractured: "I don't know why they sent me here. I'm not crazy. I don't remember doing it. I don't know. I just don't remember what happened." But there were things he could recall and he offered these rambling and odd details, which seemed to merge different events into a single narrative: "[My] wife and I were separated and I called her up. She was pregnant. [Her] mother got on the phone and said the baby was dead. I went up to see her and told her I would be back for the funeral. I was on acid at the time they arrested me in Salisbury. I think they picked me up; they said I had a pistol on me. I don't know. I promised my wife I'd be back for the funeral; I asked them in the jail if I could go, they said no. I was on a trip from acid in the jail. I remember the bars

---

3 Again, one possible theory for this bullet wound is a ricochet type scenario when he was firing the gun that night.

swaying. The next thing I remember was being picked up by the police in a motel in Delaware. Flew me back to the Maryland Pen in a helicopter. They told me I had killed two policemen; I don't believe them. I told them I did not kill anybody. I don't know what they are trying to do. This occurred in December 1968. I was pushing the stuff in jail to the colored people. The guy was bringing a little cocaine and a lot of acid in and I was selling it to them and I took two trips myself. The last trip was the one that I don't remember. The bars were waving at me and the next time I woke up [I was] in [a] Delaware motel being arrested."

Joseph also told Dr. Addison that he felt Sheriff Sam Graham had belittled him by spilling his food on the floor and by making him cut his hair in front of his girlfriend, Donna. There is no other testimony to corroborate these events; however, Sheriff Graham did not allow long hair in his jail and required haircuts for his inmates. Joseph complained that these incidents further frayed his already tense nerves and so he took a hit of acid. At that point, he said, everything went sideways. The bars began to sway. He said he was moved to another side of the jail but he continued to ask for his release so he could attend the baby's funeral. Then nothing ... until he awoke in a motel in Dover.

Drug use was customary for Joseph and he freely admitted to regular use of narcotics, hallucinogens, and alcohol as well as selling marijuana from time to time. He said that while he was at the penthouse prison he was taking acid on sugar cubes and occasionally snorting cocaine, telling the staff at CTPSH that his friend used a box of candy to bring it in. Some of his acid trips were black holes, moments in which he said he had no memory or recollection, but he denied having delusions or hallucinations when not on a trip. One psychologist noted that Joseph appeared to escape into drug use because he struggled to "face his anxiety and self-contempt," but the drugs only served as a temporary stopgap. They didn't fix the root issues. The only time he revealed any sort of paranoid ideations was when he complained that Dr. Ido Adamo, one of the psychiatrists, along with other staff at Clifton T. Perkins State

Hospital were sadistic, giving him thorazine, and doing things to him that they shouldn't be. In his medical chart, the staff wrote that he was receiving 50mg of thorazine twice a day, which is a standard dose. Dr. James Addison noted this sense of paranoia, but wrote that he didn't feel Joseph was psychotically paranoid.

When Dr. Addison tried to probe into his sexual history, Joseph remained guarded, saying *I'd rather not talk about that*. He confirmed the first time he had sexual intercourse was when he was thirteen-years-old and said it was with a 39-year-old woman who had picked him up when he was hitchhiking.[4] He did not brag about his sexual experiences, and it is possible that he was uncomfortable with the topic. Joseph did speak of Donna Blair Campbell, though. He told Dr. Addison that he was worried about her because she was being accused of bringing the gun into the jail, which Joseph said wasn't true. He put that blame squarely on the shoulders of Erick Thomas Irwin. The whole mess was tiresome to him; he told the doctor, "I just want to get out."

At first, Joseph was described as "pleasant" and "cooperative," but that veneer quickly disappeared. He was initially admitted to Ward 3 where, within days of his arrival, the nursing staff described him as being hostile to the point of needing to be secluded. Once out of isolation, he got into an altercation with another patient who struck Joseph in the face. He began to complain of hearing voices and having headaches, which was not what he related to the doctor upon his admission. On February 5th, he was moved to Ward 8 where he became less active and was often found sleeping on the floor. The nursing staff noticed his behavior fluctuated; they noted at times he was happy and easy-going, but could also turn belligerent and disagreeable, loud and bothersome. On February 23rd, he said he was going to kill himself if he wasn't released. Joseph complained of pain, primarily in his back and in his eyes, which he said caused him to be unable to see. A doctor prescribed a medication

---

4 In his first admission to CTPSH in 1965, he said his first experience was with a woman at the Maryland Training School for Boys.

for him, but Joseph wouldn't take it. Five days later, he struck a patient on Ward 7 for seemingly no reason at all; for this, he was placed in seclusion again—this time for three days.

When Joseph was in a talkative mood, he spoke about being found incompetent. This was a red flag for the staff and it was noted in his chart. When Dr. Ido Adamo spoke with the Bartholomey family, they asked him about Joseph's mental state at the time of the murders, but Adamo did not answer, offering only that he wasn't in a position to render that kind of assessment. That determination would be made during a medical conference with other staff members near the end of the admission. Meanwhile, Joseph continued to be aggressive. On March 14th, he was struck again by another patient after getting into a verbal spat in the dining hall. The next day, he threatened to hurt Dr. Ido Adamo for upsetting his mother, Dolores.

On March 19th, a psychologist gave Joseph a series of tests: an IQ test, an inkblot test, and a color pyramid test. This was the day after Joseph's 22nd birthday. By now, he was used to having spent holidays and birthdays inside an institution. On the Wechsler Adult Intelligence Scale, he again scored within an average range. His full scale IQ was 98, his verbal was 102, and in an unusual shift this time, his performance score was 93, now within an average range. The doctor did note: "While his contact with reality is adequate, he has to use a considerable amount of energy to keep it so. At times his thinking borders on autistic, and his social judgment is faulty." The remainder of the testing revealed to the psychologist a young man who was "extremely lonely" who "not only sees the world about him as cruel and threatening, but who also sees himself as fragile and vulnerable. His feelings are easily hurt and he constantly expects something terrible to happen to him." When it didn't, then Joseph would self-sabotage. This was the relentless and ruthless cycle of his life and now two men were dead because of it.

On March 26th, 1969, the medical team met for Joseph's final conference. Seven doctors—including Dr. Ian McKay, Dr. Ido Adamo, and Dr.

James Addison—as well as three staff members reviewed all the notes, reports, and testing done since his arrival. Their determination was that Joseph's diagnosis was severe antisocial personality disorder with drug dependence and that he was responsible at the time of the alleged offense. He was once again deemed competent to stand trial for his actions and discharged on Sunday, March 30th, 1969. Joseph was taken back to the Maryland Penitentiary where he would wait for his murder trial.

The next day, at 10:00 p.m., a corrections officer found Joseph hanging in his cell. He had tied his bedsheet around his neck and had hung it from the top rungs of the cell's bars. The officer grabbed the sheet, which loosened, and Joseph tumbled to the floor. Still alive and conscious, Joseph was taken to the infirmary where he was kept overnight. He survived and remained incarcerated at the Maryland Penitentiary.

Once again, Joseph was disconnected from the outside world. Life continued on without him. In April, Sirhan Sirhan was convicted of RFK's murder and given the death penalty. The Stonewall Riots broke out on June 28th, becoming a rallying symbol for the LGBTQ community's fight for equality. The Apollo 11 astronauts landed on the moon. Charles Manson and his family went on a killing spree. Musicians and fans gathered for a festival in Woodstock, New York. The summer of 1969 was one for the history books. And Joseph missed it all.

As the fall approached, he was readying himself for trial and there was a plot twist in the making: despite the findings of the Clifton T. Perkins State Hospital team, Joseph was going to plead not guilty by reason of insanity.

– THE MURDER TRIAL OF JOSEPH JAMES BARTHOLOMEY, JR. –

EARLY OCTOBER 1969
CHARLES COUNTY, SOUTHERN MARYLAND

Because Joseph had killed the sheriff and the jailer of Wicomico County, his attorneys sought a change of venue, believing that their client would not be able to receive a fair trial on Maryland's Eastern Shore. And so, the murder trial was moved to Charles County, Maryland—a county made famous when another young killer with moody eyes and dark hair tried to escape justice. After murdering President Abraham Lincoln in Ford's Theater on April 14th, 1865, John Wilkes Booth fled through the forests and swamps of Charles County, just south of Washington, D.C., before being shot and killed in a barn in Virginia. Booth's accomplices, like Charles County resident Dr. Samuel Mudd, were brought to trial. Several of them were hanged for their roles; others were given prison sentences. Justice was served. Or maybe not entirely. Just four years later, President Andrew Johnson pardoned Dr. Mudd for his role in the assassination and he was released from prison. He moved back to Charles County where, fourteen years and nine children later, Dr. Samuel Mudd died of pneumonia at age forty-nine.

Now, a hundred years later, the murder trial for 22-year-old Joseph J. Bartholomey, Jr. began on a picturesque autumn morning. Temperatures were in the mid-70s as the sun shone brightly on the historic Charles County Courthouse. On that Monday, October 6th, Alfred

Truitt and Richard Pollitt from the Eastern Shore led the prosecution and Joseph's defense was led by Baltimore attorney, James F. Garrity, who also had an assistant. The Honorable J. Dudley Digges of Charles County presided.

By the time of the trial, Judge J. Dudley Digges was a twenty-year veteran of the bench and was revered for his depth of knowledge, pragmatism, even temperament, and steady handling of his courtroom. When he was named to the circuit court in February 1949, he was the youngest judge in Maryland's history at just thirty-seven years old. (His father had also been a judge.) Digges was considered a serious jurist who took pride in writing his opinions that carried a "literary polish," according to another judge who was close to him. Years after the Bartholomey trial, in May 1974, he wrote his most significant opinion in the case to disbar former Vice President and Maryland Governor Spiro Agnew for tax evasion. This excerpt reveals the sharpness of his pen: "It is difficult to feel compassion for an attorney who was so morally obtuse that he consciously cheated for his own pecuniary gain the government he swore to serve, completely disregarding the oath he uttered when he was first admitted to the bar, and absolutely failing to perceive his professional duty to act honestly in all matters." That opinion was so famous that when Judge Digges died of cancer in 1983, newspapers from Maryland to California wrote of his passing and his work. A lifelong Democrat, Catholic, and bachelor, Judge J. Dudley Digges lived for the law.

This Bartholomey case would be no different. Court began at 10:00 a.m. and the first order of business was to combine the four charges—the escape, the assault with intent to murder Ralph Pusey, and the first degree murders of Albert Kelly and Samuel Graham—into one trial. Next, out of a prospective pool of more than a hundred possible jurors, three men and nine women were selected and seated. This task took up most of the morning hours, and now the lunch hour was upon them. Judge Digges gave the jury strict instructions about not speaking to anyone about the case. He told them to be prepared that the trial could take several days. Then, he excused the jury and court recessed for lunch at 12:43 p.m., but it was a quick one as they were back in session at 1:45 p.m. Judge Digges expected efficiency.

Each side was allowed time for their opening statements. Wicomico County State's Attorney Alfred Truitt rose to speak. His mind was one of a singular determination. Alfred sought justice for Sam and Albert. At home, his family saw his quiet resolve as he prepared for the trial. When he got in the car to head for Charles County, his wife, Clara May, stood at the door and shouted, "Give 'em hell!" And that was exactly what he planned to do.

Truitt told the jury he had known the murdered men and that Sam Graham, the sheriff, had been a "close personal friend." This was a simple, straightforward case, he stated, as he began to walk them through a detailed summation of the events of the night of December 8th, 1968. "After we prove these facts to you, we will respectfully ask you for a verdict of guilty on all counts," said Alfred Truitt.

James Garrity was ready for the defense's opening remarks. Born in Los Angeles but raised in Baltimore, Garrity had attended the prestigious Baltimore City College before graduating with a bachelor's degree from Duke University. When he attended the University of Maryland School of Law, he was president of his class and, in June of 1960, he graduated with a law degree. The young Democrat made a few unsuccessful attempts to get into politics in 1962 and 1963, but in early 1965, he was named as one of ten assistants to Maryland Governor Theodore McKeldin. The late summer days of 1965 saw James Garrity acting as an assistant state's attorney and handling a wide variety of cases, including a rather grim inquiry of a mother who had sewn her dead infant into a couch cushion. Now he found himself at the defense table beside Joseph Bartholomey.

Garrity pointed to the rather obvious reason he was standing in front of them—no lawyer from Wicomico County would represent his client. Both Garrity and his assistant were court-appointed and they had asked to move the trial because they wouldn't have been able to find a suitable jury. Instead, the defense placed its hopes for a fair trial on this Charles County jury. James Garrity did not argue the facts of the case as laid out by Truitt, but rather he pivoted to the defense's main point: Joseph J. Bartholomey, Jr. was insane. He asked the jury that, while they listened to the prosecution's case, to keep an open mind about his mental condition, saying "... it is not whether Mr. Bartholomey here is guilty of the crimes that he is charged with, but it is after we present our case on the insanity issue, whether the State then has proved beyond a reasonable doubt that Mr. Bartholomey was sane at the time."

The stage was set.

The first witness called by the prosecution was Dr. Peter Boolukas, a pathologist at Peninsula General Hospital. Dr. Boolukas offered his medical qualifications to the court: degrees from Dartmouth College and the University of Basel in Switzerland with required residency experience. He testified that he performed the autopsies of Samuel Graham and Albert Kelly on Monday, December 9th, 1968 and his illustrations were entered into evidence.

Kelly, he said, died of a gunshot wound to the head. The bullet entered the back of his head on the right side, just above his right ear and went directly through his brain before lodging itself in the left frontal lobe. There was a second gunshot wound. This one started in Kelly's back on the left side, entering the left lung through the center vertebra and came to rest in the right lung. This caused internal bleeding, roughly "a little more than a quart of blood[1] in each chest space." Both injuries were catastrophic. Dr. Boolukas testified he was able to remove both bullets from Kelly's body.

The autopsy of Graham was more complicated because there were multiple gunshot wounds to contend with. In his testimony, Dr. Boolukas said he believed the one that caused Graham's death was the one that entered Graham's chest from the left side, which passed through

---

1 The average adult human body contains between five and six quarts of blood.

the left lung and his aorta and his right lung, and came to rest in the soft tissue of his right side. This caused significant internal bleeding, "which amounted to a least two quarts of fluid in each chest space." This was a catastrophic injury. There was a second bullet wound that showed an entry point in Graham's chest from the front and went through the left lung and stopped in the soft tissue of his back on the left side. A third bullet was found in Graham's left armpit. A fourth bullet entered Graham's lower left abdomen at a downward angle and came to rest in the area near his rectum. There were two additional gunshot wounds to the front of Graham's left leg, which were connected by a single track, but Dr. Boolukas was unable to determine which was the entry and which was the exit. A final possible gunshot wound was found on the top of Graham's left foot but this laceration did not contain a bullet. Dr. Boolukas suspected these three leg wounds could have been from the same shot as these wounds were in alignment.

Truitt asked about time of death.

The doctor said, "I didn't try to pinpoint it, but it was at least twelve hours because the rigor mortis was developed."

Dr. Boolukas testified that he removed a total of four bullets from Samuel Graham's body and turned over these bullets, along with the two removed from Albert Kelly's body, to Corporal Samuel Reed Chaffey of the Maryland State Police.

Garrity's cross-examination of Dr. Boolukas was benign. He asked about the difference in entrance and exit wounds and the doctor explained that exit wounds tend to be larger. Garrity asked about the lacerations found on Graham's legs and whether or not Dr. Boolukas could pinpoint if those were gunshot wounds or not. The doctor said, based on what he saw, he could not say with full certainty what caused those particular wounds.

Next, Alfred Truitt called Chief Deputy John Walston to the stand, who testified that Joseph James Bartholomey, Jr. was in the Salisbury jail on the night of the murder. To that point, the prisoner logs of the jail as well as Joseph's robbery warrants were entered into evidence. The prosecution continued, laying out their case with three more witnesses who had been in the penthouse prison that night: Donald Leon Dashiell, Ralph Anthony Harmon, and Ralph Lee Pusey. Donald Leon Dashiell, the trustee, told the jury what he saw that terrible night: he had been sitting with Albert Kelly at the desk, he saw Joseph Bartholomey with the gun, he ran to get the sheriff, he saw Albert Kelly fall, he took the elevator to get help. Ralph Anthony Harmon, the juvenile prisoner, confirmed Donald Dashiell's testimony. Under cross-examination, James Garrity asked Harmon if another prisoner had also come out of his cell to escape, but Harmon said that wasn't so. Garrity appeared to be suggesting Joseph hadn't acted alone, but that implication went nowhere. Ralph Lee Pusey, now a deputy with sheriff's department, testified to the entire chain of events as he saw them: he had coffee with Sam, he spoke to Albert, he went down to the trustee's cell, he heard gunshots and came running, and then he saw Joseph, who fired a shot at him.

The afternoon's proceedings were happening faster than Alfred Truitt had expected and he asked to approach the bench. Some of his evidence, he explained to Judge Digges, was still in Pikesville. This vexed the expeditious judge: "I have been trying to tell you we all move much faster here than we do other places. I tried to point these things out to you." Special prosecutor Richard Pollitt saved the moment by asking if they could put on a different witness who may be recalled at a later time. Judge Digges agreed.

The next witness was Maryland State Police Corporal Samuel Reed Chaffey. He recounted the night: MSP received the call for help, he arrived at the courthouse, he saw Graham and Kelly's bodies as they were being taken to the hospital, and he went up to the jail and noted the arrival of other law enforcement officers. This was it for now; Chaffey would return to the stand later.

The prosecution called Deputy Bud Fowler to the stand. Fowler gave his brief account: he was in the basement when Donald Dashiell came to get him, he saw the bodies of Sam and Albert on the floor, he saw Dorothy Graham and Ralph Pusey, and he did a cursory search before being called away. After Deputy Fowler stepped down, another prisoner took the stand. Vincent Horsey had been in the juvenile cell that night with Ralph Harmon, but now he was an inmate at the Maryland Correctional Institution for Men at Hagerstown serving a ten-year sentence for assault and robbery. Vincent twice had to be asked to speak louder. He testified that he and Ralph Harmon had been sitting on the bunk and smoking when he heard Joseph Bartholomey tell Albert Kelly to open the door: "Said if he don't he would kill him." Vincent told the jury he saw Joseph reaching around the door and firing the gun at the sheriff. On cross-examination, James Garrity questioned Vincent about a statement he allegedly made to the police about someone else participating in the events of that night. This was similar to the question he asked Ralph Harmon about another prisoner coming out of a cell, but Vincent Horsey categorically denied any other person's involvement in the murders. It was Joseph Bartholomey and Joseph Bartholomey alone.

Maryland State Police Detective Sergeant Robert Weir was next to take the stand for the prosecution. Alfred Truitt was ready to narrow in on how Joseph was caught, but the defense objected at the start of his testimony. The issue was the probable cause for Joseph's arrest. The prosecution needed to establish it, but the defense twice objected, likely because Weir was not the arresting officer. To settle the matter and to ensure the jurors would not hear anything prejudicial to the case, Judge Digges sent the jury out of the room at 3:30 p.m.

With the jury out of earshot, Alfred Truitt returned to Detective Sergeant Weir who then testified that he had spoken with Erick Thomas Irwin after the escape. He explained that Joseph and Erick were friends and that it was Erick who took Joseph to Dover, Delaware and got him situated in a motel there. Because of this development, Weir reached out to law enforcement in Dover.

Alfred Truitt stopped him there and called the next two witnesses who were police officers from Delaware. One testified about deducing that the motel the Maryland authorities were looking for was the Capital City Motel based on Erick's description; the other testified that he went to the motel, found the owner, confirmed that a "John Davis" was lodged in Room 22, called for Joseph to come out, and then arrested him. All this testimony was to prove there was probable cause to arrest the man in Room 22 who turned out to be Joseph Bartholomey.

Alfred Truitt was moving through his witness list at a rapid pace, but he had hit a snag. An important witness was not yet there. Once again, he approached Judge Digges and apologized for how fast this part of the trial is going. He told the judge that he needed the ballistics expert from the Maryland State Police, Sergeant Russell Wilhelm, who had the bullets and gun. This witness, Truitt told the judge, was already on his way and could arrive at 5:00 p.m. Judge Digges acquiesced and announced a recess until then. He also told Truitt and Pollitt that he fully expected the prosecution to wrap up their case by the end of the day.

Judge Digges indeed ran a whistle-stop courtroom.

• • •

At 5:19 p.m., court was back in session and the jury was seated to hear testimony. Alfred Truitt recalled Maryland State Police Corporal Samuel Chaffey to the stand. Now, he testified about receiving the bullets from Dr. Peter Boolukas during the autopsies as each one was recovered. He labeled each one as they were given to him, testifying that he "placed them in some tissue paper and placed them in the glass container and put a rubber stopper on top and made my mark on top." He said he gave them to MSP Sergeant Robert Burkhardt on December 12th, 1968. The bullets were entered into evidence.

During James Garrity's cross-examination, he asked Chaffey about the chain of custody. "You said you maintained possession of these vials until December 12th, Corporal?"

"Yes, I did."

"Where specifically?"

"In my personal possession."

"You mean at home?" asked Garrity.

"With me when I went to work and home when I was home."

"In other words, they were on your body?"

"That is correct, sir."[2]

The next witness was a Delaware State Police lieutenant who testified about going into the motel room and finding the front panel missing from the wall air conditioning unit. When he peered inside, he saw the gun. The lieutenant tagged the weapon, photographed it, put it in a bag, and turned it over to MSP Sergeant Burkhardt. The .22 caliber H&R revolver was entered into evidence.

The prosecution then called Maryland State Police Sergeant Robert Burkhardt to the stand. He identified the bullets as the ones given to him by Corporal Chaffey and that he placed those bullets and the gun into a cigar box, which he delivered to the ballistics expert, Sergeant Russell Wilhelm, at the Maryland State Police Headquarters in Pikesville on December 12th, 1968.

Now it was time for the final witness who would tie those bullets to that gun. After offering his extensive background as a ballistics and firearms expert, Sergeant Wilhelm testified that the bullets and gun presented in court were the ones given to him by Sergeant Burkhardt. He gave a lengthy explanation of the ballistics process for the jury and announced his findings: the bullets that killed Albert Kelly and Samuel Graham came from that .22 H&R revolver.

That concluded the State's case and the prosecution rested.

Judge Digges reminded the jury again they were not to discuss the case and court was dismissed at 5:47 p.m. The defense would start in the morning and what a spectacle it would be.

---

2 Again, this exchange highlights how the chain of custody was maintained for the bullets in this case. Today, it is handled differently, but this would not have been unusual for the time.

Marylanders awoke to jubilant headlines on the morning of Tuesday, October 7th. The Baltimore Orioles captured the pennant by sweeping the Minnesota Twins and were headed to the World Series. Not even the gray skies, with clouds blotting out the sun, could dampen the spirits of Marylanders. But that day, unusually warm and overcast, felt like a storm was brewing. And maybe it was.

Court began at 9:30 a.m. with defense attorney James Garrity requesting a moment to speak with his assistant and they left the courtroom for a short while. When they returned, Garrity asked to approach the bench and made a motion for the judgment of acquittal in every count. Judge Digges flatly denied the motion.

Garrity's first witness of the day was Dolores Bartholomey and she told the court she was Jimmy's mother. (He was still Jimmy to her.) She gave an abridged account of their family's troubles: how her marriage was happy at first but then it collapsed, how young Jimmy was repeatedly moved around, and how the fights and arguments created an unstable situation for everyone involved. But there was no real way, within the confines of a trial, to make the jury fully understand just how broken and difficult his early life was. Just recounting it was hard for Dolores; the defense attorney told her to take her time while also gently asking her to speak up. She recounted how Joseph Sr. left the family, how Shirley and Jimmy asked for him, how she struggled to make ends meet, and how Leona and Michael Bartholomey stepped up to help. She spoke about the times Jimmy saw the devil in the sky and appeared afraid, telling Dolores, "The devil is after me." She testified that she did not know where her son was the year that Joseph Sr. left him at Ms. Redman's boarding house. She knew he was at the Maryland Training School for Boys, but Dolores didn't know how long or how many times or even for what reason. As a teenager, she said, "Jimmy was the type of boy that I loved him, but you couldn't get close to him and at the age of fifteen he was starting to run the streets. He was pretty hard to handle."

Just as Garrity began to ask her about Joseph's relationship with his half-brother, Ethan, the prosecution objected. Alfred Truitt sensed that the trial was now approaching the question of Joseph's sanity. Both lawyers approached the judge's bench, only this time, it was the defense caught off guard by the speed of the trial. Garrity told Judge Digges that he hadn't expected to get to this portion of his case until Wednesday and one of his doctors couldn't make it until 11:30 a.m. This irritated Judge Digges and earned everyone an admonishment: "Gentlemen, I tried in every way possible to warn you all to have these witnesses here. I can't lock a jury up in the jury room [for] hours while you all are—"

Garrity interrupted him to say another doctor could likely get there sooner.

Judge Digges asked, "What do you expect the doctors to say?"

"The doctors say he is insane."

"Very well, we'll take a recess." And with that, Dolores stepped down from the witness stand and Judge Digges told the jury to retire to the jury room for the time being. This again reveals the care Judge Digges was taking with the case and the jurors. He would hear the testimony first to be sure it would not prejudice the jury.

At 10:47 a.m, while the jury remained in the jury room, James Garrity called psychiatrist Dr. Stephen H. Kaufman to the stand. Educated at Johns Hopkins University and the University of Maryland, he had worked with an array of mental health issues including psychosis, schizophrenia, and severe personality disorders. Having established the doctor's qualifications for the court, Garrity moved onto the doctor's assessment of Joseph Bartholomey's sanity.

Dr. Kaufman testified that he had seen Joseph a total of seven times: six times in September 1969 and once on October 2nd, just four days before the murder trial was to start.

"Doctor, could you state in your own opinion and with reasonable medical certainty whether the defendant, Joseph James Bartholomey, Jr., was suffering from a disease, mental disease, or defect on December 8th, 1968?"

"I believe he was suffering from a mental disease at the time of December 8th, 1968."

"And could you state, Doctor, whether as a result of this mental disease or defect he lacked substantial capacity to appreciate the criminality of his act and lacked substantial capacity to conform his conduct to the requirement of law?"

"I think that he was unable to either appreciate the criminality of his offense or to make his behavior conform with the requirements of law," Dr. Kaufman testified.

Swiftly, Alfred Truitt was on cross-examination.

"Doctor, what is your diagnosis?"

"I diagnosed Bartholomey to be paranoid schizophrenic."

Truitt repeated the diagnosis twice; Kaufman confirmed it twice.

"Were any tests administered to him?"

"By me?" Kaufman asked. "No. No specific tests."

Truitt then asked the doctor to explain what a paranoid schizophrenic was.

"Well, I think it is difficult to define but I will do my best. I think it would be a person that would have a severe disorganization in his personality such that the different elements of the personality would not be well coordinated and one in which the chief symptoms would be having delusions or hallucinations. Delusions being a fixed false belief that can [not] be challenged or changed no matter how much the facts of reality would indicate it."

This was the first time the specific diagnosis of schizophrenia had been applied to Joseph and Truitt seized on that. "Are you telling us that [schizophrenia] is a step removed from an antisocial personality?"

"Well, I would think it is more than a step."

Truitt pressed the doctor. "Well, how far removed is it?"

Kaufman offered a differentiation: "a paranoid schizophrenic condition would be a very severe psychiatric illness" whereas an antisocial personality would not have "any delusions or serious disorganization of the personality."

Truitt asked about drugs and Kaufman confirmed that Joseph Bartholomey had a history of drug use. Then, he asked the doctor to explain the manifestations that he saw in order to conclude that Joseph was a paranoid schizophrenic.

"I think there are a number. One is that he has a very strong delusional system."

Here, the defense objected. Garrity didn't like the prosecution probing for any testimony that might rebut the insanity plea, but Judge Digges overruled him. Twice.

Dr. Kaufman began to explain what made him diagnose Joseph as a paranoid schizophrenic, and for the first time, Joseph's political ideology is presented publicly. The story he had told the staff at Clifton T. Perkins State Hospital about his wife and their dead baby and doing LSD and cocaine as a result of his despair and frustration had been abandoned. There would not be a single mention of any of that in this trial. Instead, Joseph had latched onto something new, something political.

Dr. Kaufman said, "He feels that the world has been taken over by the Communist[s], that the police, the judges, that most teachers in his life, that [his] stepmother are Communists or Communist agents. He feels that President Nixon is a Communist, and it is his destiny to kill Nixon, to save his country. He has the idea that there are fifty million Chinese being infiltrated into this country to take over all the cities of America. ... In the course of talking to him, he had strong beliefs that the guards at the Maryland Penitentiary, where he was, were trying to kill him, that he was afraid to sleep at night for fear of being sprayed with mace and being taken out and hung, that they frequently take people off the street at night and drown them."

Joseph Bartholomey, the Communist slayer.

The doctor continued on, saying that he believed Joseph was a paranoid schizophrenic because, during their conversations, Joseph seemed to believe newspaper articles were meant just for him and that the guards were trying to get information out of him. Dr. Kaufman felt Joseph's responses were out of proportion and inappropriate. Beyond that, the doctor factored in Joseph's previous hospitalizations and strange behaviors, his lack of close relationships, and his mother's history of mental illness and hospitalizations.

Alfred Truitt homed in. Joseph had been married. Joseph had lived with Donna for several months. Were these not close personal relationships?

Dr. Kaufman shored up his statement, "… I don't think there has ever been one based on any kind of mutual trust or any kind of openness in the relationship … there is a certain superficiality about them and if things tend to get closer or intimate he would tend to back away or get out of the situation."

"What is his prognosis?" asked Truitt.

"Very poor."

With that, Truitt had no further questions. Dr. Kaufman was dismissed temporarily, although Garrity would recall him later. Judge Digges brought the jury back in at 11:07 a.m. Once settled, Garrity recalled Dolores Bartholomey to finish her testimony. She said Joseph appeared to both like and reject his half-brother, Ethan, and testified to Joseph's violent outbursts: he had threatened her with a knife, he had thrown a knife at Dolores's brother, and he had told her he was going to kill someone. She confirmed that both she and Joseph had been admitted to Crownsville State Hospital. This caused a brief objection from the prosecution, but they were overruled. Dolores recalled Joseph's apparent hostility to the Catholic faith.

Garrity asked her, "Did you ever have any religious pictures in your house?"

"Yes, sir, I have a picture of the Last Supper over my table. … Jimmy would come up and he would sit at the table and he would look up at the picture and make fun of it."

"What would he say?"

"He would look up and he would say, 'Oh, he is eating his last supper again.'"

"What was your reaction?"

"I would look at him and I would just say, 'Jimmy, please, please do not say that. You are going to get punished some day.'"

"Were there any other instances regarding any religious objects or pictures?"

"Yes, sir. One night Jimmy came in and he had two pictures in his wallet and he said, 'Mother, I want you to see these.' And when I looked at them, the one picture of Jimmy was out in the cemetery and he had his hands pinned back at a cross and then the other picture, he was laying in a casket like he was dead."

Alfred Truitt had no questions for Dolores Bartholomey and she was allowed to step down. The next witness was Betty Bartholomey, Joseph's stepmother. She spoke about meeting her now-husband and his children, but when Betty got to the part about Ms. Redman's boarding house, Joseph called out from the defense table, "Communist home. It is a communist home."

The court ignored his outburst and Garrity continued with his examination of Betty Bartholomey. Like Dolores, she recounted the way Joseph was shuttled around from one house to another. (In her testimony, she also called him Jimmy. He remained Jimmy to his family.) She said she had asked Leona and Michael Bartholomey to take him in.

Garrity probed a little deeper. "Are you saying that you two didn't get along too well?"

Betty admitted to being high-strung and feeling like her stepson was too much for her to handle. "I feel, Mr. Garrity, that I was sometimes putting great pressures on Jimmy at his age with a young baby around and being my first one and trying to adjust to a new baby and his being there and trying to adjust ... Jimmy seemed very jealous of the baby and this is one of the reasons that we felt he would be maybe better off at the aunt and uncle's home."

She also testified that he was sent to the Maryland Training School for Boys where his bad behavior continued. At one high school, he was expelled because he ripped the plumbing out of a boys' bathroom. Not only was he being re-homed regularly, he was constantly running away. Betty told the jury, "Police were called and we would have to warn them. He went to Ohio, Michigan, and different places, Philadelphia, and each time we would be called and we would have to wire money and be at a train [station] when they would return him and it just kept things in a general uproar in the home."

The next witness for the defense was Shirley, Joseph's older sister, who was working as a clerk typist in Baltimore. She testified to the turbulence in their home during their childhood: "Well, my mother and father ... they were always arguing and I remember my father was running around. He was never at home and a lot of the times he was drunk. ... I remember one day he was just gone. Jimmy and I were both real little and on Saturdays we used to sit and wait for him to come ... a lot of times he would just never show up." She told the jury that she and her brother felt their father was ashamed of them, recalling a time when he and Betty made remarks about their lack of manners. Of her time living with Joseph Sr., Shirley was blunt: "Then finally we had to move from [Victory Villa] because my father used to go out nightclubbing and we would be left alone in the house until three or four o'clock in the morning and I think the neighbors just reported it. ... [Betty] never lived there but a lot of mornings, we would wake up and find them together."

Garrity asked about their broken home and Shirley said, "[Jimmy] always wanted to be close to my father. He always looked up to him. And he decided to stay—."

Joseph interrupted, "Shut up. I don't want to hear no more."

Judge Digges told the defense to keep moving along.

Shirley tried to help the jury navigate through their back-and-forth upbringing, especially her brother's. Then Garrity got to his behavior. Shirley said, "He was always trying to scare my mother. Jimmy couldn't get close to anybody. He couldn't accept love and I think because he was hurt by so many people, rejected by people, and he would scare my mother and he would threaten my little brother with a knife ... and he was always getting in trouble in the school."

Their parents did not help her when she had to handle Jimmy alone. She testified about a time when Dolores was having a nervous breakdown and Jimmy was acting up: "... I was being called home from work because he was threatening Ethan and I called my father and asked my father if he would please come over. I begged him to help me with my brother. He told me to take a frying pan and hit my brother on the head and knock him out and call the police. He said they would put him away somewhere." After his arrest, Shirley said she was told Jimmy had tried to commit suicide.

Garrity asked her, "Shirley, do you remember an incident about the second grade, Jimmy's second grade?"

She did. They were in school together at St. Catherine's. There was a Halloween party for the first and second graders. She dressed him up like a little girl, but the costume backfired. He "got hollered at for it" and the school made Shirley take him back home and put him in boys' clothing again. "Jimmy was hurt by this and he never forgot it and he felt like we were trying to make a fool out of him," she said.

After Shirley was excused, James Garrity approached the bench to ask for a brief recess. It was getting close to lunch. But Judge Digges, ever efficient, told him to put on another witness instead.

The defense called Donna Blair Campbell, Joseph's girlfriend, to the stand. She was still an inmate at the Maryland Correctional Institution for Women and had not yet had her own trial. Her attorney was present to keep her from saying anything that might incriminate her. Garrity began with how they met in June of 1968 in Ocean City, Maryland, and immediately, her attorney objected. Garrity explained he was working his way toward her testimony about the time Joseph slashed his wrists at a party. Donna had been there and saw it happen. Her attorney allowed it.

"We were at a place I was staying down there during the summer and Joe was there and he tried to kill himself."

Garrity asked, "How?"

Donna must have been nervous because her testimony was disjointed and slightly confusing: "Well, he slit his wrist, all up his arm. He had to be rushed—they tried to get him to the hospital but the hospital wasn't close enough. They said the only one would be in Salisbury or something. So they had to take him—they put him in a car. He was real pale and they took him to some kind of Naval place and they were like Navy guys. I don't know what the exact name [of the place where he was taken] is called, but right there in Ocean City on Baltimore Avenue and they had a doctor come and carry Joe. He said he would die if it was his arm was all cut up and he was bleeding real bad. It was a lot of blood."

On cross-examination, Alfred Truitt began to inquire about their relationship. After an initial objection by her attorney, Truitt was able to get Donna to say that she and Joseph were dating and had been for about a month prior to the suicide attempt. Her attorney limited any lines of questioning after that and she stepped down. Anyone hoping to learn her role in the murders would be disappointed.

By this point on the second day of the trial, Judge Digges was ready to recess for lunch and he let the jury go at noon.

• • •

At 1:03 p.m., court was back in session and James Garrity called Leona Bartholomey to the stand. She was working as a secretary and living in a new home in Pasadena, Maryland. Garrity began by asking Leona, once again, to explain the turbulence of Joseph's childhood to the jury. She recounted the numerous moves he experienced and her involvement and how Dolores and Joseph Sr. helped—or didn't—along the way. She explained how Jimmy was unsettled and constantly misbehaved, especially the night she found him crawling on all fours in her bedroom. "I couldn't go back to sleep practically all night, but he never did that after that," she remarked. "But it scared me so bad I was kind of worried after that, you know."

Truitt had no questions for Aunt Leona.

The defense then called forward a corrections officer from the Maryland Penitentiary who found Joseph hanging by his bedsheet after his return from Clifton T. Perkins. Garrity asked him about that night.

"The first part of the day there was nothing unusual. He was talking with other inmates on the tiers and the only thing unusual that did happen that night with Bartholomey was that [at] my 10:00[p.m.] count I found him hanging by the cell bars on top and he had the sheet tied around his neck and [cell] bar, which I yanked the sheet and he fell down."

"Was he conscious or unconscious; could you tell?"

"He was in a daze. He couldn't have been hanging very long."

"I see. What did you do, Corporal?" asked Garrity.

"I notified the desk where the Captain of the shift could be notified. On our shift, we are not allowed in the cell until the Captain comes into the wing and the Captain came on down and the door was opened. The inmate was carried over to the institutional hospital for treatment and kept overnight for observation."

"I see. Did you say how he was hanging, what he was hanging by?"

"By his neck."

Alfred Truitt, on cross-examination, asked about "the hole" or the punitive segregation unit and if Joseph had ever been placed there.

The corporal said, "The hole is for observation mostly, where an uncontrollable person can be observed by two different wings at regular intervals." He then confirmed that Joseph had been in "the hole," but he could not remember the dates. No one had any further questions and the officer stepped down.

Here, the defense announced their next witness: Joseph J. Bartholomey, Jr. And this would be anything but boring. Earlier that day, Dr. Stephen Kaufman had presented Joseph's Communist ideology while he was on the stand, but the jury had been out of the courtroom for that. Now, for the first time, Joseph himself would explain the political motive behind the murders of Samuel Graham and Albert Kelly and he would not stop there.

James Garrity opened with an easy line of questioning. He wanted to make sure Joseph understood that he did not have to testify in this trial. Joseph said he understood.

"Why did you want to take the stand?"

"Well, in 1963, May 4th to be exact, I was kidnapped by police." He said they kidnapped him from his home and took him to Crownsville State Hospital. (Here, he is referencing the events at his great-grandmother's house that led to his arrest and his subsequent psychiatric admission.)

"Why did they do this?" asked Garrity.

"Well I have been—I found out in 1963 that the Russians, the Communists, were trying to take over this country and—."

Garrity interrupted him to ask how he heard this information.

"Yes. I was told by somebody special that nobody knows but me. And I am the only one that can talk to him."

"Why is that?"

"Because they trust me. I am a Democrat and we got to [get] rid of Communism."

Garrity continued. "Who says we—what do you mean we got to get rid of Communism?"

"The voice that talks to me."

"What voice?"

"Special. People trying to get rid of this Communism."

"When do you hear this voice?" Garrity asked.

"Just at urgent times when they need me to do things."

"Well, what do you mean at urgent times? What was the last urgent time; do you recall?"

"Yes. I was in [a] cell in Wicomico County Jail and they told me that the Sheriff was going to kill me, was going to get me because I exposed him as a Communist."

There it was. Joseph had now testified that the reason he had killed Samuel Graham and Albert Kelly was because he believed they were Communists. He continued on, saying that the voice told him that Graham intended to harm him and that Graham didn't like him. Graham cut his hair and threw coffee on him, Joseph told the jury. And then he offered a doomsday prediction: "I am out to stop all this Communism. If we don't by '72, the world will be done for."

"I beg your pardon?" Garrity asked.

"By May 4th, 1972. The world will be destroyed if I don't stop this Communism."

"How will it be destroyed?"

"The Communist Chinese and the Russians blow us all up."

"Have you had any experience with these Communist Chinese and Russians?"

Joseph was primed. "You had better believe it. They almost turned me into a Chinese down in Ocean City one time." He continued to explain to his defense attorney that the "Narcotics Agency" was out to get him because they were Communists and they had infiltrated every state police, county police, and city police agency and even had judges and corrections officers in their midst.

"Why do you say they are all Communists?"

"Well, like, they lock[ed] me up and tried to steal my brain," Joseph said. "Because they know I got intelligence and I am out to expose the scheme that is going on."

Garrity pushed him on the "scheme." Was it the government?

Joseph said that President Nixon was the head of the Communist party in America.

"Well, what about Nixon? What would you do?"

Joseph, having already announced two political murders, was about to claim a failed plot to assassinate Richard Nixon. "Well, see the voice told me to get him. So I had a 30-30 rifle and a box of—."

"When did you have a 30-30 rifle?"

"This summer past, not this summer, the summer before." (The summer of 1968.) "And [I] had a box of shells and a telescope and I had to get a boat, a cabin cruiser, and Nixon has a home near the water and I had to take the boat down there and then shoot him and then I could be the leader and expose all this Communism."

In that moment, the jury must have recalled the specters of political assassins John Wilkes Booth and Lee Harvey Oswald and James Earl Ray and Sirhan Sirhan. Was Joseph J. Bartholomey, Jr. the same kind of man?

Garrity asked if he knew where Nixon's waterfront home was located.

"It is in California," he said.

As stunning as this admission was, there is no evidence that Joseph tried to assassinate Richard Nixon. Did he have a rifle in the summer of 1968? That is unknown, but he did get access to a number of guns during the robberies in November 1968. However, what Joseph did not seem to know was that Nixon purchased that house in California sometime in 1969.

Joseph told the jury a disconnected story of the torture he said he received at Perkins and Crownsville: "They did it at Perkins twice, stuck wires on my head and make me drink stuff and tried to get to my brain. Down in Crownsville, they would throw me in a room with no bed or nothing, and be real cold in the wintertime, no heat, and open the windows up and laugh ... When I went to Perkins last time, a boy broke a chair leg off and they blamed it on me and threw me in a room and I had my mattress up against the door and a guard came in and kicked me in the face and told me to keep my mattress back against the wall. And they found out the boy did it, the boy admitted he did it and the doctor said,

'I'm keeping you in there; you ain't no good.' He said I caused trouble and I told him I was going to cause trouble until I exposed all of them."

Garrity asked, "What do you mean exposed all of them too?"

"Yes, he is one of the Communists right there."

"Mr. Truitt?" asked Garrity.

"No, that doctor. Yes, he is too."

Here, Alfred Truitt interjected: "I'm a Democrat like you are."

Joseph snapped back, "No, you are a Communist."

"Why do you say Mr. Truitt is a Communist?" asked Garrity.

"He is working for the State."

"Do you have anything else for the State?"

Boy did he ever. "I got a speech I have been preparing for a long time. I would like to read it. I started preparing it a long time ago but I just finished it in my cell in the Penitentiary. They kidnapped me and put me there and I ain't committed no crimes and they put me in the Penitentiary and everybody else there did something. I didn't do nothing except what I am supposed to do."

Garrity asked him what he meant by that.

"I have to get rid of certain people. I have to eliminate them. They have to be eliminated," Joseph said. He spoke of the Vietnam War and how we are killing Communists there and that it was his duty as a Democrat to expose the Communists and "get this country back on its feet." He went on a tirade about Nixon: "When Nixon took over, he raised the tax and now people can't even buy food without spending all their money, can't do nothing."

Then it was time for Joseph's prepared speech that would expose everything about everyone. The prosecution offered an objection, but Judge Digges allowed it. Joseph's grandiloquence was about to begin.

"I got this speech here and I am going to prove to you that people like him and him and him, what they are doing to us. This is 'Declaration of Independence.' Take heart, brothers. They who have conspired to imprison you are more criminal that you could ever be. To all in this courtroom, the Communist Judge, the Communist District Attorney and all Communist police within, and you all know who I am talking about, to my Democratic friends in our fight for freedom and to all the people throughout the world. Yes, I know I shall be persecuted for my fight for freedom. As a Democrat, freedom fighter I was ridiculed, laughed at, spat upon and arrested on trumped up charges. While being in Wicomico County Jail, they, the Sheriff, Samuel Graham, and his deputy, Albert Kelly, had my hair cut off and laughed at me, trying to get my brain. They were trying to steal my brain. I know—excuse me—and transplant in its place a Communistic brain.

"Being a man of superior intelligence, I saw through their scheme and saved myself in time. I know that these Communistic jailers were trying to poison me in various ways but I have learned early in life how to see through all these schemes. They separated me from the other inmates in [the] Wicomico County Jail so they could kill me without leaving any witnesses. They did not fool me, not even for one minute because the voice of great known came to me and told me of these plans. I have done my best to try to save the United States, but so far I have failed and I am sorry. I did not get a chance to kill Nixon as I was told to do and my Democratic friends I ask you to forgive me. We all know that Nixon is a Communist and that he will lead the United States into destruction by May 4th of 1972. That is if he is not eliminated, which I think he will be. Even though I am the great man I am, I have failed in my duty to life so far. We all know that. Communist[s] have taken over the United States. They control the Government, except for J. Edgar Hoover, and that is because he is too old, he is a good man. They control the States, especially the hospitals and they control all the police departments.

"Excuse me. I am hoping they have not taken over all the newspapers so this great speech may be printed for all Democrats to read. As when I was kidnapped and shipped to Crownsville, May 4th, 1963, I learned fast and expertly how all police have turned Communist. My futile attempt to escape were always stopped as I was overwhelmed, time and again by these Communist police. I have strained daily to keep this country from being sick. Many of my friends turned against me and become [sic] a traitor. As in 1965 after escaping from Crownsville, I was again kidnapped and sent to Perkins. There they attached wires to my head trying to steal my thoughts. I have been through a lot to try and show the Democratic people of the United States how the Communist[s] are taking over our country, but to no avail all eyes seem blinded except mine. So now here at this great trial to all citizens I say come forth and help me destroy these Communists for it is either now or never. This, my people, is all I have to say to you. I have also discovered while sitting here listening to these Communist lies that I have more, even I myself, than I thought existed.³ My friends of great knowing, come rally behind me and let's destroy these Communist police. And we will get them sooner or later."

Joseph's bizarre speech was finally over. Garrity had no further questions and it was now Alfred Truitt's turn to square up with the man who had murdered his friend.

"When was it that you got this 30-30? You say the summer before last?"
"Yes, sir."
"And those, your instructions then were to kill Nixon?"
"Yes, sir."
"What was the reason you were to kill Nixon?"
"He was head of the Communist party."
Truitt countered, "Well, he wasn't President in '68, was he?"
"He was running for Presidency."
"When did you get this in '68, this rifle?"
"I got it — I don't remember the month. It was in the summertime."
"Were you also instructed to eliminate Samuel Graham and Albert Kelly?"
"I am instructed to eliminate all Communist agents."

---

3 This sentence reads oddly, but it is the verbatim line from the trial transcript. It is unclear what he "discovered" while sitting there.

"Well, did you eliminate Samuel Graham and Kelly?"

Joseph didn't miss a step. "Yes, I did. I eliminated him thoroughly."

"That is all." Truitt was done.

Now that Joseph had testified to his political motivations and ideations, James Garrity was ready to cement the insanity plea with three expert witnesses. First, he called Dr. Norman H. Bradford, Assistant Professor of Medical Psychology at the University of Maryland, to the stand. Although he was trained as a child clinical psychologist, he did have experience with adult patients and held a teaching position at Johns Hopkins University.

Garrity asked Dr. Bradford if he had seen Joseph; he had, he said, just within the last month. He had administered two psychological tests, and based on those results, he found Joseph to be a person with definite feelings of sadness and a distaste for the world around him. He thought Joseph had probably felt that way for a long time. The doctor said Joseph was vulnerable, impulsive, and given to moments of exaggeration.

The defense attorney asked Dr. Bradford for a diagnosis.

"My diagnosis is a schizophrenic reaction, paranoid type. I think that is the most appropriate way to put it, but that is the diagnosis we would have to choose in our diagnostic name. I would say he is a person who is a paranoid psychotic."

"Could you explain that any further, Doctor?"

"I think it is a person who tends to be most of the time feeling vulnerable, feeling that the world is hostile, feeling that he is alone, must be guarded in order to protect himself, feeling beyond or better, feeling bottled up, incapable, as he has in the past, of being damaged, he will be damaged again if he is not careful and guarded."

Garrity asked Dr. Bradford for his professional opinion regarding Joseph's mental condition on the night of December 8th, 1968. The prosecution objected but was overruled by Judge Digges.

Dr. Bradford answered, "In my judgement, it was the condition on that date; yes."

The defense was done with Dr. Bradford.

Now, Alfred Truitt was up. "Is it possible, Doctor, that this man could be faking?"

"I don't think he was, no."

"Is it possible?"

"Yes, it is possible."

"Do you know his previous history, of the mental institutions having been in and out of?"

"Yes."

"And is it not possible he could have learned the routine having been in and out of those places?"

Dr. Bradford dismissed the idea.

"But it is possible?" Truitt pressed.

"Yes."

On redirect, James Garrity asked if it was probable that Joseph was faking and Dr. Bradford answered that he didn't think it was very probable that Joseph was faking his mental illness.

Next, Dr. Stephen Kaufman returned to the stand for the defense. This time the jury would hear his testimony. He testified again that he had seen Joseph on seven different occasions while he was an inmate at the Maryland Penitentiary. His first visit was September 11th, 1969; the last was just a few days before the trial began. Over the course of these interviews, Dr. Kaufman said he found Joseph to be "a severely disturbed person."

Garrity confirmed that the doctor had the reports from Crownsville and Perkins as well as the Maryland State Police. He asked, "Tell the Court and jury, please, what your findings were."

"Well, I found Mr. Bartholomey to be a very disturbed man from a psychiatric point of view. I felt that his personality was not well integrated, that he had severe disturbance in his thinking and that he had some evidence of hallucinations, of the auditory type."

"What do you mean hallucinations of auditory type?" asked Garrity.

"He would hear voices. I think he described something about that in court, but he described hearing voices and that he wouldn't know at times whether the voices would be coming [from] inside of his brain or outside and sometimes they would switch. ... He described one situation in reference to that where he said in Ocean City, in the summer of '68, voices told him to leave Ocean City and they also told him to get Communists and he feels that he betrayed the voices in a way by not listening to them [and] staying in Ocean City and that he had not done all that he could do to rid this world of this Communist menace. Also, as I say, he has, in my opinion, severe thinking disorder."

"What do you mean by that, Doctor?"

Dr. Kaufman explained that Joseph believed in things that most people would find absurd or strange. In his delusions, he thought a higher power was speaking only to him and directing his actions.

Garrity continued. "Could you give an example of some of these delusions?"

The doctor referred to his notes here: "... he had the belief that the Communists are taking over the world, that police and judges—"

"They are," interrupted Joseph. Again.

Disregarding his own client, Garrity asked Dr. Kaufman to continue.

Dr. Kaufman repeated the Communist ideology: Everyone was a Communist. His teachers. His stepmother, Betty. President Nixon. Millions of Chinese Communists were infiltrating America. By 1972, the Communists will have taken over the country. There was also the paranoia that the prison guards were trying to hurt him, which was why he refused to sleep at night. He thought they might come in and mace him or hang him or drown in the river.

Garrity pressed for more examples of Joseph's delusions.

Dr. Kaufman then relayed a conversation he'd had with Joseph on September 19th. Joseph was ruminating on Communism. He said he was glad to see Dr. Kaufman because he thought "they" might have gotten him, but then, as if to double-check, Joseph asked the doctor if he was a

Communist. The Communists were everywhere, Joseph warned. When Dr. Kaufman asked about the trial and what Joseph thought might be the outcome, Joseph told him, "I think they are going to execute me." And then Joseph went on a tangent about Jackie Kennedy and Bobby Kennedy before circling back to Nixon, telling Dr. Kaufman, "And they will get me. All I wish [is that] I killed Nixon because he is a Communist. I can't be sure about Agnew. Maybe he is and maybe he isn't. But he is from Maryland and that is in his favor."

Further delusions, Dr. Kaufman said, were evident. Joseph told him about the experience he had when he believed he was turning Chinese: "His skin was becoming yellow, his eyes were becoming like a Chinese [person's] and he felt that he had to stop it and was pulling at his skin and pulling at his hair and he believed that the Chinese were going to then take him to China and tap his brain and get his thoughts from his mind and use his thoughts to betray America and make a fool out of him in front of his parents and relatives and ridicule him." Dr. Kaufman pointed out, "[Joseph believes] the wool is being pulled over everybody's eyes and he is the only one that knows the truth about what goes on in this world."

"Doctor, would you say he was suffering from a mental disease or defect December 8th, 1968?" asked Garrity.

"Well, I believe when I evaluated him, he was suffering with a severe mental illness and he still is."

"When do you believe this might have started?"

Dr. Kaufman said he believed this mental illness started in childhood. Here, Garrity and the doctor spent a few moments reviving Shirley's testimony about when she dressed him up as a little girl with lipstick for Halloween and how this incident of humiliation and ridicule might be evidence of his mental health concerns emerging in childhood. But could Joseph be faking all this? Dr. Kaufman said, based on his years of experience working with psychotic people, he did not think Joseph was faking. In fact, he thought that it would be a pretty hard thing for

Joseph to do. Joseph's elaborate ideas about Communism and how those beliefs were intertwined into his life pointed to a deeper issue and not something easily faked.

"What would you say that mental disease is?"

"I would label it paranoid schizophrenic." Dr. Kaufman said this label of paranoid schizophrenic meant generally that there was a disorganization of his personality ... that if Joseph were a puzzle, his pieces wouldn't quite fit together. Then add in the paranoia of his Communist conspiracy theories. Dr. Kaufman testified that he did not think this type of mental disorder could or would develop within a few months. Therefore, as Garrity questioned him further, it was possible that he was a paranoid schizophrenic on or before the murders.

When it was time for Dr. Kaufman's cross-examination, Alfred Truitt seized upon the topic of Joseph's hallucinations, specifically the one about turning Chinese. He asked, or rather reminded, Dr. Kaufman that Joseph had taken LSD that summer and asked, "So this was a hallucination induced by drugs, right?"

Dr. Kaufman agreed, stating that Joseph believed LSD allowed a person to see the truth.

"But this is one of the hallucinations to which you have referred in making up your opinion that he is a paranoid schizophrenic, right? And this one hallucination is induced by drug?"

"Yes."

Truitt continued, "Well then, what other hallucinations ... did you base your opinion on?"

"Well, I didn't see him or hear him hallucinate. He did describe to me—."

"Then it was all subjective. He is telling you?"

"Yes. Yes. I based my opinion very little on his description of the hallucination," said Dr. Kaufman.

Truitt switched his line of questioning and asked the doctor to explain what he meant by the lack of integration of Joseph's personality.

"Well, what I mean by that is that ... with him there are certain elements where his emotional states wouldn't necessarily go along with the condition he is in or what he is talking about. For example ... when Mrs. Bartholomey was testifying and crying, he was laughing. He was smiling. He frequently would smile to me when talking to me about his problems and seemed very unconcerned ... even [when] talking about being executed. He mentioned that he might well get the gas chamber and they would turn the gas chamber on and off so he would die slowly over a three-year period and [Joseph] kind of chuckled and giggled with that. This [is] what I mean by not integrated. If I had such an idea I think I would be rather scared."

Truitt changed course and asked one last question: had he administered any of his own tests? Just interviews, Dr. Kaufman confirmed.

James Garrity called his third and final doctor to the stand: Dr. Stanislav Groff, a world-renowned psychiatrist from Czechoslovakia.[4] By the time of the trial, Dr. Groff was teaching psycho-pharmacology and psychotherapy part-time at Johns Hopkins University. He said his main field of interest was hallucinogenic drugs like LSD. Several times in his testimony, he was asked to speak louder.

Dr. Groff testified that he had seen Joseph in the Maryland Penitentiary twice in the recent weeks leading up to the trial, and like Dr. Kaufman, he based his findings solely on his interviews with Joseph. The first interview centered around his drug use and his experiences with LSD. "There was a very interesting thing which I found in his sessions.[5] ... they were mostly bad trips and it has been our experience that this is always indicative of pre-existing pathology in the person. In other words, [the negative experience] is not produced by the drug, but the drug brings up something that is in the personality already. So that when we see people having difficult reactions or having some prolonged

---

4 The former Czechoslovakia is now the Czech Republic and Slovakia.

5 Dr. Stanislav Groff said that the term "session(s)" was used to refer to patients using LSD under medical supervision; when not under medical supervision, the frequently used term is "trip(s)."

reactions or psycholeptic complications, it is always a borderline personality structure; in other words, [a] pre-psychotic condition."

Garrity asked Dr. Groff if the focus of the interview shifted.

It did, he said, but not at first.

"Oh, he didn't talk to you about that first?" Garrity was referring to Joseph's Communist ideations.

"No, it took some time." Dr. Groff then stated his impression was that Joseph had a significant degree of personality disturbance before the drugs and that continued drug use could have accelerated that disturbance.

The second interview that Dr. Groff had with Joseph centered around his "delusional" way of thinking—this massive Communist plot. Garrity asked the doctor if he thought Joseph was suffering from a medical defect on the night of the murders and Dr. Groff agreed that he had a mental disease.

"Paranoid schizophrenia?"

Dr. Groff answered, "Yes. Again, it is very difficult to say for sure, but it is very probable from what we know about the dynamics of this disease."

Garrity asked the doctor if he believed Joseph had the capacity to understand the criminality of his actions that night. Did he know what he was doing was wrong?

"Provided that the manifestation of the disease were already there to the degree which we see it today or even to a lesser degree, I think that it severely impaired his ability to appreciate the criminality," Dr. Groff said. Further, he added that Joseph saw himself as leading a war against this country's enemies, and to that end, Joseph would see his actions as worthy of a medal, not a prison sentence.

"In other words, he would not be able to appreciate the criminality of his act then?" asked Garrity.

"He would not be able."

The prosecution did not have any questions for Dr. Groff, and with that, the defense rested its case.

Judge Digges ordered a short recess at 3:05 p.m.; less than half an hour later, they were all back. Alfred Truitt had two rebuttal witnesses, both psychiatrists. Judge Digges was moving this case along.

The prosecution called Dr. Robert H. Sauer to the stand. He was a staff member at Clifton T. Perkins State Hospital as well as the clinical director at another psychiatric facility in Maryland. Dr. Sauer was one of the staff members on the medical committee in March 1969 that determined Joseph's diagnosis was severe antisocial personality disorder with drug dependence and that he was responsible at the time of the murders.

Truitt asked the doctor to explain to the jury the process used by the medical committee after a patient has been admitted, but before he could answer, Joseph yelled out, "Kidnapped! Not admitted." He was once again ignored.

"Well, after a patient is admitted to Clifton T. Perkins State Hospital, they undergo initial evaluation on admission, are then assigned to a staff psychiatrist for detailed work-up and are also assigned to a psychologist who gives them a battery of psychological tests and seen by a social worker and physical examination, laboratory examination, including a brain wave, electroencephalogram. All this information is then gathered together and presented at a medical staff conference, at which the psychiatrists are present and consider all this data and interview the patient following presentation of this data." Dr. Sauer also testified that they obtained information from other institutions where Joseph had been.

Alfred Truitt wanted to get at the heart of the matter: did Joseph Bartholomey have the ability to discern right from wrong on the night of the murders? Was there such a mental defect as to keep him from understanding the criminality of his actions?

Dr. Sauer testified, "It is my opinion that at the time he was not suffering from a mental disease or defect of such severity that would cause him to lack substantial capacity to appreciate the criminality of his conduct or conform his conduct to the requirements of law."

Truitt asked the doctor what they meant by the diagnosis of antisocial personality disorder with drug dependence.

"I mean a personality disorder which is a deeply engraved, maladapted way of relating to society, manifested by strong antisocial traits ... lack of conscience, impulsiveness, poor judgment, callousness, a heedlessness toward life, and an inability to learn from past experience. This would describe what is popularly called a psychopath."

James Garrity began his cross-examination by pointing out that Dr. Sauer had never personally examined Joseph. Dr. Sauer acknowledged that he had not done a formal examination of him, but he reiterated that he had been a part of the staff conference and had agreed with the other doctors who were present about their collective opinion of Joseph.

Twice during this part of Dr. Sauer's testimony, Joseph interrupted—once to call him a Communist. The court continued to ignore him.

Garrity came back to the Clifton T. Perkins staff conference report where another doctor stated that Joseph had "paranoid ideation." He asked Dr. Sauer, "Do you agree that this is paranoid ideation there?"

"Oh, yes. I think Mr. Bartholomey has never been able to trust anyone." But the doctor declined to say that these paranoid ideations were reaching or had reached a psychotic level.

"And what paranoid ideas does he have, Doctor?"

"Well, he was very paranoid about the police, in Salisbury, felt they were definitely out to convict him for this ... that they were out to get him. Now this would be considered paranoid, although I thought there were certainly a realistic element in it."

Garrity had Dr. Sauer read for the jury a part of the Perkins report that documented Joseph's belief that Dr. Ido Adamo was trying to harm him by putting him on thorazine. Didn't Joseph feel that there was a threat to his life and safety?

Dr. Sauer would not take the bait and insisted that Joseph and Dr. Ido Adamo didn't like each other and that this aversion became intense on Joseph's end. Dr. Sauer had seen thousands of patients in his career. This wasn't unusual.

Back to the report, Garrity asked, "It states there he denied delusions and hallucinations. Did he have any discussion with you about delusions and hallucinations; do you know?"

"Well, he certainly did not mention any of these things that were brought out in court today about a Communist plot. That is all entirely new to me. This is the first time I heard it."

Garrity asked Dr. Sauer to explain his belief that Joseph's paranoid ideations were not at psychotic levels. The doctor responded that paranoia is relative with varying degrees: a person who trusts everyone would be considered naive while a person who trusts no one because he believes that others are going to kill him would be a delusional, paranoid person.

Garrity recollected for the doctor that Joseph believed he was being framed. Wasn't that true?

"At the present time, he did."

"Let me ask you this, Doctor; is it possible for a person to have delusions and hallucinations and not talk of them?"

"Yes, very possible."

James Garrity circled back to Joseph's claim that Dr. Ido Adamo had put him on thorazine.

Dr. Sauer said, "His reference there to some thorazine. I am not personally familiar with what he did receive. However, I know he was involved with several fights with other patients so it seems likely that he may have been given some tranquilizers to calm down."

"As a matter of fact, wasn't he administered thorazine the whole time he was there?"

Dr. Sauer said again that he wasn't aware of it, but it was possible. Then, in maneuver reminiscent of a Matlock "gotcha," James Garrity had the doctor read from Joseph's discharge summary from Clifton T. Perkins: "Patient provocative in his relationship with other patients but showed no psychotic symptoms. Had to be on thorazine, 50 milligrams B.I.D. until 3/30." Joseph indeed had been placed on thorazine, which lead Garrity to ask: if a doctor wanted to figure out if his patient was having delusions or hallucinations, would they put the patient on thorazine?

To that, Dr. Sauer said, "No, I wouldn't do that."

"What would be the effect if you did? Why wouldn't you put him on thorazine?"

"Well, it might stop the hallucinations."

Hoping to leave some questions in the jury's mind about the possibility of Joseph's hallucinations, Garrity was finished with his cross-examination of Dr. Sauer. Now, the prosecution opted to redirect and Alfred Truitt asked to have the entirety of Joseph's record from Clifton T. Perkins State Hospital entered into evidence, not just the snippets the defense had had the doctor read.

James Garrity immediately objected to this, but then withdrew it.

The next rebuttal witness for the prosecution was Dr. Herman Reiner, a psychiatrist and the Clinical Director at Clifton T. Perkins State Hospital. He had received his medical training in Switzerland before coming to America where he worked as a psychiatrist in North Carolina, Iowa, and Ohio before settling down in Maryland in 1965. Dr. Reiner had been involved in the examination and evaluation of Joseph Bartholomey when he was at Clifton T. Perkins.

For Dr. Reiner's testimony, special assistant prosecutor Richard Pollitt took the lead. "Doctor, based on all these things which we have mentioned, were you able to form an opinion with reasonable medical certainty as to whether or not on December 8th, 1968, as a result of a mental disease or defect, Joseph Bartholomey lacked [a] substantial capacity to appreciate the criminality of his conduct or to conform his conduct to the requirements of the law?"

"My opinion was that Mr. Bartholomey did not suffer from mental disease or defect of such severity as to cause him to lack [a] substantial capacity to appreciate the criminality of his conduct or to conform his conduct to the requirements of law."

"What was your diagnosis, Doctor?"

"My diagnosis was antisocial personality with drug dependence."

Richard Pollitt had no further questions.

James Garrity asked Dr. Reiner how regularly he saw Joseph, and Dr. Reiner responded that said he would see him as he made his rounds, that he and Joseph would chat from time to time. Then Garrity asked about the diagnosis reached by the staff conference, which was antisocial personality with drug dependence.

"Doctor, do you agree with Doctor Addison that there were no delusions or hallucinations exhibited by the patient?"

"Yes, I definitely do."

"And what do you base that on, Doctor?"

"Because I am basing it on the patient's tendency to malinger mental disease."

"What do you mean by that, Doctor, specifically, please?"

"He was hospitalized before at Crownsville. He was hospitalized at our hospital. He has never mentioned any of these delusions that I heard mentioned here today. That was the first time that I heard about it." While it was possible for a person to have delusions and hallucinations and not speak of them, Dr. Reiner's opinion was that this didn't apply to Joseph, saying, "On the ward, he tried to impress upon the attendants that he was very sick and that he hoped to be incompetent." This impression was written down by the nursing staff and submitted to the staff conference.

Garrity asked Dr. Reiner to find that particular item in the conference notes and he did: "Mr. Bartholomey talks a great deal and tries to be impressive. He speaks of getting found incompetent."

But the defense pressed the doctor to read further from the staff conference notes. Dr. Reiner obliged and testified to the following notes: "Sometimes he would talk aimlessly in circles", "On January 31st, 1969, he became very hostile and had to be secluded", "Mr. Bartholomey constantly complained of hearing voices and having headaches. He received no tranquilizers while on Ward 3", and "His behavior appears to fluctuate. At times he appears to be hallucinating."

"And you stated there was no evidence of hallucinating, didn't you, Doctor?"

"Yes, because anybody can make believe he is hallucinating."

Garrity then brought up Joseph's threat to kill himself while at Clifton T. Perkins on February 21st, 1969.[6] Wasn't that significant?

Dr. Reiner replied, in his opinion, Joseph had a tendency to malinger his mental illness. "That wasn't only my impression. It was the general impression of every member of the medical staff."

James Garrity quickly moved on. Couldn't a diagnosis of antisocial personality with drug dependence be paired with paranoia? Dr. Reiner allowed this point and said it would not be inconsistent for someone with an antisocial personality disorder to have paranoia as well. Garrity next revisited the issue of Joseph being given thorazine and asked Dr. Reiner a similar series of questions that he had posed to Dr. Sauer. "And if you were trying to determine whether a person was having delusions or hallucinations, would you administer thorazine?"

"The amount of thorazine he started to get March 8th is minimal."

"That doesn't answer my question."

"At night. I wouldn't hesitate. He was getting it at night because he was apparently restless at night." Dr. Reiner held firm that Joseph was receiving the thorazine at night to help him sleep because the hospital staff did not like to give possibly addictive drugs like barbiturates to patients. The thorazine, at a 50mg dose, was deemed a better choice.

Garrity asked if they couldn't have tried another drug, but Dr. Reiner batted that away, saying his history of drug use prevented that option. It would not have been their protocol. Their exchange was testy and, at one point during Dr. Reiner's testimony about the thorazine and paranoia, Joseph shouted out to the doctor, "You are showing your communism!"

After that, James Garrity had no further questions.

Richard Pollitt opted to ask a few more questions on redirect. He wanted to revisit Dr. Reiner's statements about how the staff felt Joseph was malingering his illness, but James Garrity objected several times.

---

6 According to the documents from CTPSH, this occurred on February 23rd.

Eventually, Judge Digges overruled the defense and Dr. Reiner was allowed to answer, "I personally had the feeling, very strong feeling, that he was attempting to malinger mental illness."

"What do you mean by the word 'malinger,' Doctor?"

"Wanting to appear to be mentally ill in order to perhaps, to be found mentally ill and not to be responsible at the time of the alleged offenses."

Pollitt scored his point, but Garrity wouldn't let it rest there. On redirect, he asked, "As a matter of fact, Doctor, it is your opinion he was mentally ill, isn't it?"

"My opinion?"

"Yes."

"Oh, no. He was not mentally ill."

"Antisocial personality, Doctor?"

"It is not a mental illness."

"Did you give any other opinion at the staff [conference]?"

Dr. Reiner said, "Yes, it was recommended that he could be considered for transfer to Patuxent Institution to be evaluated as a defective delinquent."

"I see," said Garrity.

"And patients that are mentally ill don't go to Patuxent."

Neither James Garrity nor Richard Pollitt had any additional questions and Dr. Reiner was excused. The jury had now heard all the witnesses for the prosecution and the defense. Alfred Truitt asked to approach the bench.

"Could we inquire how long we plan to go tonight?"

"I was hoping we could finish tonight. Did you have any other idea?" Judge Digges had his foot on the proverbial accelerator. He wanted to finish the case and so did James Garrity. Alfred was surprised, but agreed that the prosecution was also done. But it was getting late in the day and once the jury heard there would be a long break and then closing arguments, the foreman said they would prefer to start fresh in the morning.

"Very well," said Judge Digges. One can imagine the swift judge was disappointed, but nevertheless he relented and court was adjourned at 4:56 p.m.

• • •

The third day of Joseph J. Bartholomey, Jr.'s trial began on Wednesday, October 8th at 9:30 a.m. Everyone was ready to proceed and the jury was brought in. Judge Digges began with lengthy remarks to the jury by advising them about the four charges—the escape, the assault on Ralph Pusey, and the murders of Samuel Graham and Albert Kelly—and how to consider each one. He carefully walked the jury through how the law should and should not be applied and what "beyond a reasonable doubt" meant. He then explained to the jury, that under Maryland law, the difference between murder in the first degree and murder in the second degree is premeditation and that any murder committed while attempting an escape from any prison or jail in the State of Maryland is automatically considered murder in the first degree.

The heart of the defense's case was that Joseph Bartholomey was insane and the judge addressed this point with the jury: "The Legislature provided that a defendant is not responsible for criminal conduct and shall be found insane at the time of the commission of the alleged crime, if at the time of such conduct, as a result of mental disease or defect, he lacks substantial capacity either to appreciate the criminality of his conduct or to conform his conduct to the requirements of law. ... Furthermore, the term mental disease or defect do not include an abnormality manifested only by repeated criminal or otherwise antisocial conduct." This was a crucial difference.

Judge Digges told them to approach the problem before them by weighing the opinions of the doctors and experts and consider the evidence as it has been presented to them. Theirs was a heavy burden, but an important one and they should take their responsibility with the utmost seriousness. Two men were dead and another life was hanging in the balance. Then, Judge Digges ordered a short recess at 10:44 a.m.

Eleven minutes later, court was back in session and now it was time for the prosecution's closing statement. Special prosecutor Richard Pollitt rose to address the jury. He began by going over each of the four charges, confidently assuring them that the State had met the burden of proof.

For the escape charge, the State had to prove beyond a reasonable doubt that he was lawfully detained in the jail; for this, Pollitt reminded the jury of the five warrants issued by a Wicomico County judge charging him with various crimes and because of these warrants, he was arrested and held in the jail. This, Pollitt explained, meant that Joseph was indeed lawfully detained and the evidence provided showed that he had escaped his legal confinement.

Next was the assault with intent to murder charge for Ralph Pusey. Pollitt explained that by taking a shot at Ralph Pusey in the hallway, Joseph had assaulted him, and had that bullet hit Ralph Pusey and he died, then this would be an instance of murder in the first degree, just like with Albert Kelly and Samuel Graham.

On the cases of first degree murder for Kelly and Graham, Richard Pollitt explained to the jury that the State had to prove three things: that someone was dead, that Joseph Bartholomey had been the killer, and that there was premeditation or that it happened during an escape attempt. All three of those, Pollitt told the jury, had been proven to them beyond a reasonable doubt. Albert Kelly and Samuel Graham were dead. Multiple people saw Joseph Bartholomey do it. In court, Joseph even admitted to murdering them. And with regard to premeditation, Pollitt said that they had already proven he was lawfully detained in the Wicomico County Jail and had escaped, so this fact alone met the burden of proof for first degree murder. But beyond that, Pollitt explained that Joseph had time to consider his actions, meaning he had premeditated the murders.

Richard Pollitt revisited the testimony of each of the State's witnesses as he made his points and reminded the jury of the exact events of the night of December 8th, 1968. There was no question as to what happened and who did it. The only question that remained for the jury, he said, was whether or not Joseph Bartholomey was legally sane when he committed these acts. And as Judge Digges had said, if the only manifestation was repeated criminal acts or antisocial conduct, then the defendant did not suffer a mental disease or defect. Pollitt reiterated, "Bearing in mind, ladies and gentlemen, it is not every defective delinquent or emotional disturbed person who is legally excused. He must meet certain requirements at the time of the act to be entitled to be legally excused or committed for serious crime. ... He may be [a] defective delinquent, he may be emotionally disturbed, but he is still legally responsible for his acts."

Consider the testimony of Joseph's family, Pollitt implored the jury. "The fact he struck his mother, the fact he ran away, the fact he was a bully in school sometimes apparently, the fact that he was sniffing glue, the fact that he threw a knife at his uncle or whatever it was, these are the things that are repeated criminal or otherwise antisocial conduct, which are not the type of insanity that excuses a person to put him on the street to do it again."

Pollitt's argument was that Bartholomey was an antisocial person just as the doctors from Clifton T. Perkins State Hospital had said. His jealousy over his siblings was normal; being embarrassed about being dressed up as a little girl was normal. Even his suicide attempt in Ocean City with Donna Campbell was not evidence of abnormality because he was admittedly on LSD at the time.[7] His suicide attempt in the jail was also not evidence of insanity. Pollitt took aim at the defense team's doctors and their claims about his insanity, pointing out how recent all their examinations had been and how they had to speculate on when it had started for Joseph. They were not certain, Pollitt told the jury.

---

7 The suicide attempt in Ocean City and the LSD trip when Joseph said he was turning Chinese are always talked about as two separate events in the trial testimony and the medical documentation. Here, Pollitt appears to put them together.

Richard Pollitt went back to the doctors at Clifton T. Perkins State Hospital and their testimony that they had never heard Joseph talk about Communist plots and his desire to kill President Richard Nixon. These doctors and nurses and staff members saw Joseph daily for two months, not just a few times. He reminded the jury of Dr. Herman Reiner's testimony that they believed Joseph was malingering his mental illness. His diagnosis was antisocial personality disorder, but he was also sane.

The special prosecutor ended his remarks with this: "As to what was his condition on December 8th, we say on that date Joseph James Bartholomey, he didn't shoot Samuel Graham and [Albert] Kelly because they were Communist, he shot them because they were performing the duties which they should have been performing and he knew enough that he had done wrong to get himself a motel room under an assumed name. He knew he had done wrong. He was not insane and he should be found guilty of murder in the first degree. The punishment, to be given, is not your problem. That is the responsibility of His Honor, Judge Digges. You must be convinced. We think you are convinced beyond any reasonable doubt that he committed these crimes, that at the time he was not legally insane, not the point that he can be excused."

Richard Pollitt had delivered a convincing closing argument.

Now it was the defense's turn. James Garrity began with an odd opening about jury instructions and finally meandered his way toward the evidence at hand. Had the State proven Joseph was legally detained? He wasn't so sure because the warrants said he was to be arrested, but no one had given testimony that he was arrested. But he was willing to let this point slide because he wanted to focus on whether or not the prosecution had proven that his client was sane on the night of the murders. To this end, he reviewed the testimony of his expert witnesses and how they testified to Joseph having delusions and hallucinations as well as a long term history of such. He pointed to Dolores's testimony that Joseph said he saw the devil as a little boy. Garrity reminded the jury that Dr. Kaufman had speculated that his condition started around the second grade; a serious mental condition, such as schizophrenia, would not simply evolve in a single night.

Leaning heavily on the expertise of his witnesses, James Garrity emphasized the way these independent experts arrived at their observations. His doctors actually spoke with Joseph and evaluated him, giving him tests and interviewing him unlike the prosecution's doctors who were just part of the staff conference. The doctor who evaluated Joseph at Clifton T. Perkins was Dr. James Addison and he was not called to take the stand. Garrity pondered: why was that? Would his testimony not stand up to scrutiny? Would he have changed his mind or given another opinion that would have been helpful to the defense? James Garrity harped on this point several times while also criticizing the Clifton T. Perkins team for not having proper dates on their charts and for not having the police report.

He asked the jury to take into consideration what Joseph's family reported and how that meshed with the testimony of the defense's experts. Joseph's repeated criminal acts and antisocial behavior were not the whole picture. Garrity asked how could they find out if he was having delusions or hallucinations if they were medicating him with thorazine twice a day? Joseph was insane, he said, and then repeated Dr. Stanislov Groff's testimony that "yes, he did have a disease or defect on December 8th, 1968 and he did not appreciate the criminality of that at the time." To that point, Garrity recalled for the jury that Dr. Stephen Kaufman had testified that Joseph was unable to conform his behavior to the requirement of law because of his mental disease or defect.

Garrity took issue with Richard Pollitt mentioning LSD during the suicide attempt in Ocean City and he wanted to be sure the jury understood this correctly. No one testified that Joseph was on an acid trip when he slashed his wrists and had to be rushed to the doctor. He also had a problem with Dr. Reiner's testimony that the team felt Joseph was malingering because Dr. Reiner only had a passing personal experience with Joseph. And again, he asked, where was Dr. Addison?

As he wrapped up his remarks, James Garrity implored the jury to see that, in Joseph Bartholomey, they were looking at a young, paranoid man who had been made to suffer the indignities of humiliation and constant rejection by his family, a sad case of a person who never had any real love or affection in his tender years, a defendant who was the culmination of so many terrible situations and events and experiences that he was no longer sane. "There is a man's life in your hands really and you have to take this into consideration when you weigh the facts and see whether the burden, beyond a reasonable doubt, has been met."

James Garrity sat down. He had done what he could for Joseph.

The last word would belong to Alfred Truitt. In his rebuttal, he thanked the jury for their patience and consideration on behalf of the prosecution and the defense. Their job, although a civic responsibility, was to uphold the laws of Maryland and that was serious work. Then, Alfred Truitt took aim at the defense's case. First, James Garrity said no one testified that Joseph Bartholomey was arrested, but Truitt told the jury that he had been arrested by Salisbury Police Detective Jerry R. Mason. A small point, but in a trial like this, a smart lawyer covers them all.

He wanted to make clear that Joseph Bartholomey was sane and he had been considered sane for some time. And to that point, Alfred Truitt had one last reveal, a stunner that would have made Perry Mason proud. He reminded the jury that the defense had frequently referred to the Clifton T. Perkins State Hospital material. In those documents, there was a doctor who also happened to be involved in Joseph's 1965 stay at CTPSH after he had escaped from Crownsville. This doctor, Dr. M. J. Pescor, had been present at both staff conferences: the one in 1965 and the one in 1969. Truitt explained to the jury that, at the staff conference in 1965 to see if Joseph was capable of standing trial for the crime of assaulting a police officer, the presiding opinion was that he was a sociopathic personality who was competent to stand trial and responsible for his actions. Dr. Pescor had twice agreed with the diagnosis, *both before and after* the killings of Samuel Graham and Albert Kelly.

Immediately, James Garrity objected: whether or not Joseph was competent to stand trial in 1965 was not in play for this trial.

Alfred Truitt did not back down and reminded the court that these documents were already in evidence. Dr. Pescor had agreed with the diagnosis of sociopathic personality in 1965 and he agreed again with the diagnosis of antisocial personality and drug dependence in 1969. Truitt hammered away at this crucial detail: "Four years later, same diagnosis. He is antisocial. He is antisocial. We will agree with that." Truitt then read from a Crownsville report: "His memory was quite good. His stream of mental activity was good. He denies any hallucinations." Following that, Truitt quoted a Clifton T. Perkins nurse's report: "Patient is very loud and hostile verbally. Patient tries to keep ward in uproar. Patient is trying to play insane when ward personnel are around him. To other patients he acts normal."

Truitt emphasized that Joseph was antisocial, a defective delinquent. These people are a danger to society so what would happen if they found him insane? Well, Truitt informed the jury, he would be committed for confinement to a state hospital where, after some time, he could apply for release. "We respectfully ask you ladies and gentleman to find him guilty on all counts and sane," said Alfred Truitt.

The closing statements were finished and now the attention turned back to Judge Digges as he instructed the jury on the possible verdicts and that they must be unanimous. They were to remain as one body—no separation—while they had lunch at a nearby restaurant. Upon their return, they would begin deliberation.

At 3:00 p.m., the jury was back in court, ready to begin the task ahead of them. The foreman asked Judge Digges if they could have the medical reports and the judge allowed it with neither side objecting. Then the jury filed out. Alfred Truitt and Richard Pollitt, Sam's old friends on the side of the prosecution had delivered a solid case. There was no doubt there. And James Garrity had presented the best possible case given what he had in front of him. All they could do now was wait.

Five hours and eighteen minutes later, the jury had reached a verdict. Everyone was called back to the courtroom and Judge Digges gave strict instructions that there was to be absolutely no demonstrations or outward remarks of any type as they proceeded.

The clerk of the court addressed the jury foreman and asked him for their verdict. The jury foreman announced they found Joseph J. Bartholomey, Jr. sane and guilty on all four charges. The verdict fell like a sledgehammer.

Dolores Bartholomey began to scream.

Joseph turned and yelled, "Get your fucking arms off her, cop! Don't put your arms on me! Get your fucking arms off me! You are a motherfucker!"

A young woman in the audience, possibly his sister, Shirley, also cried out.

Joseph was still screaming, "Get your hands off me, you motherfucker! Get your hands off me!"

Once Joseph was quieted, the defense asked for a formal poll of the jurors and each agreed to the verdicts of sane and guilty on every count. Then James Garrity said, "If Your Honor please, the defendant will file a Motion for a New Trial."

"Very well, gentlemen, the defendant is in your custody until further order of the Court. Remove him from the courtroom."

Shirley called out to her brother, "Jimmy, we will get you out of there someway. My brother is sick and he needs help. He shouldn't be punished. He is sick."

"Very well, Mr. Sheriff, assist the lady from the courtroom." Judge Digges was done with these outbursts and reclaimed control of his courtroom. He turned his attention to the jury, thanking them for their service and expressed the gratitude of the people of Wicomico County. And with that, the jury was dismissed with one last note: their payment slips would be mailed to them by Mr. Mudd, a name that harkened back to another murder in another century.

THE MURDER TRIAL OF JOSEPH JAMES BARTHOLOMEY, JR.

• • •

Joseph Bartholomey would learn his fate in the hours before America rang in the new decade. On December 30th, 1969, two and a half months after the trial and the guilty verdicts, Alfred Truitt, Richard Pollitt, and James Garrity were back in court along with Joseph's family to hear Judge J. Dudley Digges rule on sentencing. Two of the crimes for which he was found guilty—the murders of Albert Kelly and Samuel Graham—carried the possibility of the death penalty. That mortal decision rested with Judge Digges alone.

Each side would have a chance to make a few remarks.

As Truitt rose to speak, he understood the enormity of the moment. This was his second death penalty case. His first was the 1958 murder of Salisbury police officer Henry T. Stephens by Johnnie Brown[8]. After Brown's first trial, which resulted in a guilty verdict and a death penalty sentence, Brown's court-appointed lawyers, Salisbury attorneys Vaughn E. Richardson and Richard Pollitt, appealed the decision and won. (Vaughn Richardson would soon defend Joseph's friend, Erick Irwin.) The appeal judges ruled that the jury had not been properly questioned about whether or not racial bias could influence their decision. Stephens was White; Brown was Black. Alfred Truitt replaced the prosecutor from the first trial, but the outcome was the same for Johnnie Brown. He was guilty and sentenced to die in the gas chamber by Judge E. McMaster Duer. After that trial was over, Johnnie Brown was driven back to the Maryland Penitentiary in Baltimore by none other than Sheriff Samuel A. Graham.

Now Alfred Truitt stood in front of another judge to ask for the death penalty again ... for another man who killed two officers of the law ... for the man who had killed his friend.

He noted that the facts were clear and undeniable and that this was a case that had weighed on their minds. Two lawmen had been mur-

---

8 This case was mentioned in an earlier chapter, "A Tempest Draws Near."

dered, which Truitt noted that even in places where capital punishment had been abolished, the killing of an officer was a warranted exception. "This is a cold, calculated, planned, schemed murder of two people of authority, one of whom was shot in the back." Truitt reminded the court that Joseph had been found guilty of all charges, and ended his commentary by saying, "As I say, I intend to be brief, but I think in consideration of all these elements, the State would respectfully ask the Court for the maximum penalty."

James Garrity arose to address the court. He too must have felt the heavy burden of knowing Joseph's life was hanging in the balance. He told Judge Digges that in his nine years of practicing law, he had never been involved in a case where the death penalty had been imposed. He didn't believe in the death penalty and he didn't believe it protected society from crime. Statistics bear out that the death penalty is not much of a deterrent, he said, and the tide of popular opinion was turning against it as a form of punishment. And he went back to his central premise: Joseph was not of sound mind. He cited the psychiatrists who stated that both his condition and prognosis were very poor. "It is a wonder that in all these years something wasn't done by some court along the way about this, put him in a more maximum-security institution where he would not elope, where something possibly could be done for him. This is the more noble aspect of penology and rehabilitation."

But, Garrity acknowledged, there was very little chance of rehabilitation for Joseph. His only hope was for the mercy of the court. "To me, perhaps because maybe I didn't give enough to this defendant, maybe I wasn't eloquent enough or clever enough to give him as much as perhaps someone else could have; to the State because maybe they pushed too hard for the taking of someone else's life ... I plead with Your Honor that God will have mercy on our souls."

Judge Digges asked Joseph to stand. "In addition to what has been said, is there anything you want to say before the Court determines the sentence in these cases?"

Joseph, true to form, stood and said, "No, I don't think it would really make any difference to knock myself out."

"Very well, if you have nothing further to say you may be seated."

Judge Digges echoed Alfred Truitt's comments that the case had weighed heavily on his mind, too. He'd been on the bench for twenty years now and he had overseen death penalty cases and said he would be in favor of abolishing capital punishment. The defense may have felt a small flicker of hope in those words, but not for long. The judge said he had to consider the case and the law before him. "In the intervening two or three months, I have not only considered the matter, I have read and re-read and read again the detailed investigation of the Parole Department made at my request, in an effort to seek some justification for my not imposing the supreme penalty." However, upon review of the facts of the case—"and how horrible they are"—lead him to only one, hard decision.

For the escape charge, Judge Digges sentenced Joseph to ten years. For the charge of assault with intent to murder of Ralph Pusey, he gave Joseph ten years. And for the charges of first degree murder in the killings of Albert Kelly and Samuel Graham, Judge Digges sentenced him to death in the gas chamber.

PART IV

– DONNA AND ERICK –

Joseph Bartholomey had faced his judge and jury and knew his fate. He would die in the gas chamber. But what of his co-conspirators, Donna Blair Campbell and Erick Thomas Irwin? Donna was nineteen when she was arrested at her parents' home in Baltimore for her role in the double homicide. Erick was around twenty-one when he, too, was arrested at his parents' home. They were both initially held in the same penthouse prison where Joseph had killed Graham and Kelly, but their trials had to wait until Joseph's was finished.

• • •

Erick Thomas Irwin's lawyer was Vaughn E. Richardson, a popular attorney in Salisbury. On December 27th, 1968, weeks after the double homicide, he petitioned the Wicomico County Circuit Court to have Erick sent to Clifton T. Perkins State Hospital for evaluation. Was his client insane on or about the night of the murders? Judge William W. Travers approved the petition and on New Year's Eve 1968, the newly installed Wicomico County Sheriff Eugene Carey delivered Erick to Clifton T. Perkins State Hospital.

There, he was given a battery of physical and psychological tests. His IQ scored 111, which placed him on the above average intelligence scale. Erick also admitted to some drug use. Ultimately, like Joseph, the staff concluded he was not insane and released him from their custody. On February 28th, 1969, Erick was transferred back to the Wicomico

County Jail. But unlike Joseph's lawyers, Vaughn Richardson did not seek a change of venue for his client. Erick sat in the penthouse prison for the remainder of 1969.

On Monday, January 12th, 1970, Erick Thomas Irwin went to trial in Judge Travers's courtroom for the charge of aiding Joseph in his escape. For this crime, he was found guilty and given the maximum of ten years in prison with credit for time already served. He'd been incarcerated for 400 days. The other charges against Erick—breaking and entering, grand larceny, and conspiracy to murder—were all placed on the stet (or inactive) docket.

Wicomico County State's Attorney Alfred Truitt told the court and all present that despite helping Joseph escape, Erick had been honest and forthcoming with law enforcement; he had not hindered the investigation and he had been cooperative. Truitt also stated that as far as he could discern, Erick had not known about the shootings when he picked up Joseph. The fact that the gun used to kill Graham and Kelly came from Joseph and Erick's burglary is not mentioned in the reporting of Erick's trial.

Vaughn Richardson offered a small excuse for his client's behavior. He said that Erick had been at the University of Maryland when he became involved with a protest group. This caused his grades to drop, forcing him to enroll at Chesapeake College in Wye Mills, Maryland. When Judge Travers asked Erick to explain what this protest group was all about, Erick told him it involved protesting the Vietnam War and racial discrimination.

"It all appears very foolish to me now," he told the judge.

"Your sentence would have been much worse, if you had been convicted of being an accessory. You're very lucky."

And Erick Thomas Irwin was lucky indeed: by June 1971, he was out of prison, gainfully employed, and engaged to a young brunette from Salisbury. They married that summer, had a child, and by all accounts, he never made another headline. Erick Thomas Irwin died on January

30th, 1994 and was buried in small graveyard in Worcester County, Maryland. He was forty-six.

• • •

After a few weeks in the penthouse prison, Donna Blair Campbell's attorneys filed a petition to have her moved to "a more appropriate facility." She was unable to make the $95,000 bond, a grand sum in 1969.[1] On January 7th, 1969, her Baltimore attorneys, Norman N. Yankellow and Joseph Rosenthal, asked State's Attorney Alfred Truitt to get Judge William W. Travers to sign the petition. Three days later on January 10th, 1969, Judge Travers signed the petition and Donna Campbell was moved from the Wicomico County Jail to the Maryland Correctional Institution for Women in Jessup, Maryland. Her new home was not far from the Maryland House of Correction or "The Cut" where her boyfriend had spent eight months in 1966.

The Maryland Correctional Institute for Women had been built with funds from the Works Progress Administration in 1939. The first female prisoners arrived at the small campus on October 1st, 1940. By the 1960s, the inmate capacity was around 235 although it was designed for a population of 185. Most of the women were serving short sentences; roughly half were drug users. The layout of the prison was simple: two cottages, an administration building, a chapel, three ancillary buildings for canning, power, and storage, and a small chicken house with open spaces between them. The two-story cottages, Horigan and Lane, were designed similarly with a kitchen, dining room, and a recreational area with individual rooms on both floors.

Upon her arrival, she was admitted to the Horigan Cottage and placed under an initial quarantine. This was where all new inmate admissions were sent. It also had the hospital and a craft room for the inmates to work in. The women sewed flags and made hospital garments;

---

[1] $95,000 in 1968 is roughly equivalent to $870,000 in 2025.

in the summer, they worked a fifteen-acre garden and canned the vegetables. The other inmate dormitory, Lane Cottage, had the library and a small school room. Donna Campbell was granted recreational privileges once she was released from quarantine and volunteered for housekeeping duties. She was a model inmate during her stay at Horigan Cottage and worked as a clerk in the Administration Building and continued her housekeeping tasks. Donna kept herself out of trouble.

On October 29th, 1969—three weeks or so after the conclusion of Joseph's trial in Charles County—her attorney filed a motion to move her trial too, arguing that Donna could not get a fair trial in Wicomico County. On March 5th, 1970, Judge William Travers signed off on the request allowing for her trial to be moved to Howard County Circuit Court where Judge James McGill would oversee her trial.

Six months later, on March 23rd, 1970, Donna sat down at a typewriter. "Dear Sir," she began, "I am awaiting trial in your circuit, I have been incarcerated since December of 1968, since the constitution assures every defendant a quick and speedy trial, I am hereby requesting your aid in seeing Justice met. There are three defendants in this case, two, who have already been to trial. Being ignorant to the legal procedures I place this letter before you, hoping you will gain me some relief. Please let me know if you received this letter; Sir; Sincerely I am: Donna Blair Campbell."

The next day, she asked to be transferred to Lane Cottage and that request was granted. The day after that, she got a letter from Judge McGill saying he had received her letter.

Donna began working as a resident teacher and started participating in group therapy sessions that were conducted by the prison's psychologist. She completed an eight-week Planned Parenthood course and served two terms as a member of the resident council. Her mother and father were allowed to visit her twice a week. Her file noted only one incident of odd behavior. During a visit with her family, for reasons unknown, she became hysterical, crying and screaming, and she had to be taken to a segregation area until she calmed down. Once she regained her composure, she went back to Lane Cottage.

By mid-May 1970, she still had not heard anything more from Howard County Circuit Court regarding her trial so she contacted Judge McGill again. This time in neat handwriting with blue ink on white legal-sized paper, she again asked for her trial to be placed on the docket. Her letter was received two days later. A trial date was set for June 8th and then it was postponed until July 7th. Donna's mother even sent a letter to the judge asking for her daughter's trial. She begged the judge to let them know if the July 7th date would stand firm. Her daughter's eighteen-month stay in prison had been terrible hardship for the family and all they wanted was a trial date. She wrote that she was certain of her daughter's innocence.

The postponement held and Donna Blair Campbell went to trial in Howard County Circuit Court on Tuesday, July 7th, 1970 at 9:45 a.m. with Judge James McGill presiding. She had been incarcerated for 574 days. After all this time and despite her mother's earnest belief in her daughter's innocence, Donna pleaded guilty to aiding Joseph's escape. She denied slipping the gun in the box of candy to Joseph Bartholomey; rather, she said that Erick Thomas Irwin had been the one to hand over the box of candy, concealed in his jacket. Her defense attorneys told the court that she had no previous criminal history and were able to produce a number of character witnesses, including a priest and a nun. Judge James McGill gave her a suspended five-year sentence and five years of probation. The other charges against her—a charge of murder, of being an accessory before the murder, and of murder-conspiracy—were all dropped.

Donna Blair Campbell was free to go. She paid $136[2] in court fees and moved back to Baltimore where she got a job as a cashier clerk with a credit company, making a modest income of $375[3] a month. Her su-

---

2 $136 in 1970 is roughly equivalent to $1,125 in 2025.

3 $375 in 1970 is roughly equivalent to $3,100 in 2025.

pervisors spoke highly of her. Her probation officer wrote: "During this period of time, the subject has made an excellent adjustment to supervision. The subject reported as instructed, remained gainfully employed and was available for all home visits. All money owed has been paid in full. In view of the above, this case successfully expired as of 12-10-73." And so, on that date, the fifth anniversary of her arrest, she completed her probation and slipped into obscurity.

Throughout her incarceration, Donna Campbell regularly corresponded with Joseph Bartholomey.

– ANOTHER MURDERER NAMED BARTHOLOMEY –

APRIL 1971

Monday, April 5th, 1971 was a chilly yet sunny day in Baltimore, a reminder of the dying winter and a spring that wouldn't quicken its pace. Yet, in one northeast neighborhood near Herring Run Park, a white hot panic was spreading like wildfire. A small child was missing.

Dwayne K. Little was just four years old with big brown eyes, a sweet smile, and a cherubic face. His mother last saw him when he went outside to play at 2:30 p.m. When she went to get him about an hour and a half later, he was nowhere to be found and she immediately called the police. While the Littles were living every parent's worst nightmare, law enforcement began scouring the neighborhood near their home on Mayfield Avenue. Canine units and helicopters were brought to the scene. As the sun set near 6:00 p.m. and the temperature dipped to 45°, fear and worry for Dwayne Little only intensified.

One can only imagine the fear and the terror the Littles felt as night fell and their baby boy was still missing. Out in the cold. In the dark. Alone.

As the sun rose that next morning, the temperatures continued to plummet and fierce winds began to whip as the day wore on. Rain soaked the searchers. Hundreds of volunteers—off-duty city workers, students from nearby schools, even a Boy Scout troop—were desperate to find Dwayne Little. One police officer keeping guard near Sinclair Lane and

Parkside Drive said he had nearly a thousand people ask him how they could help out. Mothers gripped their children tightly. One mother stared down a couple of strange men until they introduced themselves as a reporter and a photographer for the *Baltimore Sun*. Everyone in the neighborhood was tense, on edge. The search continued through the morning into the afternoon and into another cold evening. The outcome looked utterly bleak.

Then, after thirty hours of searching, a break came. A neighbor recalled seeing Dwayne with an older boy from the neighborhood named Ethan L. Bartholomey. He lived two doors down from the Little family with his half-sister, Shirley, and her husband, and his mother, Dolores. At 11:15 p.m., the 45-pound body of Dwayne Little was found in the Bartholomeys' trash can under a foot of garbage. This unfathomable discovery was so grotesque that even hardened cops struggled for words.

What on earth had happened?

Immediately, police took Ethan Bartholomey into custody. Detective Patrolman Edward S. Chlan with the Homicide Division of the Baltimore City Police Department questioned Ethan in the basement of the Northeast District police station. It was a hard interview for Detective Chlan as Ethan, a fifteen-year-old in junior high school, recounted what had happened and why. Dwayne Little had wandered over to the Bartholomeys where Ethan was playing records. Dwayne picked up a puppy that belonged to the Bartholomeys, but then he dropped it. The puppy yelped loudly and this sent Ethan into a violent rage; he told Detective Chlan, "The dog started screaming just like my mother always does." He grabbed a loose pneumatic storm door closer and beat the four-year-old child. Then Ethan strangled him. After seeing what he'd done, he took the little boy out to their backyard and put him in the trash can, heaping rubbish on top of his lifeless body.

When Dolores Bartholomey was informed that her second son now stood accused of a brutal murder, she collapsed and was taken to Johns Hopkins Hospital.

Dwayne's father, Charles Little, told the *Baltimore Sun* that he had noticed that Ethan Bartholomey didn't seem to associate with kids his own age, but rather seemed to gravitate towards the younger children, saying "It was always little kids." He saw Ethan as lonely and made a point to be pleasant when he saw him in the neighborhood. And now his son was dead at the hands of that lonesome teenage boy.

Of course, the *Baltimore Sun* and other news outlets also reported that Ethan's older brother, Joseph J. Bartholomey, Jr. was on death row for two murders. Newspapers as far away as Wichita Falls, Texas and Des Moines, Iowa and Miami, Florida carried the story. Dolores Bartholomey now had two sons with three murders between them. Murder seemed to be a family affair.

• • •

On Wednesday morning, April 7th, 1971, Ethan L. Bartholomey appeared before Judge Robert J. Gerstung of the Central Municipal Court. The juvenile court system had waived its jurisdiction. His half-sister, Shirley, was there. Ethan was quiet and wore a corduroy suit. When the judge asked him if he knew why he was there, he stared back with an empty expression and said, "No."

An assistant medical examiner took the stand and said there were bruises and hemorrhages around Dwayne's neck. This pointed to strangulation, just as Ethan had told the police he had done.

Detective Edward Chlan testified about his interview with the young murder suspect. Fighting back tears, he began to describe a disturbed, isolated, and sad teenager who felt an intense bitterness towards his mother. Ethan had had trouble adjusting to life at Herring Run Junior High School and was planning to transfer to a Catholic school. From the testimony, the impression was that Ethan was possibly being bullied by the other neighborhood kids. (Based on the testimony at Joseph's trial, both Dolores and Shirley admitted that Ethan had been tormented and threatened by his resentful older brother. Perhaps the bullying had started closer to home.) Chlan testified that Ethan often kept to himself and said he felt "his mother hated him because he didn't play football and games like the other kids."

During his time on the stand, Detective Chlan, an eighteen-year veteran of the police force, had to stop and clear his throat several times. This was the kind of horrific case that would haunt a cop until his dying day. What he saw, what he heard, what he knew ... it was all beyond comprehension.

Judge Gerstung ordered a psychiatric evaluation and appointed a public defender for his case.

The Littles had lost more than they could enumerate. They lost their four-year-old boy. There would be no first day of school or graduations. His parents would never know who Dwayne was going to be. They must have clung tightly to the memories they had, always reminded there would never be more. Holidays, birthdays, and family gatherings now tainted by his absence. The "what ifs" only mounted on top of one another. Forever four, Dwayne Little was a memory trapped in amber.

For Dolores and Shirley, there had to be a sickening feeling of déjà vu. This was Joseph all over again. A broken, angry boy who had lashed out in a lethal way. Three innocent people were dead in less than four years at the hands of these two brothers. Soon, psychiatrists and psychologists would be reviewing and discussing Ethan's case the way they had with Joseph. Another Bartholomey murder trial loomed on the horizon like a storm that refused to abate.

But before Ethan Bartholomey could be held to account for this atrocity, his older brother was back in the headlines.

– THE FURMAN DECISION –

Joseph James Bartholomey, Jr., inmate #111445, was sitting on death row and waiting for his turn in the gas chamber when another inmate saved his life.

William Henry Furman was a Black man who had been convicted of home invasion and murder in Savannah, Georgia. His life had been one of hardship. He had a sixth grade education and few, if any, resources to help him combat his persistent epilepsy, intellectual disabilities, and alcoholism. The failed robbery at William Micke's house in August of 1967 was a terrible idea born in an alcohol-soaked mind. He said he had intended to steal a radio or two, but when Micke awoke, Furman got scared and ran. He fired a single shot through a closed door, but it was enough to kill Micke. Police found William Furman hiding under his uncle's porch and charged him with murder. He said it was an accident, but a nearly all-White jury found him guilty and gave him a death sentence. However, the state sent him to a psychiatric facility in Georgia instead of death row. This seemed like a nod toward a collective understanding that William Furman had appreciable challenges, both physical and mental.

In January 1972, his attorney argued before the United States Supreme Court that the death penalty was unfair and often arbitrarily applied, especially to members of the Black community as well as people gripped by poverty. And the Supreme Court agreed (in a five to four ruling) in June 1972, overturning the death penalty across the country. This is not to say that the court ruled the death penalty as unconstitutional, but that the discretionary application of it was. All death row inmates had their sentences put on hold until the states could revise their criteria and ensure they were properly and appropriately applying the death penalty. When his attorney went to visit him to tell him the news, William Henry Furman just stared back at him. He failed to grasp the gravity of what had happened in the nation's highest court. Later, he would say that all he wanted to do was stay alive.

Back in the Maryland Penitentiary, Joseph found himself as one of twenty-three death row inmates whose sentences were now on hold while the statutes were reviewed and revised. These inmates had been spared, even if only for a moment. This did not mean freedom or new trials. It meant they would be resentenced. Joseph's came in January 1973 back in Charles County Circuit Court. Judge James C. Mitchell handed down two life sentences to be served consecutively. Also spared by the Furman decision was Johnnie Brown, the man who killed Salisbury police officer Henry Stephens and who was prosecuted by Alfred Truitt in his second trial. Brown received a life sentence after having spent eighteen years on death row.

And so there it was. Joseph James Bartholomey, Jr., just twenty-six, would live out the rest of his natural life behind bars. Isolated from the world. His family. The choices he made—the lies, the schemes, the killings—had placed him here in this cold, cold cage. This was his punishment. Long days of uselessness and monotony followed one after the other as the weeks grew into months and the months into years. Forgotten. Unimportant. Lost in a system of bureaucratic purgatory where he was nothing to nobody. No peace. No comfort. Violence always lurking around a corner. Guard up. Eyes open. And then the night comes. Again and again. This was his life now.

Would the same fate await his brother?

– THE TRIAL AND SENTENCING OF ETHAN L. BARTHOLOMEY –

APRIL 1973

Three months after Joseph's resentencing, Ethan Bartholomey's murder trial began. He was seventeen-years-old now and, just like his older brother had done, he had spent the last two years at a Maryland psychiatric facility. Nine psychiatrists gave their testimony at an evidentiary hearing on April 11th and 12th about Ethan's mental state. Four said he was legally insane; five said he did not lack the capacity to understand the criminality of his actions and therefore he was *not* legally insane. Judge Anselm Sodaro of the Baltimore City Criminal Court ruled with the five, finding Ethan sane and able to stand trial.

Judge Sodaro began by noting that Ethan was a teenager of average intelligence (his IQ was given as 96) but that he was a lonely, socially awkward boy who hated his mother. "That he showed characteristics of a schizoid personality disorder; that he was not allowed to develop in a normal healthy manner principally because of his mother's constriction and suppression of his needs for activity and involvement. ... He is probably a danger to others and himself," the judge said. "The court was told that unfortunate murder act appears to have been the product of the defendant's need to manifest his hostility toward his mother and to liberate himself from the structure that was stifling his identity development."

This was a damning indictment of Dolores Bartholomey as a mother.

Both of her sons felt unloved and unwanted and it created within them a deep cavern of resentment and hostility for her. Brothers who continually descended, inch by inch, into that dark canyon and found only rage and loneliness at the bottom. In that moonless void of emotional despair, they lashed out, unfurling their brutality, and now three people were dead by their vengeful hands.

• • •

On Friday, June 1st, 1973, Ethan L. Bartholomey pleaded not guilty but agreed, through his attorney, to a statement of facts about the case. Judge Sodaro convicted him of second-degree murder and handed down the maximum sentence allowed: thirty years in prison.

When she heard the verdict, Dolores Bartholomey screamed. Dwayne Little's parents did not attend the trial.

Ethan L. Bartholomey was remanded to the Maryland Correctional Institution for Men in Hagerstown, Maryland, a massive and menacing stone-built prison that rises up like a medieval castle from the green rolling hills of Washington County. Just a single glance in its direction will conjure forward *The Shawshank Redemption*; it is easy to imagine Andy and Red walking behind those thick, gray granite walls. Construction on the prison started in 1932, when it was called the Maryland State Penal Farm. The name changed in 1964. This was not a place for the gentle-minded: one prison guard later recalled that he saw more action there than he did in Vietnam. Prison riots. Suicides. Murders. One inmate was believed to have stabbed his bunkmate thirty-six times after reading *Helter Skelter*, Vincent Bugliosi's book about Charles Manson. "Helter Skelter's Son" was written on the wall in the dead man's blood. Another prisoner had his throat slit because he was late returning a book to another inmate. Continued overcrowding and understaffing did little to ease the tensions contained within that prison of rock and mayhem. This is where Ethan Bartholomey would have to make his way.

After his sentencing, Ethan disappeared into history after one last footnote. A year after his trial, he was among thirty-four graduates who walked across the stage in the prison's auditorium as part of the Class of '74. The inmates-turned-graduates donned blue gowns and mortar boards with yellow tassels as they marched in to the familiar tune of "Pomp and Circumstance." From time to time, parents let out whoops of cheers and expressions of pride as their loved ones were handed diplomas. There were speakers for this event and one told the group, "Getting a diploma while incarcerated is a doubly good thing to do." A sociology professor gave a speech during the ceremony about self-improvement: "The moral is—give a little more and get in return a thousandfold. You cannot fill your own bucket by dipping into other people's buckets. You must fill the buckets of others. How you see yourself is how other people see you." An inmate drama group concluded with this: "If you have to hate, hate the things you should hate. When you love, love things that are important. It's up to you!"

– THE REST OF THE STORY –

The senseless murders of Wicomico County Sheriff Samuel Graham and jailer Albert Kelly came at the end of a turbulent year of political assassinations and strife as well as protests and riots over the war in Vietnam and for civil rights at home. Even Joseph J. Bartholomey, Jr. had tried to turn his crime of opportunity into a Communist political plot during his trial but failed in his attempts to convince the jury. He was no John Wilkes Booth. He was no Sirhan Sirhan.

In the 1970s and 80s, Joseph tried a few times to overturn his conviction, but it never worked. He did not have a lawyer, so he filed his post-conviction relief work himself. The petitions he wrote are surprisingly orderly and mostly factual. There was no hint of the wild conspiracy theories he once claimed to believe in; there was no more talk of Communism or killing Nixon or the world ending on May 4th, 1972.[1] His post-conviction work cited legal cases and precedents, which was impressive for a man who never graduated high school. Joseph's efforts to get out of prison were fruitless.

In June 1979, the Associated Press ran a story about the first inmate college graduation in Maryland's history. The educational program had been offered to inmates at the Maryland Penitentiary by Coppin State

---

1 On May 4th, 1972, Richard Nixon notably gave a eulogy for J. Edgar Hoover at his funeral at the National Presbyterian Church at 11:00 a.m. He also had meetings with H. R. "Bob" Haldeman and Charles Colson, two men would later be indicted for their roles in the Watergate scandal. In one of his recorded conversations that same day, Nixon said, "The American people are suckers. Getting to know you … all that bullshit." It wasn't the end of the world as Joseph had said, but the days that followed were the beginning of the end for Nixon's political career.

College.[2] Just as Ethan Bartholomey had earned his high school diploma and walked across the stage in a cap and gown, it was Joseph's turn to accept his college diploma. On Sunday, June 3rd, 1979, Joseph and several other inmates from the Maryland Penitentiary put on their caps and gowns, signifying their college graduation ceremony, which lasted about an hour. The educational program had a positive effect for the prisoners who enrolled. One inmate who was in prison for murder told the AP reporter, "I think my mother is proudest. When I talked about these things, I saw the look on her face. She was real pleased and that helped me get through the program. Being here there's not much I can do to make my mother proud of me, but going to school is a positive thing." Another inmate said, "This (education program) is a real encouraging vehicle for improving ourselves and trying to get out of here." That inmate had already served half of his twelve-year robbery sentence.

The AP reporter also spoke to Joseph Bartholomey. He told her that when the lights went out in the prison cells at 11:00 p.m. every night, he and the others who had to study would "sit by the door on the floor and read" by the hallway lights. Joseph was proud of himself for earning his degree and he spoke the first positive, recorded words about himself when he told the reporter, "I feel a lot of elation. Nobody on the outside understands what we went through. Right now, I don't think there's a man here who would ever commit another crime. Getting an education lets you look inside and see all the wrongs you did."

Maybe this is as close to self-reflection as he could get. He'd done plenty wrong in his young life, choices that resulted in him spending most of his life—more than seventy percent of it—institutionalized. Recent studies have shown that there is a high incidence of antisocial personality disorder, as high as 47% in one study, among the incarcerated. Considering the hallmarks of this disorder—a lack of guilt or remorse, aggressiveness, irritability, lying, impulsivity, failure to conform to social norms, irresponsibility, and a reckless disregard for others—may

---

2 The school was renamed Coppin State University in 2004.

provide some insight into these statistics. This is not to say that all people with antisocial personality disorder end up in prison, but many like Joseph J. Bartholomey do.

What made him the way he was? Certainly, his environmental risk factors were significant. Buried in his psychiatric files, there is a small note that might provide insight. According to a medical form filled out by Dolores during his 1965 admission to Clifton T. Perkins State Hospital, Joseph was diagnosed with scarlet fever in 1955 when he was eight years old. Modern studies have revealed a possible link between these streptococcal infections and a disorder called PANDAS or Pediatric Autoimmune Neuropsychiatric Disorders Associated with Streptococcal Infections. While there is no definitive test for PANDAS and there is no available information to suggest Joseph had it, the disorder can cause a range of symptoms in children, including mood changes like rage and irritability, compulsive and obsessive behaviors, motor problems and tics, bedwetting, hyperactivity, food aversion, sleep irregularities, and anxiety. Could such a disorder have been plaguing Joseph during this time in his life? It might explain why he struggled with bed wetting as long as he did as well as his unusual sleep issues of waking in the night and walking around, a trait observed at the Maryland Children's Center and by his mother. PANDAS is a rare condition, but if he had it, one thing is for certain: it would only have exacerbated his predicament as a young child.

During his trial, his defense team argued that he suffered from paranoid schizophrenia. There were some signs of paranoia throughout his life: at the Maryland Children's Center, he thought he heard people calling his name and he was generally distrustful of authority figures. Studies have shown that people with schizophrenia may have antisocial traits or exhibit antisocial behaviors at times. Today, a mental health professional might consider a diagnosis of schizophrenia, per the *Diagnostic and Statistical Manual of Mental Disorders,* if the person is having at least a combination of the following: hallucinations, delusions, disjointed or disconnected speech, or a presentation of being catatonic or emotionally disordered or limited in a manner that is clinically concerning. Could Joseph have been schizophrenic? While it is possible, there is more evidence to suggest he had antisocial personality disorder. First, while schizophrenia could interfere with a person's ability to discern the difference between right and wrong, Joseph always understood what he was doing was wrong. Second, there was a consistency of his diagnoses from conduct disorder as a child to antisocial personality disorder as an adult. We now understand that individuals with conduct disorder who grow up continuing these same behaviors are then diagnosed with antisocial personality disorder. They are impulsive, deceitful, irresponsible, and violate social norms; they harm without remorse. And that is certainly a portrait of Sam Graham and Albert Kelly's killer.

Joseph J. Bartholomey, Jr. died in prison on Saturday, June 14th, 2008. He was sixty-one.

. . .

In 1972, a new principal came to Wicomico High School. Young, handsome, and college-educated, Anthony "Tony" Sarbanes was the proud son of Greek immigrants who had made their life in Salisbury, Maryland and raised their three children. While Tony went into education, his brother, Paul, entered politics and his sister, Zoe, was a business woman. They were the living embodiment of their parents' American dreams.

When Tony Sarbanes walked through the doors of Wicomico High as the new principal, he soon met his two vice-principals, Frank Waller and Dorothy Graham. He already knew Mrs. Graham: Tony had attended Wicomico High School as a kid and had hoped against hope that he wouldn't be assigned to her history class because of her hard-nosed, no-nonsense reputation. Now she called him Mr. Sarbanes. He stood next to her and Frank Waller as they prepared to usher in the 1971-1972 school year. Yet, even then, even as her boss, he still could not bring himself to call her Dorothy. She was, as always, Mrs. Graham: efficient, disciplined, and steady.

But Dorothy Graham had changed. Losing her husband in such a violent, sudden, and public way had broken something in her. Was it her heart? Her spirit? Her confidence? She was struggling and Tony could see it, especially when she dealt with the students. Typically, when a student misbehaved and was sent to the office for a disciplinary action, the student would see one of the vice-principals first. Mrs. Graham had once been able to be a strict disciplinarian, but now, when a student was sent to her, she had a difficult time managing it. She held a stiff upper lip when confronting the student, but when that kid left her office, she closed the door and wept. Tony could hear her quiet sobs. Then her door would open again and her stoic mask was back in place, if only for the moment, as if her tears had never come at all. She once told Tony, "You know, I just cry over any reason."

After moving out of the courthouse, she lived alone in an apartment on Alvin Avenue, not far from the high school. She seemed afraid to go out at night, and that fear, although understandable, caused a growing strain on Tony Sarbanes and Frank Waller. They had to work all the evening school events. So Tony asked her if there was anything she might feel comfortable doing and she agreed to work the wrestling matches. On those nights, a Wicomico County sheriff's deputy would escort her to and from the games. Sam's men continued to look after her.

To Tony Sarbanes, Sam's murder had had a profound effect on Dorothy. She wasn't the same. How could she be? Dorothy appeared to recognize this too, telling Tony on several occasions, "I've lost my nerve. I'm holding you back." Even though he silently agreed with her, he could not bring himself to say it or act on it. He respected her too much. Tony made up his mind: if she was to retire, the decision would be entirely hers. He'd have nothing to do with pushing her out.

Dorothy Graham had dedicated herself to education in Wicomico County for forty years. An untold number of students had come and gone through her classroom as a history teacher and her office as vice principal. Through the highs and lows, she had made a difference, probably in ways that she didn't even realize. It was time. She made the decision to retire at the end of that school year in June 1972.

Tony Sarbanes wanted to honor her legacy of good works so, at the end of the following school year, he had the names of the four major academic awards changed to begin with her name. Now, the Academic Achievement Award was the Dorothy Graham Academic Achievement Award and so on with the other three. Tony received a note in the mail from her, thanking him for thinking of her with such a lovely tribute.

Dorothy Graham died on Monday, July 8th, 2002, a few months shy of her 93rd birthday. She had remained a widow, devoted to the memory of her late husband who had been gone for more than three decades. Joe Long, a former Maryland State Senator, wrote to the *Daily Times* that he was sorry to hear of her passing and that because of her interest in her students, she likely kept many of them from becoming juvenile delinquents, including himself. When Tony Sarbanes arrived for her funeral at Holloway Funeral Home, he was informed that Mrs. Graham had listed him as a pallbearer. He was shocked. He had no idea that she had chosen him for such a special and final gesture. And so Tony Sarbanes helped carry her to her grave at the Wicomico Memorial Park where she came to eternal rest next to her beloved husband, Sam.

• • •

After Joseph Bartholomey's murder trial, both Richard M. Pollitt and Alfred T. Truitt, Jr. continued on as highly-regarded lawyers and finished their sterling careers on the bench.

In 1972, Governor Marvin Mandel appointed Richard Pollitt to be a judge in the Circuit Court of Wicomico County. He had continued to

Judge Richard M. Pollitt

Image courtesy of the Pollitt family

practice law after the Bartholomey murder trial and even represented the town of Fruitland, Maryland for a time. By 1981, he was the chief judge of the First Judicial Circuit, and then, five years later, Governor Harry Hughes appointed him to the second highest court in Maryland—the Court of Special Appeals. He sat on that bench until he retired in 1989 and later moved to Williamsburg, Virginia where he passed away in December 1992. His obituary chronicled his family life, his career as a lawyer and a judge, as well as his dedication to a number of civic organizations. One line was dedicated to his work on Sheriff Sam Graham's case.

Public service remained the heart of Alfred Truitt's work. He continued in the role of Wicomico County State's Attorney until 1971 and then crossed the aisle and became a public defender. His daughter, Maggie, remembered a time when he had represented a man accused of killing a young, pregnant woman who had been her classmate. Upset that he was representing him, she asked him, "How is that? How could you possibly defend that man?"

Alfred came right back at her. It was a legal matter, not an emotional one. He believed in the law and that everyone should get a fair trial and proper defense. In his later years, he reveled in mentoring young law clerks, several of whom went onto be judges themselves.

In 1977, Governor Marvin Mandel appointed him to be Associate Judge on the First Judicial Circuit where he served for the next thirteen years before finally retiring. He remained married to the love of his life, the beautiful Clara May until her death in March 2015. Her passing shattered the old judge and he died ten weeks later. The morning of his death, he had been on the bench. His family and friends remember Alfred "Sonny" Truitt as a fair, honest, and loyal man who loved to tell a story, and with all he had seen and done in this life, well, there is no doubt he had plenty to tell.

• • •

The Wicomico County Sheriff's Office has evolved from a small department with eight deputies working out of the basement of the historic county courthouse, as it was in Graham's tenure, to a modern day law enforcement agency with more than ninety sworn deputies and specialized units including a Criminal Investigative Division, a Narcotics Task Force, a Child Advocacy Division, and K9. And while the growth of the department has been significant, there have only been five sheriffs to serve the county since Sam Graham's death nearly sixty years ago.

Eugene Carey served out the two remaining years of Graham's elected time. Then, William "Bill" Shockley served as sheriff for twelve years. Next came John W. Baker who died while in office in 1984 after having served just two short years. The chief deputy, Hunter Nelms, took over and then served as sheriff of Wicomico County for twenty-three years. Many credit Sheriff Nelms with pushing the department into a present era of policing. This meant that some of the older deputies, like Tommy Lewis and Bud Fowler from Graham's day, decided it was time to hang up their gun belts. Lewis stepped away to give his full focus to his family and the Salisbury Fire Department; Fowler retired in October 1987. The old penthouse prison was abandoned around this time. The department had ceased being responsible for the jail in 1970s. The sheriff, his deputies, and the prisoners of the county were all moved to another complex on the north side of Salisbury. (It seems the ideas of Joseph Egeberg, the state jail inspector who preferred regional jails over little lockups, prevailed.) Other changes came, too: in the 1990s, the name was changed from the Wicomico County Sheriff's Department to the Wicomico County Sheriff's Office to reflect that the sheriff's position is an elected one.

The current sheriff is Michael "Mike" Lewis, the son of one of Sam Graham's deputies. He was elected in 2006 and has held the position ever since, and by all appearances, it is his job until he decides to give it up. He has run unopposed in his last several elections.

Yet the memories of Big Sam Graham and Albert Kelly still remain with the department. Their photographs are displayed on a wall inside the Wicomico County Sheriff's Office. These are not just portraits of dead men. These are honored symbols to the men and women walking those halls, a reminder of their dangerous occupation. Graham and Kelly were the only lives lost in the line of duty in the department's history ... until Sunday, June 12th, 2022.

That Sunday evening, Deputy Glenn R. Hilliard was attempting to serve a warrant on Austin Jacob Allen Davidson, a twenty-year-old from Delmar, Maryland who was wanted by the Maryland State Police, the Worcester County Sheriff's Department, and the Baltimore City Police. Their encounter would have fatal consequences.

Glenn Hilliard was a much loved man. Like Sam Graham, he too was adopted. When his mother met him, she said he was tightly clutching two toy cop cars, one in each little hand. He grew up with police work as his calling, working at the Ocean City Police Department and the Berlin Police Department before transferring to the Wicomico County Sheriff's Office where, by June 2022, he was a long-standing veteran of the force. Everyone who worked with Glenn—a good-looking and smart deputy with a charming smile and a knack for tech work—would later

Corporal Glenn R. Hilliard

Image from the
Wicomico County Sheriff's Office
Courtesy of Sheriff Mike Lewis

speak of a man with an endearing personality who was always ready to help anyone in need.

That fateful Sunday, he spent the morning in church with his beautiful wife and their three adorable children. When he suited up for his 3:00 p.m. shift that Sunday, his wife felt uneasy. Call it a wife's intuition or even a premonition. While there was no obvious reason for her discomfort, it is the feeling that many spouses of law enforcement officers face. *Will they be hurt? Will they come home?* The answer only comes when their car pulls back into the driveway. And, as painful as it is true, sometimes they don't come back.

Someone called in a tip, saying that Austin Jacob Allen Davidson was hanging out in Pittsville, a small town on the eastern side of Wicomico County. By this point in his life, Austin was no stranger to hard times and trouble of his own making. He was born on November 27th, 2001 to young parents; he had two sisters, one older and one younger. When he was nine years old, his mother died. His father was incarcerated. As a teenager, Austin posted photographs of his life on his social media accounts: a goofy kid with red hair, blue eyes, and a toothy smile who loved video games, football, and church. But behind the guileless photos was a lonely teenager who seemed desperate for attention and affection. A change began to manifest within him. He got into trouble for hacking and illegally modifying online video games. He bragged about an in-school suspension for being disrespectful to a teacher and using inappropriate language. In one oddly prophetic post, Austin asked his followers, "If I went to jail, what would you think I did?" The first commenter wrote, "Killing someone." When he was sixteen, his older sister died and his younger sister was adopted by a pastor and his wife. If family is an anchor that helps hold us in place, then Austin Davidson was certainly adrift.

One of his first contacts with police came four months after the death of his older sister. The Maryland State Police tweeted out his picture and said he was missing from Princess Anne, Maryland. At the age of seventeen, Austin robbed a McDonald's in Baltimore with a gun and made off with less than $1,000. He pleaded guilty and was given only probation before judgement and three years of supervised probation. This was not a wake-up call for him. In the months leading up to June 12th, 2022, he continued to commit crimes, big and small: speeding, a marijuana misdemeanor, driving without a license, assault, and second-degree burglary and possession of a firearm, which he wasn't allowed to have as a felon.

He tattooed his face with a small heart. He no longer posted Bible quotes. He flashed guns. He bounced from place to place, even living out of his car for a time. Untethered. Hardened. Violence was blossoming. That silly, beaming smile was gone, and in its place, the camera lens saw only cold, menacing stares.

Austin Jacob Allen Davidson was armed and he was dangerous.

Deputy Glenn Hilliard was dispatched to Pittsville around 8:30 p.m. and began looking for him. The summer sun had already set and the darkness of night was coming. He spotted a subject who matched the given description walking down Gumboro Road and decided to turn his car around for a better look. The subject ran into an apartment complex, hiding out momentarily in a stairwell. But as the patrol car got close, Davidson ran. Hilliard spotted him and immediately gave chase. Hilliard was gaining on Davidson, yelling for him to stop or else he'd be tased. Suddenly, Austin Davidson stopped running, but this was not a surrender. He was not giving up. He turned and fired a 9mm gun directly at Deputy Hilliard. Two rounds hit. He'd shot a cop. There could be no undoing of this act. Austin Davidson knew it. He sent a message: "I killed a cop they might kill me." And then he fled into the woods.

Another officer arrived and found Deputy Glenn Hilliard barely clinging to life. He was transported to Tidal Health Medical Center in Salisbury where he was soon pronounced dead. His murder was a profound and agonizing loss for his family and friends and for the local law enforcement community, especially the entire Wicomico County Sheriff's Office. Just hearing those words, that Glenn had been shot and killed, reduced strong men to speechlessness and tears.

The manhunt began immediately as scores of police flooded Pittsville and the surrounding area searching for the killer. For Austin Davidson, there was no way out. The sheer volume of law enforcement meant he could try to run, but he had no place to hide. He ditched his backpack of guns and ammunition in a trailer. He texted a few people. And then he turned himself in.

In the days after the murder of Deputy Glenn Hilliard, the old tensions between the Eastern Shore and Baltimore flared. Wicomico County Sheriff Mike Lewis pointed out that the Baltimore prosecutors and judge had allowed a seventeen-year-old, who had been convicted of an armed robbery, to go free in 2019. *Had he been incarcerated, Hilliard would still be alive,* said Lewis and others. The Baltimore press turned around and pointed the finger right back at the Eastern Shore for failing to jail Austin after the assault charge in Ocean City in April 2022, for which he failed to appear in court, and for a May 2022 charge of second degree burglary and firearm possession for which his trial was pending.

But the back and forth blaming, as always, made no difference. Glenn Hilliard was gone and Austin Davidson would be tried for his murder.

Hilliard's funeral was held on Tuesday, June 21st, 2022. Police arrived from all over the nation to honor a man who was adored by everyone who knew him. Glenn Hilliard, by all appearances, was an easy man to like. One after another, officers in crisp uniforms stood in front of the podium at the Emmanuel Wesleyan Church in Salisbury and broke down in tears as they recounted their fond memories of Deputy Glenn R. Hilliard. Their lips quivered and they swallowed hard against the deep swells of emotion their own words brought forward. Sheriff Mike Lewis looked out into the front row where Hilliard's family sat, dabbing the tears from their eyes. He apologized for losing Glenn. Then he called his deputies to order and posthumously promoted the fallen deputy to the rank of corporal and awarded him the Wicomico County Medal of Valor. Hilliard's family spoke of their love and their sorrow for a man that never had a cross word for anyone. *Celebrate his life,* they said, *because he died doing what he loved.* Then a deputy from Talbot County sang "How Great Thou Art" … the baritone in his voice rang through the church and stilled the air.

Outside the church, a riderless horse awaited his hearse. Helicopters flew overhead. Bagpipers played "Amazing Grace." A 21-gun-salute was followed by taps. As he was taken from the church, people lined the roads, waiting in the grass and holding flags under a pale blue sky dotted with small white clouds. The procession was long as it headed east from Salisbury to the Sunset Memorial Cemetery in Berlin, Maryland where Corporal Glenn R. Hilliard was laid to rest.

At his trial a year later, Austin Davidson's defense tried to paint him as a man on the run who was now sorry for his crimes, but the prosecution pushed back on that narrative, offering details of Davidson's boastful talk in prison about killing a cop. The trial lasted a week and the jury, deliberating for less than four hours, pronounced him guilty of murder. Wicomico Circuit Court Judge S. James Sarbanes—the son of Tony Sarbanes who had worked with Dorothy Graham and carried her to her grave beside Sam Graham—sentenced the 22-year-old Austin Davidson to life in prison without the possibility of parole.

Now, there is another portrait to hang next to Samuel Graham and Albert Kelly—Glenn Hilliard's. Three honorable men who deserved far better than to die as they did. In stories like these, the ones left behind are the ones who must face the devastation and clean up the wreckage after the monstrous storms have expended themselves. Their families, friends, co-workers, neighbors ... they are the heartbroken, carrying their grief like a heavy, heavy stone because now their love has nowhere to go. The ones left behind must carry on and remind the world of who these men were, of their legacies, of their stories. They are the ones who hold the memories now.

• • •

The killers responsible for the murders of Samuel Graham, Albert Kelly, and Glenn Hilliard have chilling parallels, almost as if they were two sides of the same coin. Joseph and Austin: twin hurricanes born fifty-four years apart who destroyed nearly everything in their path.

Joseph James Bartholomey, Jr. 21. A Baltimore kid from a broken home who started committing petty crimes only to end up killing a Wicomico County sheriff and a jailer. Lonely, hostile, bitter, and desperate for the affection he routinely rejected. It festered and he became violent. He was tried for his crimes and spent the rest of his life in prison.

Austin Jacob Allen Davidson. 20. An Eastern Shore boy from a broken home whose crimes escalated from Baltimore robbery to the murder of a Wicomico County deputy. A lost teenager who was seeking connection only to turn towards the darker side of criminality. No amount of supportive words or church outings could alter his violent course. And just like Joseph, he will also die in prison.

Could someone have intervened and altered the shape of Joseph and Austin's lives? Was there anything that could have stopped this early on ... before it became too late? Decades ago, a British psychologist named John Bowlby put forward a theory about attachment. Children in the earliest stages of development seek out attachments to their caregivers. A baby cries out and is quickly picked up by their mother, cradled and calmed; a toddler, in a moment of insecurity, holds fast to a grandparent's leg and finds reassurance and protection; a child wakes from a nightmare and is soothed back to sleep by a parent. These actions form positive and healthy emotional bonds between children and their caregivers and the development of this, argues Bowlby, is essential for our well-being. We need to understand love and nurturing; we need to feel safe and of value. Without this, our emotional development can be stunted or broken altogether. Does this theory apply in any way to Joseph and Austin? Or Ethan Bartholomey? Were their emotional and physical needs met as little children? And if not, is it possible something broke within them at an early age, something that could not be fixed?

We will likely never know and the speculation ends with knowing that, as young adults, Joseph and Austin reached a fatal point of no return and became outliers. Many people with childhood trauma and who have experienced tremendous pain and hardship do not become violent. They choose a different way forward ... therapy, love, advocacy, understanding, fellowship, mentoring. But Joseph and Austin, these twin hurricanes, once formed, set upon a deadly course of heartache and destruction. There would only be disaster. They smashed into our communities, roaring and ruthless, and left us forever changed.

And yet, somewhere, just over the horizon, lurks another.

We know it.

– EPILOGUE: GHOSTS –
MAY 2021 AND OCTOBER 2024

We speak of murder. Then we speak of ghosts. Our myths and legends, our histories told to us by grandparents and great-grandparents, our own narratives are all woven from the fibers of trauma and redemption, good fortune and misery, dastardly deeds pitted against bravery, things lost and triumphs gained, the light and the darkness of our shared humanity. We tell these stories because we *are* these stories. And in the telling, we remember who they were and consider for a moment who we are, who we might yet become. We bring to life once more the ones who are no longer here.

And now this story has been told.

The old jail is empty, but it is not open to the public. Hidden away above the courthouse, it is sealed like a tomb. No one walks the long, narrow halls. No hands grip the cold metal bars. No one keeps watch over the forsaken souls anymore. It was abandoned in the late 1980s, and like insects on a corpse, time has been eating away at it ever since. Cobwebs cling to lines of electrical conduit fastened to the low ceiling. Industrial white paint cracks and peels back from the brick walls in patches as large as a man's hand, exposing a moment in time when the penthouse prison was painted a pale, hospital green. Rust consumes the radiators and pipes. The tile floor—dirty, scratched, and stained—gives way to bare, cold concrete where loose bits of the ceiling have fallen down and come to rest. A single padlock hangs from a thick chain on a closed door. These hallways invite claustrophobia and dread. Shadows slip around corners. Whispers and murmurs. The gray bars, floor to ceiling, are the telltale reminder of its past. The cell doors are wide open and the ghosts are all let out.

It is a forgotten place, like the attic of an abandoned farmhouse decaying on a countryside road, where only the morbidly curious have cause to seek out its remains and gawk at the skeletons of dead animals and the random remnants discarded by the people who once dwelled there. The old jail is not a place for the living anymore. There are reminders of that. Graffiti left by an unknown hand in bluish-green marker on one wall recites a cryptic, rhyming message: the tale of an inmate from cell number seven being transferred to heaven before he had a chance to eat at eleven.

There is nothing left here but phantoms and echoes. Nothing but the memories of stories.

Here, in this place, sojourned sinners and saints. Outlaws, bootleggers, thieves, and murderers. Lawmen who believed in honor and duty and in the meaning behind their badges. Children. Women. White. Black. The fearful and the downtrodden. Those who gave up and those who refused to do so. These lives were fatefully intersected in moments of brutality and sorrow and never fail to reflect the damages we inflict upon one another ... damages which cannot be undone.

The old jail holds all this.

I have walked these halls. I have touched those metal bars. I have stood in the spot where the terrible events of December 8th, 1968 unfolded. Once, as I was leaving the courthouse, I met a woman who spoke in a hushed tone about the ghost of a murdered sheriff who still roams the hallways. If there was ever a place to offer up a disturbing setting for a nightmare, this would be it. This jail and the old grounds of Crownsville State Hospital.

It was abandoned in 2004 and sat in a state of decay for years. New revitalization efforts are underway and parts of the Crownsville campus have been restored, but when you cast your eyes upon the crumbling brick buildings with their barred windows dripping rust while the sagging branches of the willow trees rustle in the wind, you cannot help but believe there are souls still within. In September 2025, a beautiful memorial was erected on the grounds to pay tribute to and name 1,727 souls who died at the hospital and were buried in unmarked graves.

To say a place is haunted is to say it once held us.

The penthouse prison and Crownsville aren't the only places from this story that have been lost to time. The Maryland Children's Center where Joseph spent several months for psychiatric examination closed on September 20th, 1986. The Maryland House of Correction, or "The Cut," closed the doors on its violent history in 2007 and demolition began in 2014, but not before it was featured in HBO's popular crime drama, *The Wire*. The Maryland Training School for Boys was later renamed the Charles Hickey School, but it was mostly shuttered between 2005 and 2007. The barbarity of that institution existed before, during, and after Joseph's time. In late 2023, a lawsuit was filed by thirty-seven men who had been there as young boys and said they had been physically and sexually abused between the 1970s and into the 2000s. In March 2025, a former staff member was charged with thirty-eight counts of sexually assaulting young boys who had been at the Maryland Training School for Boys. The plaintiffs had horrific stories of systemic abuse, which is wholly consistent with what we know happened to the boys at the school. So many of those children carried monstrous traumas with them and doing so cost them dearly. They suffered PTSD. They battled drug and alcohol addiction. They committed crimes and were incarcerated again and again. The broken became the lost. One man, through his tears, told investigators, "We didn't matter. ... we didn't matter then and I don't think we matter now." Another said, "They broke me. Everything that connected me to my humanity was gone."

Clifton T. Perkins State Hospital remains as Maryland's only maximum security psychiatric center. Many of the others have gone the way of Crownsville as there was a push to de-institutionalize those who are mentally unwell. We saw the horrors and understood that this vulnerable population wasn't getting the help they needed and so we closed the doors and shuttered the windows, yet we did so without a plan, pushing those who are most in need of care into the streets and elsewhere. It is a failure twice over. And just like MTSB, Clifton T. Perkins State Hospital is also now facing its own lawsuits regarding alleged abuses and, as of April 2025, stood to lose its accreditation. More lessons left unlearned.

Almost everyone directly involved in the story of Sam Graham, Albert Kelly, and Joseph Bartholomey is gone. Even my grandfather, Bud Fowler. Seven months after I talked with him about what he remembered of the double murder, he went into the hospital. He was frail and near the end. Our family had gathered in the small room, waiting for the inevitable conclusion to his eighty-six years of life. His eyes were closed. Motionless except for his odd, ragged breaths. This was goodbye for Bud. I sat at the foot of his hospital bed and I watched his chest slowly rise and fall ... until it didn't rise again. My grandfather, Delbert Earl Fowler, died on Thursday, March 17th, 2011. The man who was born on Halloween died on St. Patrick's Day. And that little oddity always makes me smile. I never worry about seeing his ghost because if there's black coffee, pinochle, and Jesus in heaven, then he sure isn't coming back here.

Not long after I visited the jail, I made a discovery. Bud's gun, that .357 western frame single shot revolver my grandmother bought him, is still around. It lives in the private collection of Wicomico County Sheriff Mike Lewis whose own father sped away from their farmhouse to get to the jail the night Sam Graham and Albert Kelly were murdered. The stolen murder weapon, the .22 caliber Harrington and Richardson revolver, was returned to the Voigt family on December 8th, 1978—the tenth anniversary of the slayings. I have always wondered if a thing like that holds memory or if we hold the memory for it.

I have been telling this story—the story of a sheriff, a jailer, and a prisoner—for years now. It sits with me. Their photographs are over my left shoulder as I write this epilogue. They have been here this entire time. Now, their story has been told and these ghosts will remain ... with you and with me.

EPILOGUE GHOSTS — 301

If you were to step out of the elevator and turn right, this would be your view. The open metal door is the entrance to the jail. The doorway beyond leads into the sheriff's quarters. WCSO Captain Tim Robinson has his back to the camera while the author looks into the jail during a visit. (Robinson is now the chief of police in Ocean Pines, Maryland.)

Image courtesy of Patricia Gregorio, May 2021

The open metal door is the entrance into the penthouse prison. The doorway behind it leads to the sheriff's quarters. This is where Joseph Bartholomey and Sheriff Sam Graham fought on that fateful night in December 1968.

Image courtesy of Patricia Gregorio, May 2021

On the left, WCSO Captain Tim Robinson looks into a mechanical room while Sheriff Mike Lewis, right, looks at the lever box that controlled the cell doors. That is where Albert Kelly was just before Joseph Bartholomey shot him.

Image courtesy of Patricia Gregorio, May 2021

Looking into the jail, this is another view of the lever box. Just beyond it is the day room where Joseph Bartholomey was before the murders.

Image courtesy of Patricia Gregorio, May 2021

– ACKNOWLEDGEMENTS –

This book would not exist without the help of many people. They say it takes a village to raise a child … well, it also takes a village to support a writer raising a book.

I remain grateful to Albert Kelly's family: Margaret Kelley, Brooke Kelley, Lori Kelley, and Bonnie Moore. Initially, I had very little information about him, but Margaret Kelley saved the day. Her insights and firsthand remembrances were invaluable. And as if that wasn't enough, Margaret gave me a goodie bag of her peanut butter fudge, which was the best I have had in ages.

Alfred Truitt's daughters, Christine "Chris" Bozick and Margaret "Maggie" Engler, spent time with me on the phone and shared memories of their father. They helped me understand a man who was dear to them, Sam, and many others.

A few months into my research, I reached out to Wicomico County Sheriff Mike Lewis. He and then-Captain Tim Robinson sat down for interviews, shared historical documents and photographs with me, and escorted me on a tour through the old jail in May 2021. Robinson, who is now the Ocean Pines Police Chief, also acted as a beta reader for an early draft and provided me with important corrections. I hope they are happy with the final outcome here.

Several members of the Wicomico County Court System assisted me with finding and getting copies of different court filings: Robin Justice, Clerk of the Circuit Court James "Bo" McAllister, Melissa Lahey, Kristin Fissel, the PI unit, and State's Attorney Jamie Dykes. Additional thanks to Melissa Lahey for her additional assistance when we took that tour in May 2021 through the penthouse prison.

Over in Howard County Circuit Court, I owe thanks to Assistant Manager of Court Operations Joanne Musgrove and the Clerk of the Circuit Court Wayne Robey for their help in gaining access to documents there. And to the person or persons in Charles County who helped me, thank you. I'm sorry I lost your contact information years ago.

Worcester County attorney Joe Moore is a real scholar and a gentleman. Joe met with me several times and continued to answer my emails and phone calls. He was a wealth of knowledge (and stories!) and I appreciate his time, patience, and expertise.

Help with medical and psychiatric questions came from two accomplished women. Dr. Mithila Jegathesan, who is one of my dearest friends and a brilliant doctor, reviewed the autopsy information and other medical documents with me. Dr. Peregrine Kavros graciously agreed to review Joseph Bartholomey's psychiatric records and help me understand the terminology and concepts, both in the context of his time and now.

Librarians and archivists are incredible people. On this project, I owe my thanks to Aaron Horner, Ian Post, and the staff at the Edward H. Nabb Research Center for Delmarva History and Culture at Salisbury University, Tisha Chakraborty at Salisbury branch of Wicomico County Library, and Trevaughn Booker at the Maryland State Archives. With regard to archival photographs and images, I appreciate the help I received from Doug McQuirter at the Hagley Museum and Library, Ken Jones at the Baltimore Museum of Industry, Ian Post and Creston Long at the Edward H. Nabb Research Center, and Drew Culbertson of Imagn Images. My wife and IT guru, Patty Gregorio helped me re-create the blueprint of the jail and took photos of the jail in May 2021.

I consulted with Keith Cunningham of the Nanticoke Language Project about local Indigenous words and translations. He and Jennifer Kerby kindly answered my emails and I owe many thanks to the Nanticoke Indian Tribe.

There were several folks who sat for interviews and/or offered tidbits of information along the way: Cindy Bennett, Anne Collins, Joan Cooper, Aggie Culp, Gemma Hoskins, A. Kaye Kenney, Tommy Lewis, Rick Pollitt, Tony Sarbanes, and Sue Sherwood.

Writing is lonely work and writers need community in order to figure out what we're doing. I am lucky to have a circle of friends who are talented writers (and inexhaustible cheerleaders) in their own right. They read early drafts of this book and provided me with solid feedback. I appreciate each of them more than they know: Dr. Benjamin Beck, Joan Cooper, Andrew Heller, Dr. Clara L. Small, and Tony Russo. This book and I have benefited greatly from their kindness and honesty.

One of the most important relationships a writer can have is with a professional editor and I found that in Tarah Threadgill. Her editing work on the first major draft was indispensable; I am grateful for our relationship and for her sharp, technical eyes. I knew from the beginning that she was the right fit and *Into the Night* is a better book because of her efforts.

And, in closing, my greatest thanks will always be to my family.

First, I want to acknowledge my late grandfather, Delbert "Bud" Fowler, for letting me interview him about what he experienced that night. As I was writing this book, I often wished I could go back and talk to him once again.

My family is my greatest source of love and strength. I would not be the writer I am without them. My mother, Jacki, is an endless well of determination who nudges me along when I am pokey. (And I am often pokey.) My stepdad, Merrill, always offers kind words of support and encouragement to me about my writing. My little sister, Kristen, believes in me even when I struggle to have faith in myself. And my wife, Patty, is the greatest love of my life and I have no idea how I'd do any of this without her. I owe her everything. Of course, no section on thanking my family would be complete without giving praise to our sweet dog, Lima, who warms my feet while I write. What a pal.

– SOURCES AND SELECT BIBLIOGRAPHY –

For this book, I had access to a number of books, periodicals, newspaper articles, interviews, court records, photographs, maps, and other research materials.

<u>Primary Sources:</u>

My initial FOIA request to Charles County Circuit Court allowed me to obtain a copy of the entire trial transcript for Bartholomey's 1969 murder trial as well as copies of items submitted into evidence including autopsy drawings, two days of jails logs, a blueprint of the jail and sheriff's quarters, and Bartholomey's psychiatric and medical records. Other FOIA requests to Wicomico County allowed me to have access to copies of Bartholomey's appeals and post-conviction paperwork. A FOIA request to Howard County Circuit Court provided me with documents related to Donna Blair Campbell's case; my request to the Maryland State Archives afforded me docket entries for Campbell as well. These documents were extraordinarily helpful in building timelines and understanding key elements. Without these documents, this would have been a short story.

I was fortunate to be able to take two tours of the old penthouse prison and the sheriff's quarters. I took photographs and video on my second trip. I also stopped by Crownsville State Hospital and snapped several photos and videos on my cell phone before a security guard ran me off. I referred to these photos and videos often during the writing of this book.

I was able to obtain my grandfather's military records from the National Personnel Records Center at the National Archives and I had copies of Fowler family genealogy. Tim Robinson also provided me with several original documents from the sheriff's department related to both my grandfather and Sam Graham. Mike Lewis allowed me to make copies of the original signature books from Sam Graham's funeral. For information on Austin Jacob Allen Davidson, I scoured his social media profiles.

Databases and Archives:

It would be impossible to list every single newspaper article I read for this book as there are literally hundreds of them; however, I have listed many of them later in this section. To access these articles, I used newspapers.com as my resource, especially for *Baltimore Sun* and the *Daily Times*, two primary papers for this case. The *Salisbury News and Advertiser* articles mentioning Frederick Douglass's visit to the courthouse were sent to me by Ian Post from the Edward H. Nabb Research Center at Salisbury University

I used ancestry.com to get census data as well as birth and death records, marriage dates, family connections, draft cards, and grave locations. For obituaries, I used newspapers.com. I often checked locations on the Maryland Real Property Search website.

Visits to the Salisbury branch of the Wicomico County Library and the Edward H. Nabb Research Center proved fruitful to me. I found pertinent information in old phone directories, yearbooks, and maps. With regard to libraries and online databases, the Edward H. Nabb Research Center had several digital collections that were helpful as well as the United States Library of Congress Prints and Photographs Online Catalog and the online Maryland State Archives. At times, I would review a subject on wikipedia.com to look for additional references.

Interviews and Correspondences:

- Bozick, Christine "Chris". Personal interview. June 2025.
- Cooper, Joan. Personal correspondence. 2025.
- Cunningham, Keith. Personal correspondence. 2025.
- Engler, Margaret "Maggie". Personal interview. June 2025.
- Fowler, Delbert "Bud". Personal interview. August 2010.
- Hoskins, Gemma. Personal interviews and correspondences. 2024.
- Kavros, Peregrine. Multiple correspondences. 2025.
- Kelley, Margaret. Personal Interview. May 2025.
- Lewis, Michael "Mike." Personal interview and follow-up correspondences. May 2021 through 2025.
- Lewis, Thomas. Personal interview. January 2023.
- Moore, Joseph E. Personal interviews and follow-up correspondence. March 2022 through September 2025.
- Pollitt, Richard "Rick". Personal interview. December 2022.
- Robinson, Timothy "Tim." Personal interview and follow-up correspondences. May 2021 through 2025.
- Sarbanes, Anthony "Tony." Personal interview. December 2022.
- Sherwood, Sue. Personal interview. March 2023.

Books and Documentaries

American Psychiatric Association. *Diagnostic and Statistical Manual of Mental Disorders.* 5-TR. American Psychiatric Association, 2013.

Chavis, Charles L. *The Silent Shore: The Lynching of Matthew Williams and the Politics of Racism in the Free State.* Johns Hopkins University Press, 2021.

Cooper, Richard W. *Portrait of Salisbury, Maryland Thru the 1900s: The Places, the Faces, and the Times.* Gateway Press, Inc., 1994.

---. *Salisbury in Times Gone By.* Gateway Press, Inc., 1991.

Corddry, George H. *Wicomico County History.* Peninsula Press, 1981.

Devincent Hayes, Gianni, and Andy Nunez. *Salisbury Maryland: Picturing the Crossroads of the Delmarva.* History Press Library Editions, 2010.

Fishman, Joseph F. *Crucibles of Crime: The Shocking Story of the American Jail.* Cosmopolis Press, 1923.

Hylton, Antonia. *Madness: Race and Insanity in a Jim Crow Asylum.* First edition, Legacy Lit, 2024.

Moore, Joseph E. *Murder on Maryland's Eastern Shore: Race, Politics and the Case of Orphan Jones.* History Press, 2006.

Small, Clara L. *Compass Points: Profiles and Biographies of African Americans from the Delmarva Peninsula, Volume 4*. Salt Water Media, 2025.

Stevens, Todd. *Crownsville Hospital: From Lunacy to Legacy*. 2018. (A documentary film.)

Truitt, Charles J. *Historic Salisbury Updated: 1662-1982*. First, Historical Books, Inc, 1982.

Selected Newspaper Articles and Online Sources

Alder, Caroline. "'Flawed from the Inception': 167 Years of Maltreatment at the Charles H. Hickey Jr. School." *Maryland Law Review Online* 83, no. 65 (2023).

Althouse, Kitty. "'Quiet Here' Jailer Said to Wife Sunday." *Daily Times*, December 10, 1968.

American Correctional Association for the Commission to Study the Correctional System of Maryland. "A Study of Maryland State Department of Correction," 1966.

Baltimore Evening Sun. "2 Officials Go before Jury." February 25, 1969.

———. "Jury Exonerates Training School in Cruelty Case." August 28, 1951.

———. "Let Them Be Punished." December 2, 1968.

———. "Murder Suspect's Treatment Urged." April 8, 1971.

———. "The Investigation." December 14, 1968.

———. "The Jails." November 20, 1968.

———. "The Prison's Role." December 10, 1968.

———. "The Shore Jails." November 25, 1968.

Baltimore Sun. "Body of Boy Found; Police Hold Youth." April 7, 1971.

———. "FBI Searching for Escaped Mental Case." April 8, 1961.

———. "Local Matters - Frederick Douglass." February 24, 1880.

———. "Neighbor, 15, Charged with Boy's Murder." April 8, 1971.

———. "Newspaper, Sheriff Row." September 5, 1956.

———. "Patients Help to Build." December 27, 1912.

———. "Poland given Children's Post." February 22, 1959.

———. "Police Hunting 4-Year-Old Boy." April 6, 1971.

———. "Salisbury Lynching." May 27, 1898.

———. "Superintendent Faulkner Invites Investigation." November 13, 1919.

———. "The Salisbury Fire - a Maryland Town in Ashes - Estimated Loss One Million Dollars." October 19, 1886.

Bureau of Justice Statistics. "Correctional Institutions." Bureau of Justice Statistics, 2023. https://bjs.ojp.gov/topics/corrections/correctional-institutions.

Butcher, Charles. "Racial Problems at Cheltenham, Ca. February 1943." umass.edu. University of Massachusetts Amherst, Richard S. Cox Special Collections and University Archives Research Center, 2025.

Carson, Larry. "Review of Death Row Cases to Take Several Months." *Baltimore Evening Sun*, May 6, 1971.

CB. "When Club One Was the House of Welsh." Blogspot.com. Blogger, December 4, 2011. http://baltimoreskyline.blogspot.com/2011/12/when-club-one-was-house-of-welsh.html.

CBS News. "New Revelations from the Nixon Tapes." *CBS News*, July 27, 2014.

Cechini, Han. "Jury Hears from Witnesses, Sees Body Camera Footage in Day Two of Cpl. Glenn Hilliard Murder Trial - 47abc." *47 ABC*, May 2, 2023. wmdt.com.

Center for the Study of Social Policy. "Recognizing Race in Language: Why We Capitalize 'Black' and 'White' - Center for the Study of Social Policy." Center for the Study of Social Policy, March 23, 2020.

Cleveland Clinic. "PANDAS Syndrome: What It Is, Causes, Symptoms & Treatment." Cleveland Clinic, 2022. https://my.clevelandclinic.org/health/diseases/23553-pandas-syndrome.

Cumberland News. "New Maximum Security Hospital Rates with the Best." January 21, 1960.

Daily Times. "'Hot Line' to Be Installed at County Jail." January 15, 1969.

———. "'Well Done Good, Faithful Servant,' Sam Eulogized." December 12, 1968.

———. "28 for Sure ... For Turkey Feast." November 24, 1966.

———. "44 Grabbed by Police in Resort Drugs' Raid." May 27, 1968.

———. "Bob Simpson Is Running for County Sheriff." May 27, 1966.

———. "Carey Is Name [Sic] to Succeed Graham Here." December 26, 1968.

———. "County Council Names Walston 'Jail Warden.'" December 11, 1968.

———. "County Shocked beyond Belief over Slayings." December 9, 1968.

———. "Court House Closed for Kelly Rites." December 12, 1968.

———. "Courthouse Closed for Graham Rites." December 11, 1968.

———. "Forfeits on Drug Smuggling in Jail." April 29, 1967.

———. "Girl Receives Suspended Term in Escape Case." July 8, 1970.

———. "Grand Jury Recalled for Jail Slayings." December 11, 1968.

———. "Here and There." October 18, 1968.

———. "Inspector Is Critical of Wicomico County Jail." January 29, 1969.

———. "Jail Inspector Glad to Talk to Grand Jury." December 11, 1968.

———. "Jail Visiting Hours Cut to Two a Week." February 12, 1969.

———. "Man Arraigned in Turnkey, Sheriff Deaths." January 3, 1969.

———. "Man Is given Life in Death of Two Here." January 17, 1973.

———. "Mitchell Seeks Sheriff's Post on GOP Ticket." July 6, 1966.

———. "More Security Measures Are Made at County Jail." March 23, 1969.

———. "New Security Screen Being Put in Jail." January 23, 1969.

———. "Night Patrols in County Termed Crime Deterrent." June 28, 1967.

———. "Officer Keeping Watch over Cemetery in Delmar." April 21, 1968.

———. "One Indictment Returned by Wicomico Jury." March 12, 1968.

———. "People Patter." November 6, 1970.

———. "Police Killer Here Is off Death Row." June 25, 1976.

———. "Sam Graham Seeks Return as Sheriff Here." May 4, 1966.

———. "Sheriff Rejects Jail Apartment." January 17, 1969.

———. "Silent Prayers for Sheriff Here Open City Council." December 10, 1968.

———. "State Prison Official under Fire by Panel." February 25, 1969.

———. "Suspect Shot after Police Scuffle Here." May 19, 1968.

———. "The New Sheriff." December 27, 1968.

———. "The Regional Jail." December 1, 1968.

———. "Worcester Summons Two Jail Officials." January 31, 1969.

———. "Youth Arraigned in Robbery Here." December 12, 1968.

Duyer, Linda. "Salisbury's Slave Pens." Delmarva African American History, December 2, 2013. https://aahistorydelmarva.wordpress.com/2013/12/02/salisburys-slave-pens/.

Every Evening and Commercial. "Eastern Shore Items." June 20, 1877.

Ewing, Eve L. "I'm a Black Scholar Who Studies Race. Here's Why I Capitalize 'White.'" ZORA. *Medium*, July 2, 2020.

Fitzgerald, Gerald A. "Tragedy Shocks Neighborhood." *Baltimore Sun*, April 8, 1971.

Frank, Cooper. "Man Gets 10 Years for Aiding Slayer Escape." *Daily Times*, January 13, 1970.

Gaffney, Pete, and Larry K. Martin. "Fugitive Nabbed in 2 Jail Killings." *Evening Journal*, December 9, 1968.

Gates, Deborah. "Black Schools Gone, but Not Forgotten on Lower Shore." *The Daily Times*, February 27, 2016.

Geiselman, Jr., A. W. "Fee System at Two Eastern Shore Jails Provides $1 a Day for Inmate's Food." *Baltimore Sun*, November 20, 1968.

———. "Md. Inspector Doesn't like What He Sees, Assails 'Purely Warehousing Operations.'" *Baltimore Sun*, November 22, 1968.

———. "Police Lock-Ups Are Often Zoo-like with Filth, Poor Facilities, No Guards." *Baltimore Sun*, November 26, 1968.

———. "Prisoners Sometimes Not Extended Guarantees against Excessive Bail." *Baltimore Sun*, November 25, 1968.

———. "Some Eastern Shore Jails Crowded, Lack Inmate Care Programs; Many Are Dirty." *Baltimore Sun*, November 18, 1968.

———. "When Somerset Jailer, Wife Go out Their Relatives Watch the Prisoners." *Baltimore Sun*, November 21, 1968.

———. "Young Children, Teen-Agers Are Held with Adults in Eastern Shore Jails." *Baltimore Sun*, November 19, 1968.

guide.msa.maryland.gov. "Maryland State Archives - Guide to Government Records," n.d. https://guide.msa.maryland.gov/pages/history.aspx?ID=SH246.

Hanst, George. "Youth Who Killed Boy given Maximum Term." *Baltimore Evening Sun*, June 2, 1973.

Hiltner, George J. "Youth, 17, Is Legally Sane, Faces Trial in Killing of Boy." *Baltimore Sun*, April 25, 1973.

Jaime, Kristian. "Hilliard Shooter Gets Life without Parole in Slaying of the Wicomico Deputy." *The Daily Times*, July 6, 2023.

Jones, Natalie. "Delmar Man Charged in Shooting of Wicomico Deputy Faces Murder, Gun Charges." *The Star Democrat*, July 3, 2022.

Kugiya, Hugo. "37 Men Sue State over Allegations of Sex Abuse at Juvenile Justice School." *The Baltimore Banner*, December 13, 2023.

Long, Sr., Joseph J. "Dorothy Graham Was Outstanding Educator." *Daily Times*, July 31, 2002.

Lundquist, John. "Labor Program Keep Idle Hands Busy in State Prisons." *Salisbury Times*, December 10, 1958.

Mack, Kristen, and John Palfrey. "Capitalizing Black and White: Grammatical Justice and Equity." www.macfound.org, August 26, 2020.

Manchester, William. "Cruelty Charged at Training School; Supervisor Denies It, Invites Probe." *Baltimore Evening Sun*, June 29, 1951.

———. "School Charges Grow; Slander Suits Filed." *Baltimore Evening Sun*, July 5, 1951.

Mann, Alex. "Haunting Hospital Memorial Reveals Lives Once Hidden in Crownsville Graves." *The Baltimore Banner*, September 4, 2025.

Marquardt, Tom. "Tragic Chapter of Crownsville State Hospital's Legacy." *Capital Gazette*, June 13, 2013.

Maryland Department of Health. "Clifton T. Perkins Hospital - History." maryland.gov, 2019. https://health.maryland.gov/perkins/Pages/History.aspx.

Maryland Historical Trust. "WI-12 Wicomico County Courthouse." *Maryland Inventory of Historic Properties*. Maryland Department of Planning, Maryland Historical Trust, August 29, 2003. https://apps.mht.maryland.gov/medusa/PDF/Wicomico/WI-12.pdf.

———. "WI-571 Powellville Survey District." *Maryland Inventory of Historic Properties*. Maryland Department of Planning, Maryland Historical Trust, August 29, 2003. https://apps.mht.maryland.gov/medusa/PDF/Wicomico/WI-571.pdf.

Maryland Lynching Memorial Project. "Lynchings in Maryland." Maryland Lynching Memorial Project, 2024. https://www.mdlynchingmemorial.org/lynchings-in-maryland.

Maryland State Archives. "Biographies - Mary L. Nock." Maryland.gov, 2020.

———. "Black Baltimore 1870-1920, H.J. Brown, Maryland State Archives." Maryland.gov, 2001.

———. "Mary L. Nock , MSA SC 3520-12321." Maryland.gov, 2025.

McGarvie, Susan. "Attachment Theory, Bowlby's Stages & Attachment Styles." Positive Psychology, November 28, 2024. https://positivepsychology.com/attachment-theory/.

Meise, Mike. "Grand Jury Back for Jail Slayings." *Daily Times*, December 19, 1968.

———. "Hundreds of Mourners Visit Bier of Sheriff." *Daily Times*, December 11, 1968.

———. "Prisoners Held in Major Crimes Keep Jail Bulging." *Daily Times*, January 6, 1967.

———. "Prisoners to Get Big Meal Even Though Sam Graham's Gone." *Daily Times*, December 24, 1968.

———. "Weather Could Be a Factor in Voting Here." *Daily Times*, November 2, 1970.

Mettler, Katie. "Maryland's Max-Security Psych Hospital Denied Accreditation after Inspection." *The Washington Post*, April 10, 2025.

Moore, Dick, ed. "Editor's Scratch Pad." *Daily Times*, September 15, 1965.

Nall, Rachel. "How Much Blood Is in Your Body and How Much You Can Lose." *Healthline*. Healthline Media, July 18, 2017.

Nelson, Jim. "It's Lunch Time Again at Jail Here for Jurors." *Salisbury Times*, March 18, 1964.

Nixonlibrary.gov. "719 | Richard Nixon Museum and Library." National Archives and Records Administration, n.d. https://www.nixonlibrary.gov/white-house-tapes/719.

Norton, Howard M. "Maryland's Shame: The Worst Story Ever Told by the Sunpapers." *Baltimore Sun*, January 9, 1949.

Parker, Susan. "Maryland Celebrates Shore Native Frederick Douglass' 200th Birthday." *The Daily Times*, February 16, 2018.

Poland, Alan B., and Ruth Todd. "Police Nab Suspect in 2 Jail Slayings." *Morning News*, December 10, 1968.

Post, Ian. "Library Guides: Lynchings on Maryland's Lower Eastern Shore: Matthew Williams and Unknown, 1931." libraryguides.salisbury.edu, September 6, 2022.

Powell, Libby. "MCI Graduation Rites: A Day Not Easily Forgotten." *Morning Herald*, May 28, 1974.

Radoff, Morris L., ed. "Maryland Manual 1965-1966." Hall of Records, Annapolis, Maryland: The Hall of Records Commission, 1966.

Roemer, Leah. "'I Just Wanted…to Stay Alive': Who Was William Henry Furman, the Prisoner at the Center of a Historic Legal Decision?" Death Penalty Information Center, May 15, 2024.

Salisbury News and Advertiser. "Lecture Will Be Given." February 21, 1880.

———. "Marshal Douglass' Lecture." February 28, 1880.

Salisbury Times. "3 Youths Captured after Escape Here." December 20, 1951.

———. "A Matter of Trust." July 23, 1959.

———. "Attempt to Escape Jail Is Thwarted." December 2, 1929.

———. "Boys Re-Bury Woman's Skull." April 18, 1958.

———. "Corner's [Sic] Jury to Investigate Slayer's Death." December 5, 1931.

314 — INTO THE NIGHT

———. "County Jails Criticized in State Report." January 30, 1932.

———. "County Prisoners Face Work Details." October 12, 1960.

———. "December 1 Is Set as Date for Completion Court House Addition." September 3, 1936.

———. "Dedication of Court House Is Set for Feb. 27." February 11, 1937.

———. "Discharged Jail Turnkey Campaigns for GOP Sheriff." November 22, 1956.

———. "Former Deputy Gets in Race for Sheriff." February 3, 1958.

———. "Graham Is New Deputy Sheriff." September 8, 1949.

———. "Grand Jury Recall Considered in Wicomico County Jail Ruckus." October 6, 1964.

———. "Hundreds at Court House Dedication." February 27, 1937.

———. "Injured Gridder Stirs Rhubarb at Football Tilt Here." November 29, 1962.

———. "Kennedy's Visit to Maryland Nets Party $165,000." September 17, 1960.

———. "Kids Free Dogs, Sheriff Moves to Prevent It." August 14, 1959.

———. "Libel Suits against the Times Dismissed." March 21, 1957.

———. "Man, 81, Held Here in Murder of His Wife, 69." February 28, 1952.

———. "Maryland Sheriff's Assn. Hold Meeting in Salisbury." June 27, 1960.

———. "Modern New Penthouse Jail Ready." February 2, 1937.

———. "Now Jail Is Closed to News Reporters." August 21, 1956.

———. "Prison Produced Products Double within Ten Years." December 9, 1958.

———. "Prisoner Rushed to Hospital, Claiming He Ate Razor Blades." July 28, 1951.

———. "Prisoner Who Cut Wrist Hospitalized." November 18, 1960.

———. "Prisoners Escape, Commit Thefts, Return to Jail Here with Loot." March 2, 1955.

———. "Report Says Wicomico Jail Needs Cleaning." April 2, 1959.

———. "Riot Quelled at MD. Prison." October 24, 1964.

———. "Sheriff Graham Asks 2nd Term." January 24, 1962.

———. "Sheriff's Bullet Ends Independence Day Observance at Jail." July 6, 1959.

———. "Talk of Candidates Begins to Simmer in Wicomico County." January 16, 1954.

———. "Three Deputies Named on Deer Hunting Charge." November 16, 1956.

———. "Times Covered Wagon Contest Impels Interest - History of Salisbury Weaves in and out among Outstanding Dates." October 14, 1924.

———. "Two Officers Are Indicted County Jury." September 13, 1928.

———. "Two Resist Arrests by Dry Agents." October 19, 1931.

———. "W. W. Travers, Attorney and Miss Heath Are Wedded; Guarded Plans from Friends." June 28, 1934.

SOURCES AND SELECT BIBLIOGRAPHY — 315

———. "What We Have Been Missing." April 11, 1959.

———. "Wicomico County Sheriff Brings Suit against the Times." November 22, 1956.

———. "Wicomico PTA Meets, Names Committees." October 4, 1933.

Salisbury University-Nabb Research Center Online Exhibits. "Mary Layfield Nock (1903-1987) · Voices and Votes: Democracy on Delmarva · Nabb Research Center Online Exhibits." Salisbury.edu, 2025.

Sayles, Megan. "Graves of Imprisoned Black Children Inspire Reform in Maryland." *AFRO American Newspapers*, September 27, 2025.

Scarborough, Walt. "Two Are Arrested in Robbery Series." *Daily Times*, November 22, 1968.

Scharfenberg, Kirk. "Fugitive Seized through Friend." *Baltimore Sun*, December 10, 1968.

Schnittker, Jason, Savannah H. Larimore, and Hedwig Lee. "Neither Mad nor Bad? The Classification of Antisocial Personality Disorder among Formerly Incarcerated Adults." *Social Science & Medicine* 264 (November 2020).

Segelbaum, Dylan, and Cody Boteler. "Ex-Maryland Juvenile Detention Center Employee Charged with Sexually Abusing 6 Boys." *The Baltimore Banner*, March 28, 2025.

Skene, Lea. "Thousands Allege Sexual Abuse in Youth Detention Centers. It Could Cost Maryland a Huge Sum." *The Baltimore Banner*, March 21, 2025.

St. Louis Post-Dispatch. "Schooling in Prison Gives Convicts a New Outlook." June 10, 1979.

Swift, Tim. "Man Accused of Killing Deputy Was out on Light Sentence for Baltimore Crime, Sheriff Says." *WBFF*, June 13, 2022.

Tawes, David. "A History of the Wicomico County Sheriff's Office," July 26, 1995.

The Citizen. "Montevue to Lose Patients." May 26, 1911.

The News. "Supreme Court Spares 23 Maryland Prisoners." June 30, 1972.

Toadvine, Mel. "Police Pick up Man and Girl in Dual Killing." *Daily Times*, December 10, 1968.

———. "Sheriff Graham Resents Outmoded Report on Jail." *Daily Times*, December 8, 1968.

———. "Sheriff Graham, Deputy Slain; Jail Escapee Here Recaptured." *Daily Times*, December 9, 1968.

USA Today. "The Chaotic Year That Transformed the Nation." 2019.

Wagner, Peter. "Racial Disparities in the 'Great Migration' to Prison." Prison Policy Initiative. Upstate Prison Response, October 7, 2001.

Waters, Lloyd. "MCI: A Stone Castle with Many Stories." *The Herald-Mail*, January 28, 2017.

Wintrode, Brenda. "Maryland Lawmakers Seek to Honor Black Children Buried in Unmarked Graves." *The Baltimore Banner*, September 24, 2025.

Woodfield, John. "Death Penalty in Slaying of Sheriff Upheld." *Daily Times*, February 3, 1971.

Woodruff, John E. "Beating Case Under Probe." *Baltimore Sun*, March 19, 1966.

Wootten, Orlando V. "Police, Officials Pay Honor to Slain Turnkey." *Daily Times*, December 13, 1968.

———. "Prison Inspector Faces Worcester Jury's Probe." *Daily Times*, December 10, 1968.

– INDEX –

A

Adamo, Ido 210, 212, 247, 248
Addison, James 209, 210, 211, 213, 250, 257
adjustment reaction of adolescence 117
adjustment reaction of adolescence (severe) 93
Agnew, Spiro 106, 154, 177, 189, 200, 201, 205, 215, 242
Allen 47, 183
Allen Memorial Baptist Church 33
Annapolis 39, 108, 111, 121
Anne Arundel County 58
antisocial personality disorder 85, 117, 125, 126, 251, 252, 256, 283, 284, 285
antisocial personality disorder with drug dependence 246, 249, 250, 251, 259
antisocial personality disorder with drug dependence (severe) 213, 246
Arbutus 89
Arbutus Junior High School 76
Asbury Methodist Episcopal Church 33
Atlantic Ocean 5, 65, 150

B

Bailey, Levin C. 36
Baker, John W. 289
Baltimore 13, 14, 26, 37, 59, 67, 72, 73, 74, 75, 76, 78, 79, 81, 87, 88, 107, 108, 116, 120, 121, 140, 144, 146, 149, 150, 151, 161, 162, 164, 165, 182, 187, 197, 205, 206, 207, 215, 216, 229, 261, 267, 269, 271, 273, 292, 293, 295
Baltimore City College 216
Baltimore City Police Department 274, 290
Baltimore County 84, 88
Baltimore Museum of Industry 82
  BG&E Print and Negative Collection 82
Baltimore Sun 9, 18, 37, 50, 80, 81, 83, 84, 89, 111, 113, 121, 137, 161, 163, 165, 187, 197, 199, 274, 275
Bartholomey, Betty Lou Marsh 74, 75, 87, 88, 89, 90, 92, 95, 118, 123, 139, 140, 228, 229, 241

Bartholomey, Dolores Miller 67, 68, 69, 70, 71, 72, 73, 74, 75, 87, 88, 91, 92, 107, 108, 114, 115, 116, 117, 118, 122, 123, 125, 139, 207, 212, 223, 224, 227, 228, 230, 232, 256, 260, 274, 275, 276, 279, 280, 284
Bartholomey, Ethan Lyle 73, 74, 107, 125, 139, 224, 227, 230, 274, 275, 276, 279, 280, 281, 283, 296
Bartholomey, Joseph James, Sr. iii, 67, 68, 69, 70, 71, 72, 73, 74, 75, 87, 88, 89, 92, 95, 118, 123, 139, 140, 207, 223, 229, 232
Bartholomey, Joseph "Jimmy" James, Jr. i, ii, iii, 3, 67, 68, 69, 70, 71, 72, 73, 74, 75, 76, 77, 78, 84, 85, 86, 87, 88, 89, 90, 91, 92, 93, 94, 95, 107, 108, 113, 114, 115, 116, 117, 118, 120, 121, 122, 123, 124, 125, 126, 127, 136, 137, 138, 139, 140, 150, 151, 154, 155, 156, 161, 164, 168, 171, 172, 173, 174, 175, 177, 178, 179, 180, 181, 182, 183, 187, 188, 192, 202, 204, 205, 206, 207, 208, 209, 210, 211, 212, 213, 214, 215, 216, 217, 218, 219, 220, 221, 223, 224, 225, 226, 227, 228, 229, 230, 231, 232, 233, 234, 235, 236, 238, 239, 240, 241, 242, 243, 244, 245, 246, 247, 248, 249, 250, 251, 253, 254, 255, 256, 257, 258, 259, 260, 261, 262, 263, 267, 268, 269, 270, 271, 272, 275, 276, 277, 278, 279, 282, 283, 284, 285, 287, 288, 295, 296, 299, 300, 301, 302
Bartholomey, Leona 67, 68, 70, 71, 75, 76, 77, 87, 92, 223, 228, 231, 232
Bartholomey, Michael 67, 68, 70, 71, 75, 76, 77, 87, 92, 223, 228
Bartholomey, Shirley 67, 68, 69, 70, 71, 73, 74, 107, 115, 118, 123, 125, 139, 223, 229, 230, 242, 260, 274, 275, 276
Berlin 37, 52, 141, 294
Berlin Police Department 290
Betts, Marie 69

INDEX - 317

Bivalve 34, 56
Boolukas, Peter 186, 217, 218, 221
Booth, John Wilkes 68, 214, 235, 282
Boulevard TV and Radio Service 155
Bowlby, John 296
Boys Village at Cheltenham 81, 86
Bradford, Norman H. 239, 240
Brown, Arthur 38
Brown, Henry J. 13, 14
Brown, Johnnie 148, 261, 278
Brown v. Board of Education 61, 147
Burkhardt, Robert W. 175, 182, 188, 221, 222
Burnett, George F. 128
Burnett, K. King 206
Butz, E. M. 9
Byrd, John 12
Byrd's Tavern 10, 12

C

Cambridge 96, 97, 111, 163, 185
Campbell, Donna Blair 150, 151, 154, 155, 156, 178, 187, 188, 203, 204, 205, 210, 211, 227, 230, 231, 255, 267, 269, 270, 271, 272
Capital City Motel 177, 179, 221
Carey, Eugene McLaughlin 200, 201, 202, 203, 267, 289
Caroline County 162
Catholicism 7, 67, 71, 74, 76, 95, 122, 197, 215, 227, 275
Catonsville 59, 108, 109, 111
Cecil County 17
Chaffey, Samuel Reed, Jr. 175, 186, 188, 218, 219, 221, 222
Charles County 214, 215, 216, 217, 270
Charles County Courthouse 214
Charles Hickey School 299. See also Maryland Training School for Boys
Chavis, Charles L. Jr. 39, 40
Chesapeake Bay 5, 165
Chesapeake Bay Bridge 150
Chesapeake College 268
Chestertown 17, 162
Children's Aid Society 75
Chincoteague Island, Virginia 129

Chipman, Charles H. 190
Chipman Cultural Center 13
Chipman, Jeanette 190
Chlan, Edward S. 274, 275, 276
Cleveland, Grover 30
Clifton T. Perkins State Hospital 120, 121, 122, 123, 124, 125, 126, 127, 136, 139, 167, 207, 208, 209, 210, 211, 213, 226, 232, 235, 238, 240, 246, 247, 248, 249, 251, 255, 256, 257, 258, 259, 267, 284, 299, 300
cocaine (coke) 121, 140, 151, 154, 208, 210, 226
Colson, Charles 282
Commercial Personal Loan Company 22, 25
Communism/Communist(s) 37, 226, 228, 233, 234, 235, 236, 237, 238, 241, 242, 243, 245, 247, 248, 256, 282
conduct disorder 93, 94, 117, 285
Conley, James 48
Coppin State College / Coppin State University 282, 283
Corddry, George 146
Courts
    Central Municipal Court of Baltimore 275
    Circuit Court of Baltimore County 118
    Circuit Court of Charles County 215, 278
    Circuit Court of Howard County 270, 271
    Circuit Court of Wicomico County 26, 27, 55, 61, 267, 287, 294
    Circuit Court of Worcester County 119, 198
    Court of Special Appeals of Maryland 288
    Criminal Court of Baltimore City 107, 279
    First Judicial Circuit Court 33, 204, 288, 289
    Juvenile Court of Baltimore 88, 89, 93
    Orphan's Court in Somerset County 47
    Peoples Court of Wicomico County 32, 133, 182
    Supreme Court of Maryland 86
    Supreme Court of the United States 277
Crisfield 6, 7, 152
Crisfield, John W. 11
Crisfield Times 50
Crownsville 108
Crownsville State Hospital 58, 67, 107, 108, 109, 110, 111, 112, 113, 114, 115, 116, 117, 118, 119, 120, 123, 124, 136, 227,

233, 235, 237, 238, 240, 250, 258, 259, 298, 299
Crucibles of Crime: The Shocking Story of the American Jail 16
Cunningham, Keith 11, 20

D

Daily Times 104, 106, 129, 131, 133, 153, 154, 156, 160, 161, 164, 165, 166, 181, 182, 183, 184, 185, 187, 190, 194, 198, 201, 202, 203, 204, 287
Dallas, Robert 182
Dashiell, Donald Leon 33, 34, 36, 40, 41, 142, 171, 172, 173, 174, 219
Davidson, Austin Jacob Allen ii, 290, 291, 292, 293, 294, 295, 296
Delaware 5, 9, 177, 179, 180, 193, 210, 220, 221
Delaware State Police 179, 195, 222
Delmar 42, 99, 133, 153, 290
Delmarva Peninsula 5, 9, 16, 32, 33, 46, 104, 134, 146, 149, 178, 186, 193
Democrat 46, 47, 55, 62, 104, 105, 106, 153, 154, 186, 215, 216, 233, 236, 237, 238
Diagnostic and Statistical Manual of Mental Disorders (DSM) 93, 94, 126, 284
Digges, J. Dudley 215, 216, 219, 220, 221, 222, 223, 224, 226, 227, 229, 230, 231, 236, 239, 245, 246, 252, 253, 254, 255, 256, 259, 260, 261, 262, 263
Disharoon, Albert L. 155, 156
D.J. Elliott Crate and Basket 35
Dorchester County 33, 163
Douglass, Frederick 13, 14, 15, 23, 38
Dover, Delaware 177, 179, 182, 210, 220
Dover Police Department 179
Duer, E. McMaster 193, 204, 205, 261
Duffy, Ralph C. 19
Duffy, Thelma 193
Dykes, Emerson 51

E

Eastern Shore i, 10, 11, 14, 19, 20, 33, 37, 39, 56, 61, 102, 118, 140, 150, 153, 154, 161, 162, 163, 164, 165, 197, 198, 199, 205, 214, 215, 293, 295

Eastern Shore Public Service Company 61
Eastern Shore State Hospital 111
Easton 16, 21
East Salisbury Elementary School 42
Eden 47
Edgemere 73, 74
Edgemere Elementary School 74
Edward H. Nabb Research Center for Delmarva History and Culture at Salisbury University 8, 9, 17, 22, 24, 28, 29, 31, 32, 43, 53, 57, 97, 132, 134, 149, 191, 192, 202
Egeberg, Joseph D., Jr. 161, 162, 163, 164, 165, 166, 193, 197, 198, 199, 202, 203, 290
Eisenhower, Dwight D. 200
Elliott, Daniel J. 35, 36, 37
Elliott, James 36
Epstein's Department Store 73
Esquire Club 42
Essex 74, 139
Esther Loring Richards Children's Center 75
Evening Journal 180

F

FBI 45, 46, 121, 152
Ferndale Police Department 90
Fierst, Mack Wilson 121
Fishman, Joseph F. 16, 17, 18
Fletcher, Elbert L. 82, 83, 84
Fort Dodge, Iowa 1, 2, 129
Fourteen Holy Martyrs 76
Fowler, Delbert "Bud" Earl i, 1, 2, 3, 4, 129, 130, 131, 132, 154, 159, 161, 167, 168, 174, 176, 177, 189, 193, 219, 220, 289, 300
Fowler, Elizabeth "Libby" Mills 2, 3, 4, 129, 130, 131, 159, 176
Frederick 108
Fruitland 48, 101, 130, 201, 288
Furman, William Henry 277, 278
Furr, Emily 102, 103, 129, 153, 190

G

Garrity, James F. 215, 216, 217, 218, 219, 220,

221, 222, 223, 224, 226, 227, 228, 229, 230, 231, 232, 233, 234, 235, 236, 238, 239, 240, 241, 242, 243, 244, 245, 247, 248, 249, 250, 251, 252, 256, 257, 258, 259, 260, 261, 262
Geiselman, A. W., Jr. 161, 162, 163, 164, 165, 166
Gerstung, Robert J. 275, 276
Gladden, Herbert 194, 195, 196
Glenn L. Martin Aircraft Company Plant 68, 71, 73
Goldsborough, T. Alan 33
Gordy, John L. 104, 105
Gordy, Marvin 142
Gordy, William S. Jr. 33
Graham, Alphonso "Al Capone" 154, 155, 156, 205
Graham, Dorothy Holliday 3, 23, 24, 25, 26, 52, 57, 100, 130, 144, 146, 159, 174, 175, 176, 193, 220, 285, 286, 287, 294
Graham, Ella 21
Graham, George W. 21
Graham, John Tubman 21
Graham, Leah 21
Graham, Samuel "Sam" Adams i, ii, 3, 4, 20, 21, 22, 24, 25, 26, 27, 33, 41, 42, 43, 44, 45, 46, 47, 48, 52, 53, 55, 56, 57, 58, 59, 60, 61, 62, 96, 97, 98, 99, 100, 101, 102, 103, 104, 105, 106, 128, 129, 130, 131, 132, 133, 134, 135, 145, 152, 153, 156, 161, 162, 165, 166, 167, 168, 169, 171, 172, 173, 174, 175, 176, 182, 183, 184, 185, 186, 187, 188, 189, 190, 191, 192, 193, 194, 195, 196, 197, 198, 199, 200, 201, 204, 205, 207, 210, 215, 216, 217, 218, 219, 220, 222, 233, 234, 237, 238, 239, 253, 254, 256, 258, 261, 263, 267, 268, 282, 285, 286, 287, 288, 289, 290, 295, 300, 301
Gray, Mervin 138
Great Fire of 1886 8, 9, 27
Green Mount Cemetery 68
Gregorio, Patricia 170, 301, 302
Grier, Frederick A. 40
Groff, Stanislav 244, 245, 257
Guarino, John 147
Gunpowder Falls River 82

Gwynns Falls Leakin Park 121

H

Hagerstown 18, 99, 220, 280
Hagley Museum and Library 80
  Dallin Aerial Photography Collection 80
Haldeman, H. R. "Bob" 282
Hampden 72
Harmon, Ralph Anthony 171, 172, 219, 220
Harrington and Richardson 172, 188, 222, 300
Havre de Grace 90
Hebron 22, 23, 24, 25, 26, 46, 52
Hebron Elementary School 42
Hennessey, Kenneth 167, 171
Henry, Daniel Kenneth 53, 141, 147, 148, 149, 182
heroin 155
Herring Run Junior High School 275
Herring Run Park 273
Hilliard, Glenn R. ii, 290, 291, 292, 293, 294, 295
H. Lay Phillips Construction Company 142, 143, 145
Holland Island 33
Holland, Nicholas 40
Holliday, Edith Dashiell 23
Holliday, George 23
Holliday, Joshua Lee 23
Holliday, Linwood 23
Holloway Funeral Home 189, 193, 287
Hoover, J. Edgar 237, 282
Hopkins, John 68
Horsey, Vincent 171, 172, 173, 220
Hospital for the Negro Insane of Maryland 108. *See also* Crownsville State Hospital
House of Refuge 79. *See also* Maryland Training School for Boys
Hughes, Harry 288
Humphrey, Hubert 154
Humphrey's Lake 10, 15
Huston, Solomon T. 13, 14, 23
Hylton, Antonia 108, 115

I

Independent 62, 154

Iowa 1, 2, 129, 249, 275
Irwin, Erick Thomas 154, 155, 156, 177, 178, 179, 187, 188, 203, 204, 205, 208, 211, 220, 221, 261, 267, 268, 271

J

Jackson, Ethel Holliday 23, 24, 25
Jackson, Robert 24
Jefferson School of Commerce 155
Jessup 101, 120, 136, 207, 269
Johns Hopkins Hospital 26, 111, 274
Johns Hopkins University 224, 239, 244
Johnson, Andrew 214
Johnson, Benjamin A. 33
Johnson, Patsy 40, 41. *See also* Petta, Pasquale "Patrick" Anthony
John Wesley Methodist Episcopal Church 13. *See also* Chipman Cultural Center
Jones, Francis "Freddy" Grant 132, 133

K

Kaufman, Stephen H. 224, 225, 226, 227, 233, 240, 241, 242, 243, 244, 256, 257
Kellam, John 101
Kelly, Albert Lee i, ii, iii, 3, 4, 141, 142, 143, 144, 145, 169, 171, 172, 173, 174, 175, 176, 183, 186, 187, 188, 189, 194, 195, 196, 197, 199, 204, 205, 207, 215, 216, 217, 218, 219, 220, 222, 233, 234, 237, 238, 239, 253, 254, 256, 258, 261, 263, 267, 268, 282, 285, 290, 295, 300, 302
Kelly, Annie 141
Kelly, Henry P. 141
Kelly, Howard 141, 142, 143
Kelly/Kelley, Alvin Lee 142, 143, 144, 145
Kelly/Kelley, Bonnie 144, 169
Kelly/Kelley, Brian 144, 169
Kelly/Kelley, Margaret Palmer 144, 145, 196
Kelly, Milton 141, 143, 145
Kelly, Nellie Mae Shockley 142, 143, 144, 145, 169, 171, 195, 196
Kelly, Preston 40, 141, 143
Kelly, Ralph 19, 141, 143
Kennedy, Jackie 242
Kennedy, John F. Jr. 62, 146, 149
Kennedy, Robert F. 148, 149, 205, 213, 242
Kennedy, Ted 205
Kent County 163
Kent General Hospital 180
King, Garfield 35, 37, 41
King, Martin Luther, Jr. 146, 147, 148, 149

L

Lacks, Henrietta 110, 111
Lacks, Lucile Elsie Pleasant 110, 111
Lane, William Preston 113
Lee, Euel 37
LeMay, Curtis 154
Lewis, Arlie 142, 143
Lewis, Michael "Mike" 175, 290, 291, 293, 294, 300, 302
Lewis, Thomas "Tommy" 175, 176, 177, 190, 192, 193, 289
Lewis, William 132, 175, 176, 177, 193
Lincoln, Abraham 11, 214
Little, Charles 273, 275, 276
Little, Dwayne K. 273, 274, 275, 276, 280
Littleton, Charles 45, 46
Littleton, Mary 45, 46
Loch Raven 78, 79
Long, Joe 153, 287
LSD (acid) 140, 150, 151, 154, 155, 207, 209, 210, 226, 243, 244, 255, 257
lynch/lynching 35, 37, 38, 39, 40, 41, 147, 148

M

Madness: Race and Insanity in a Jim Crow Asylum 108
Malcolm X 146, 149
Mandel, Marvin 193, 287, 289
Manson, Charles 151, 213, 280
Mardela Springs 171, 183
marijuana (weed) 140, 150, 151, 155, 210, 292
Marine Police 194
Mars Super Market 87
Martin, W. Paul, Jr. 189
Maryland 4, 5, 10, 11, 14, 17, 19, 20, 30, 33, 39, 40, 45, 47, 50, 59, 60, 62, 67, 71, 78, 79, 89, 90, 98, 99, 106, 108, 109, 110, 111, 112, 113, 114, 118, 120, 121,

123, 136, 138, 139, 149, 153, 154, 155, 177, 178, 182, 185, 188, 189, 193, 197, 198, 200, 205, 214, 215, 216, 221, 230, 231, 242, 249, 253, 258, 268, 269, 279, 280, 282, 285, 288, 290, 292, 294, 299
Maryland Children's Center 89, 90, 91, 92, 93, 94, 117, 284, 299
Maryland Correctional Institution for Men 99, 220, 280
Maryland Correctional Institution for Women 230, 269
Maryland Cup Company 118, 122, 136
Maryland Department of Corrections 161, 163
Maryland House of Correction 30, 43, 58, 101, 120, 136, 137, 138, 139, 209, 269, 299. *See also* The Cut
Maryland Penitentiary 143, 182, 187, 205, 206, 207, 210, 213, 226, 232, 236, 240, 244, 261, 278, 282, 283
Maryland School for Boys 79. *See also* Maryland Training School for Boys
Maryland State Penal Farm 280. *See also* Maryland Correctional Institution for Men
Maryland State Police 45, 56, 58, 61, 99, 106, 121, 133, 137, 174, 175, 179, 182, 186, 187, 188, 194, 195, 218, 219, 220, 221, 222, 240, 290, 292
Maryland State Sheriffs' Association 60
Maryland Training School for Boys 44, 70, 78, 79, 80, 81, 82, 83, 84, 85, 86, 87, 89, 91, 92, 93, 94, 95, 107, 108, 123, 124, 167, 171, 211, 223, 229, 299, 300
Mason, Jerry R. 147, 148, 181, 182, 258
McDaniel College 23. *See also* Western Maryland College
McGill, James 270, 271
McKay, Ian 207, 208, 212
McKeldin, Theodore 216
Meise, Mike 190, 192, 194
Mel Toadvine Collection 22, 43, 53, 97, 191, 192, 202
Messick, Joyce 132
Methodist 7, 13, 20, 26, 33
Metropolitan Transition Center 182. *See also* Maryland Penitentiary

Michaels, Lou 153
Micke, William 277
Middle River 69, 71
Middlesex 88
Middlesex Elementary School 74
Miller, Charles 73, 74, 75
Miller, Eleanor 73, 74, 75
Mitchell, Edward Dempsey 51, 52, 53, 105, 106
Mitchell, James C. 278
Montevue Hospital 108
Moore, Dick 185
Mudd, Samuel 214
Muskie, Edmund 154

N

Nanticoke River 20, 34
Nelms, Hunter 289
Nelsons Memorial Church 26, 52, 194, 195
New Hope 141
Nixon, Richard M. 62, 154, 205, 226, 234, 235, 236, 237, 238, 241, 242, 256, 282
Nock, Mary 56, 62, 153, 193
Nock, Randolph 36
Norfolk, Virginia 35, 129
Norton, Howard M. 111, 112, 113

O

Oates, Reginald 121, 122
Ocean City 98, 118, 119, 124, 140, 149, 150, 155, 156, 230, 231, 234, 241, 255, 257, 293
Ocean City Police Department 290
Official Detective 50
Orient Hotel 30
Oswald, Lee Harvey 235
Owings Mills 111

P

PANDAS or Pediatric Autoimmune Neuropsychiatric Disorders Associated with Streptococcal Infections 284
Parks, Donald A. 33, 40, 142
Parsonsburg 51, 175
Parsons, Harrison "Smoke" 61
Pasadena 123, 231
Patterson Park 107

Patuxent Institution 252
Payne, Leslie J. 174
Peninsula General Hospital 23, 26, 36, 59, 96, 99, 175, 176, 186, 217. See also Tidal Health Medical Center
Pennsylvania 9, 139, 151, 200
Pennsylvania Railroad 25, 27, 46
penthouse prison. See also Wicomico County Jail
Pepersack, Vernon L. 137, 138
Perkins, Clifton T. 121
Pescor, M. J. 258, 259
Petta, Pasquale "Patrick" Anthony 40. See also Johnson, Patsy
Phillips, G. Murray 36, 38, 40
Pikesville 61, 62, 188, 219, 222
Pilchard, William 136
Pittsville 141, 142, 152, 185, 291, 292, 293
Pocomoke 7, 60, 162
Pocomoke River 141
Pollitt, Agnes "Aggie" 47
Pollitt, Jesse M. 27, 33, 42, 45, 46, 47, 48, 49, 50, 51, 52, 53, 55, 56, 61, 103, 166, 193
Pollitt, Josiah Wesley 47
Pollitt, Richard Malone 46, 47, 48, 50, 193, 204, 205, 215, 219, 221, 249, 251, 252, 254, 255, 256, 257, 259, 261, 287, 288
Pollitt, Rick 48, 101
Poplar Hill Correctional Camp 34, 60, 138
Powellville 141, 142, 143
Prettyman, Daniel 193, 198
Prince George's County 60
Princess Anne 11, 12, 24, 155, 204, 292
Purnell, Roscoe 58
Pusey, Ralph Lee 168, 169, 173, 174, 215, 219, 220, 253, 254, 263

Q

Quantico 12, 20, 21, 22, 34, 56, 60, 138
Quantico Creek 20
Queen Anne's County 17, 162, 163

R

Radcliffe, George L. 33
Ray, James Earl 146, 235
Reagan, Ronald 106
Red Bird 8, 12, 15, 16, 17, 18, 19, 28, 30, 37
Redman, Bertha F. 72, 73, 208, 223, 228
Red Men's Hall 48, 50
Reed's Drug Store 101
Reiner, Herman 249, 250, 251, 252, 256, 257
Republican 48, 51, 53, 55, 62, 96, 105, 106, 154, 201
Richardson, Gloria 149
Richardson, Vaughn E. 99, 261, 267, 268
Riordan, Bill 153
Ritchie, Albert C. 19, 39, 40, 68
Robinson, Tim 301, 302
Roosevelt, Franklin D. 2, 19, 27
Rosenthal, Joseph 269
Rosewood Center 111, 112

S

Salisbury 4, 5, 6, 7, 8, 9, 10, 11, 13, 14, 15, 16, 19, 23, 25, 26, 27, 35, 36, 37, 38, 39, 40, 44, 45, 47, 49, 50, 52, 53, 56, 60, 61, 62, 100, 120, 129, 130, 131, 132, 133, 142, 143, 147, 148, 151, 154, 155, 156, 159, 168, 175, 178, 179, 181, 182, 184, 187, 189, 198, 204, 205, 209, 218, 231, 247, 261, 267, 268, 285, 290, 293, 294
Salisbury Fire Department 6, 40, 135, 289
Salisbury High School 23, 61, 190
Salisbury News and Advertiser 14, 96
Salisbury Police Department 40, 56, 99, 100, 106, 134, 147, 148, 152, 156, 174, 181, 182, 183, 192, 194, 195, 258, 261, 278
Salisbury State College 201. See also Salisbury University
Salisbury State Teachers' College 47. See also Salisbury University
Salisbury Times 19, 22, 24, 30, 33, 34, 35, 39, 44, 46, 49, 50, 51, 52, 53, 62, 98, 102, 104. See also Daily Times
Salisbury University 3, 47, 201
Sanford, John "Jack" L., Jr. 165, 197, 198, 199
Santo Domingo 44
Sarbanes, Anthony "Tony" 285, 286, 287, 294
Sarbanes, S. James 294
Sauer, Robert H. 246, 247, 248, 249, 251
schizoid personality disorder 279

schizophrenia 224, 225, 226, 227, 239, 243, 245, 257, 284, 285
Severn River 115
Sharptown 44
Shockley, J. Merril 58, 99, 100, 101
Shockley, William "Bill" 51, 132, 203, 289
Silver Dollar Tavern 101
Simpson, Oliver "Bob" 104, 105
Sinai Hospital 67
Sirhan Sirhan 148, 213, 235, 282
slaves/slavery 10, 12, 15, 21, 38, 109
Smethurst, Raymond S. 156
Smith, Carol 123, 139, 140, 151, 207
Smith, Joseph W. T. 27, 55, 61
Smith, Russell P., Jr. 97, 98
Smyrna, Delaware 9
Snow Hill 11, 136, 198, 199
sociopathic personality 258, 259
sociopathic personality, antisocial reaction 120, 125
Sodaro, Anselm 279, 280
Somerset County 11, 47, 155, 163
Southern States Cooperative 48
Springfield Hospital Center 109, 111, 112
Spring Grove State Hospital 59, 80, 108, 109, 111, 120
Star-Democrat 16
St. Catherine's 230
Stephens, Henry T. 148, 261, 278
St. Peter's Episcopal Church 5, 6, 7
St. Philip's Episcopal Church 20
Sunset Memorial Cemetery 294
Sykesville 109, 111

T

Talbot County 7, 14, 162, 294
Tawes, J. Millard 120
Taylor, Rex A. 57, 193
The Cut. *See also* Maryland House of Correction
The Silent Shore: The Lynching of Matthew Williams and the Politics of Racism in the Free State 39
thorazine 115, 207, 211, 247, 248, 249, 251, 257
Tidal Health Medical Center 293. *See also* Peninsula General Hospital
Toadvine, Mel 165, 166
Toadvine, S. Frank 5, 6, 8
transient personality disturbance situation 117
Travers, Maude Larmore Heath 24, 25, 26
Travers, William W. 24, 25, 26, 184, 193, 204, 205, 206, 267, 268, 269, 270
Truitt, Alfred "Sonny" T. Jr. 53, 54, 55, 56, 60, 61, 62, 96, 101, 106, 133, 153, 181, 182, 184, 185, 193, 204, 205, 215, 216, 217, 218, 219, 220, 221, 224, 225, 226, 227, 228, 231, 232, 236, 238, 239, 240, 243, 244, 246, 249, 252, 258, 259, 261, 262, 263, 268, 269, 278, 287, 288, 289
Truitt, Christine 101, 185
Truitt, Clara May 54, 55, 62, 216, 289
Truitt, Dallas G. 184
Truitt, Margaret "Maggie" 185, 288

U

United States Air Force 200
United States Army 2, 33, 118, 129, 130, 131, 143, 159, 161, 200
United States Army Signal Corps 53
United States Naval Air Station (Corpus Christi, Texas) 129
United States Naval Auxiliary Air Station (Chincoteague Island, Virginia) 129
United States Navy 2, 129, 130, 161, 231
United States Park Police 193
University of Maryland 47, 224, 239, 268
University of Maryland School of Law 55, 216
USS Coral Sea 129

V

Valliant, Jeremiah 56
Veditz, Thomas 133, 175
Victory Villa 71, 229
Vietnam War 146, 201, 236, 268, 280, 282
Virginia 5, 35, 98, 129, 214, 288
Voigt family 300. *See also* Voigt Hobby and Sports Shop
Voigt's Hobby and Sport Shop 154, 155, 188

W

Wallace, George 154
Waller, Frank 285, 286
Walston, John 101, 133, 189, 193, 218
Walter C. Thurston Jr. Photograph Collection 8, 9, 17, 28, 31, 32, 132, 134, 149
Ward, Charles 117, 118
Warwick's Hardware 155
Washington County 280
Washington, D.C. 13, 45, 101, 121, 146, 205, 214
Washington, D.C. Police 193
Waters, John 78
Webster, Preston Lee 155, 156, 205
Weir, Robert D., Sr. 133, 175, 179, 220
Western Maryland College 23, 24, 26, 54. *See also* McDaniel College
Western Shore 149, 150
Westminster 18
Westside Community Center 56
White and Leonard 28
Whitehaven 23
White, Norman 51
Wicomico 11. *See also* Wighcocomico
Wicomico County 4, 5, 10, 11, 12, 13, 19, 20, 21, 26, 27, 28, 33, 40, 41, 47, 48, 50, 51, 56, 59, 61, 96, 104, 105, 106, 128, 131, 132, 141, 153, 168, 184, 185, 186, 190, 197, 199, 201, 202, 214, 216, 234, 254, 260, 270, 287, 289, 291
Wicomico County Bar Association 30
Wicomico County Council 106, 128, 183, 189
Wicomico County Courthouse i, ii, 3, 5, 8, 9, 10, 12, 13, 14, 15, 19, 27, 28, 29, 30, 31, 32, 33, 34, 35, 37, 38, 41, 47, 49, 55, 101, 103, 132, 135, 145, 147, 149, 152, 154, 167, 168, 170, 174, 175, 176, 177, 181, 184, 193, 195, 204, 219, 286, 289, 297, 298
Wicomico County Jail iii, 3, 4, 28, 30, 31, 32, 33, 43, 44, 45, 47, 48, 49, 50, 58, 59, 98, 99, 100, 101, 102, 104, 120, 128, 129, 133, 134, 135, 145, 152, 153, 156, 161, 162, 163, 165, 166, 167, 168, 169, 171, 172, 173, 174, 175, 177, 178, 179, 181, 183, 187, 188, 189, 190, 193, 199, 201, 202, 203, 204, 207, 208, 209, 210, 211, 218, 219, 237, 254, 267, 268, 269, 289, 290, 297, 298, 299, 300, 301, 302
Wicomico County Sheriff i, 3, 19, 36, 38, 40, 45, 53, 106, 165, 267, 282, 293, 295, 300, 302
Wicomico County Sheriff's Department ii, 3, 27, 32, 33, 41, 46, 56, 61, 104, 105, 128, 131, 142, 149, 159, 188, 189, 192, 201, 219, 286, 290
Wicomico County Sheriff's Office ii, 289, 290, 291, 293, 301, 302
Wicomico County State's Attorney 36, 42, 53, 55, 60, 96, 106, 133, 153, 181, 204, 216, 268, 269, 288
Wicomico High School 23, 24, 25, 26, 52, 53, 57, 96, 97, 130, 132, 144, 146, 154, 159, 193, 201, 285, 286
Wicomico Hotel 29
Wicomico Memorial Park 194, 196, 287
Wicomico River 11, 15, 23
Wicomico Theater 98
Wighcocomico 11. *See also* Wicomico
Wilhelm, Russell 221, 222
Wilhelm's Tavern 69
Williams, Matthew 35, 36, 37, 38, 39, 40, 41, 147, 148
Wilmington, Delaware 6, 7, 43, 180
Winters Quarter Country Club 60
Wise, Helen 36, 37
Wootten, Richard S. 183
Worcester County 11, 37, 51, 127, 136, 162, 163, 165, 197, 199, 269
Worcester County Sheriff's Department 290
Worcester County State's Attorney 197, 198
Works Progress Administration / Work Projects Administration 2, 27, 269
World War I 33
World War II 53, 71, 143, 161, 185, 197
Wye Mills 268

Y

Yankellow, Norman N. 269